Learning
and
Loving It

RUTH GAMBERG

WINNIEFRED KWAK

MEREDITH HUTCHINGS

JUDY ALTHEIM

with
GAIL EDWARDS

LEARNING AND LOVING IT

Theme Studies in the Classroom

Heinemann • Portsmouth, New Hampshire
OISE Press • Toronto, Ontario, Canada

HEINEMANN EDUCATIONAL BOOKS, INC.
361 Hanover Street   Portsmouth, NH 03801-3959
Offices and agents throughout the world

OISE PRESS
252 Bloor Street West   Toronto, Ontario, Canada M5S 1V6

The authors wish to thank the following for permission to reprint their work:
    The photos of the Dalhousie University Elementary School are reprinted courtesy
of Carlos Cacola, Meredith Hutchings, Winniefred Kwak, and David Middleton.
    The photo of children with architect Martin Giddy from the *Halifax Mail-Star* and
the photo of chili lunch sales, also from the *Halifax Mail-Star*, are reprinted courtesy
of The Chronicle-Herald.
    The drawings and writings of the children involved in the various theme studies
are reprinted courtesy of the children and their parents. Thanks to Eyra Abraham,
David Altheim, Nicholas Bain, Wren Baker-Toombs, Allison, Bronwen, and Lesley
Bennett, Paul Blaauw, Sula Buckland-Nicks, Alaine Camfield, Raju Chelluri, Matthew Edgar, Bridget and Mary Fyfe, Bryan Garland, Johannes Graham, Erinn Haley,
Andrew Isenor, Lisa Kirk, Jessica Lane, Daria and Sarah Manos, David Mitchell,
Harriet Mitchell, Jesse and Noah Morantz, Matthew Richman, Troy Schwab, Rebecca
Silvert, Julia Watt, and Amanda York for their work that is reproduced in this book.
    Every effort has been made to contact the copyright holders and the children and
their parents for permission to reprint borrowed material. We regret any oversights
that may have occurred and would be happy to rectify them in future printings of
this work.

Front cover photo by Winniefred Kwak.

Library of Congress Cataloging-in-Publication Data

Learning and loving it: theme studies in the classroom / Ruth Gamberg
    . . . [et al.], with Gail Edwards.—1st ed.
        p.   cm.
    Bibliography: p.
    ISBN 0-435-08454-2
    1. Unit method of teaching.   2. Curriculum planning.   I. Gamberg,
Ruth.   II. Title: Theme studies in the classroom.
LB1029.U6L43 1988
375'.001—dc19   87-28559
                                                                CIP

Canadian Cataloguing in Publication Data

Main entry under title:

Learning and loving it

(Curriculum series ; 56)
1st ed.
Bibliography: p.
ISBN 0-7744-0316-0

1. Unit method of teaching.   2. Curriculum planning.
I. Gamberg, Ruth.   II. Ontario Institute for Studies
in Education.   III. Series: Curriculum series (Ontario Institute for Studies in Education) ; 56.

LB1029.U6L43 1988   375'.001   C88-093220-1

Printed in the United States of America.
10 9 8 7 6 5 4 3

Contents

Acknowledgments   vii

I. THE THEME STUDY APPROACH   1

   1. Introduction   3
   2. Theme Study: What It Is and How to Do It   9

II. LARGE-SCALE THEME STUDIES   31

   3. Around the World in Sixty Days: A Theme Study about
       Houses with the Middles (Ages Six to Eight)   33
   4. The History of Buildings: A Theme Study with the Olds
       (Ages Eight to Ten)   54
   5. Building Learning, Learning from Building: The Olds and
       Middles Cooperate—With Impressive Results   87
   6. From Stones to Bricks: A Study of Housing with the Youngs
       (Ages Five and Six)   135

III. SPECIALIZED THEME STUDIES   147

   7. Chili Enterprise Ltd.: A Minitheme Involving Lots of
       Math and All the Children   149
   8. Encouraging Children to Act Up: The Whole School
       Becomes a Theater   171

IV. YES, BUT WHAT ABOUT . . .   195

   9.   What about "The Basics"? And Other Sundry Matters   197
  10. What about Evaluation?   216
  11. What about Discipline?   223
  12. Theme Study—Can Anybody Do It?   231

Notes   241

Acknowledgments

This book is very much about cooperation. Studying themes means the children must cooperate in order to learn, and in so doing, they learn to cooperate. In addition, many of their lessons in cooperation come from others who assist them in countless ways. We thank those people on the children's behalf.

First, thanks are due to the Dalhousie University Department of Education for general support. We are especially grateful to Mary Crowley, Jessi Metter, Joe Murphy, Carol Nasr, Mary Schoeneberger, Lynne Simpson, and Anne Wood, the professors and parents who sat on the School Committee during the year that most of the theme studies described in the book were carried out. They not only determined policy and made decisions, but also always encouraged program ideas and efforts. Thanks also to Eileen Dale, Ivona Zwicker, and Susan Crowell who helped with many of the boring but necessary details of running the school. And where would we have been without the services of Ruth Slaunwhite and Keith Cranidge who not only constantly cleaned up our messes but also took an active interest in the children?

Then there were the many people who taught the children lessons in cooperation by contributing freely of their time, expertise, services, and materials in order to enrich the children's theme studies. For the playhouse study, construction workers at several sites never seemed to tire of answering questions. After reading and listening to the children's proposals, Martin Giddy granted them a building permit to build the playhouse. Thereafter, Jan Erik Kwak helped cut the lumber to size, and Gordon Parsons, along with several parents, picked up saw and hammer to help the children build, using materials donated by parents, Friis Fencing and Construction Ltd., Fuller Thomas Construction Co. Ltd., and Piercey's. Jurgen Mueller, master glassblower, helped the children with their study of the history of building by teaching them about glass and glassblowing in the past and in the present. The Halifax City Regional Library displayed the major product of that theme study—the model castle that the children made. The math minitheme received a boost when the university's Chemistry Department hired the children to cater a lunch, and thus Chili Enterprise was born. The Education Department followed suit, thereby doubling the children's clientele. The play minitheme study was helped along by Dianne Milligan and Barbara Richman, who have always videotaped the plays, and by David Middleton, who took photos during rehearsals.

More generally, our theme studies have received the cooperation of Carlos Cacola and Paul Chislett, who have always obliged us by taking photos; Ted Coffin, who has reliably provided whatever audiovisual equipment we have needed; and the

Halifax and Dartmouth Regional Libraries, which have allowed us prolonged use of so many materials. Most of all, parents have been supportive in general, and many, too numerous to name, have provided concrete assistance by accompanying us on field trips, by lending their expertise and supervision to our cooking ventures, by donating materials, by locating films, by suggesting visitors, trips and books, by giving presentations, by helping with construction of the playhouse, and by performing any number of other useful tasks.

Speaking now for ourselves, we would like to thank still others who, in numerous ways, have helped us put together this book. Thanks are due to Ann Brimer, whose financial support made it possible for the study on the playhouse to be written. She and Ann Manicom, along with several teachers from other elementary schools—Sandra Bishop, Reta Boyd, Mary Osborne, Helen Stewart, Sumitra Unia, and Sheila Wainwright—read the playhouse study and offered suggestions. Herb Gamberg read the manuscript and made other contributions as well. Eileen Dale is to be thanked for her prompt and efficient typing and her patience with us. We are grateful, of course, to our families for their support and flexibility throughout our many hours of work.

We would be remiss if we did not thank the children. Those involved in the particular theme studies cited in this book were: Eyra Abraham, David Altheim, J. B. Anderson, Caleb and Wren Baker-Toombs, Elisa Baniassad, Allison, Bronwen, and Lesley Bennett, Paul Blaauw, Jamie and Rebeccah Bornemann, Sula and Naomi Buckland-Nicks, Caoimhe Butterly, Alaine Camfield, Raju Chelluri, Jesse Cox, Jamie Crocker, Matthew Edgar, Bridget and Mary Fyfe, Johannes Graham, Shawn and Tiffany Hahn, Andrew and Elliott Isenor, Lisa Kirk, Jessica Lane, Jess MacGillivray, Simon MacKenzie, Stephen-John MacLean, Trevor MacLean, Matthew MacWilliam, Daria and Sarah Manos, Ian McDonnell, Alexis Milligan, David Mitchell, Jesse and Noah Morantz, Caitlin Morehouse, Ariel Nasr, Adam Nonamaker, Kabir Ravindra, Matthew Richman, Zachary Ryan, Troy Schwab, Rebecca Silvert, Alison Simpson, Jason Sperker, Daniel Waldron, Christopher and Julia Watt, and Amanda York. While there are too many others to name, we want to acknowledge and thank all the children who have attended the school for their energy, initiative, and diligence and for their willingness to take risks. In using our ideas and developing them further, the children have shown enthusiasm and imagination that serve as a continual source of inspiration.

I

THE THEME
STUDY APPROACH

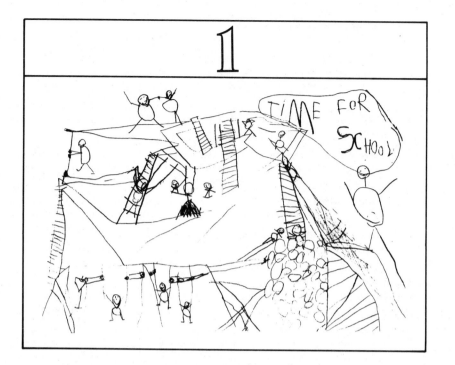

Introduction

We are living in conservative times. Belt-tightening, cutbacks, and a return to what are considered traditional truths have become contemporary watchwords. Education has not escaped this conservative shift. Throughout the continent, the trend in education reflecting this move is summed up in the slogan "back to basics." This short phrase says a great deal. It suggests that education is now off track and that we must return to a golden age of the past. It also implies that the schools are focusing on the wrong things, on peripheral and inconsequential learnings, commonly referred to as "frills," rather than the central and important issues, the "basics."

Since the back-to-basics mood tends to reject approaches to curriculum development such as the one explored in this book in favor of traditional approaches, let us examine this mood more closely. Let us look at the assertions contained within the back-to-basics slogan as well as at some of its less obvious but very real and dangerous implications.

The first question that comes to mind is: when exactly was this golden age of quality education and high academic standards? The answer is not at all clear. For example, no one complained in the 1940s and early 1950s. Yet in 1950–51, 65 percent of the students who took a standardized English examination at the prestigious University of Toronto failed it.[1] Then, a few years later, a great hue and cry went up declaiming our low educational standards as Sputnik entered the scene: "We must get back to the basics." However, since times were prosperous, "the basics" in the late 1950s and the 1960s meant, at least in part, innovation, taking chances, and trying new things. By the mid-1960s and early 1970s, there was an upsurge of lively debate, with people trying to define appropriate educational objectives and practices. These debates infused the atmosphere of the schools and universities and involved not only students, teachers, and others whose workday revolved around the school, but the general public as well.

The noteworthy point about these debates is that they were all highly critical of precisely those traditional educational outlooks and practices to which we are now being urged to return. What were these educational outlooks and practices? Why were they so sharply criticized in the latter half of the 1960s and the early 70s? What were books with titles such as *How Children Fail, Death at an Early Age, Education for Alienation, Schools Against Children,* and *Crisis in the Classroom* saying that turned the interest and attention of ordinary citizens to the school system?[2]

According to the critics, the educational system was not educating. It was not helping children become interested, active, knowledgeable, and independent thinkers and doers. Through such thought-deadening instructional methods as drill and rote memorization and such common school practices as I. Q. tests, standardized tests, and streaming,* all carried out in an atmosphere of authoritarianism, the schools were training rather than educating. They were training children in two ways, namely, to be passive, accepting, and obedient receptacles for facts, and to "know their place" in society.

The schools were competitive places that produced either successes or failures. The successes were usually middle-class students who went on to colleges or universities, while the failures were generally from working-class or poor backgrounds. In school, the "failures" were labeled, streamed, and stigmatized by a system that created victims and then blamed the victims for their problems. All of this, of course, led to alienation and the motivation to leave school at the earliest possible moment. It was due to this constellation of factors as well as to many others, such as the class, race, ethnic, and gender bias of teaching materials and the middle-class identification of school personnel, that led the critics to pronounce: schools greatly contribute to the unequal opportunities in society and hence are elitist, serving merely to reproduce the social class system.

The challenge went out to transform the schools, to create a stimulating and open environment where all children could develop to their full potential. The

---

* Streaming refers to those school practices such as the so-called ability grouping that is done in many elementary schools and the program specialization in the high schools that serve to provide students with extremely different school experiences and therefore different kinds of opportunities in life. There is a very high correlation between streaming and social class membership, with children from lower socio-economic backgrounds commonly being placed in lower streams in school and those from higher socio-economic backgrounds commonly being placed in higher streams. Through such means as this, socio-economic inequalities are perpetuated by the schools.

response to the challenge was innovations in curriculum, new instructional materials, changes in school practices, and even new designs for school buildings. Some of these changes made a difference, but most did not. Although there were serious efforts by some teachers and administrators, not all innovations were carefully thought through; a great many were not fully understood by those who were to implement them, while others were superficially accepted and tried only in piecemeal fashion.

Today, while there remain some scattered, residual benefits from those exciting days of educational experimentation, the schools have, by and large, sunk back into the old traditional outlooks and practices. It is rather ironic that at a time when the criticisms and innovations of the recent past have mostly disappeared, usually silently, we are nevertheless bombarded with the urgent directive to "go back to basics"—back, essentially, to where we already are.

Why, then, the big fuss?

> We don't have to look very far to notice that the current "back to basics" movement coincides with the gradual withdrawal of State resources from public education, as well as from all other social services, in a period of general economic dislocation . . .[3]

At bottom, it is economic, far more than educational, considerations that account for the back-to-basics trend. There is no question that an education system is in serious difficulty when, as is now the case, arguments that are essentially of an economic nature are mistaken for educational ones.

It is true; these are tough economic times. It is also true that such times call for a thorough grounding in the basics. These certainly include the three Rs that we hear so much about from the back-to-basics advocates. But there are other basics as well that, unfortunately, they tend to take rather lightly—namely, the ability to think, to question, and to evaluate so that children might learn to deal intelligently with the world in which they live. Such basics require engagement with information, ideas, and issues, engagement that can be accomplished through the theme study approach. Briefly stated, theme study, as we mean it, is student centered and emphasizes a coherent and holistic approach to learning through the study of broad themes rather than compartmentalized subject areas. This approach provides teachers with an effective way to raise standards, assuming we are referring to standards that derive from the most basic of the basics—the development of critical thinking. Theme study represents a major departure from traditional approaches to curriculum.

Perhaps a word is in order about the school where all the theme studies described in this book were conducted. Located in Halifax, Nova Scotia, Dalhousie University Elementary School (D. U. E. S.) was designated as a "Center of Excellence: 1985–87" by the U.S. National Council of Teachers of English for its theme studies program. The school is part of a university Department of Education and is situated on the campus in a building it shares with the Department. It is a small school with only thirty-six children ranging in age from five to ten; they are divided into three groups based on a combination of age, and social and intellectual maturity. While there are exceptions, as in all schools,

- the "Youngs" are generally five and six years old (Primary/ Kindergarten),
- the "Middles" are generally six to eight years old (grades 1 and 2),
- the "Olds" are generally eight to ten years old (grades 3 and 4).

The program is developed and implemented by three teachers, one of whom is full-time while the other two are half-time. In addition, there are specialist French and music teachers who provide programs in their respective areas.

It is a private school with some financial support from the university's Department of Education. Administration of the school is the responsibility of a committee composed of nine members with equal representation from the faculty of the Department of Education, the teachers, and elected parents. This committee oversees policy pertaining to the day-to-day operation of the school and coordinates the special use that is made of the school because of its affiliation with a teacher education center: observation, teaching practice, and research undertaken by prospective teachers who are studying in the Education Department and others.

The children generally come from middle-class, although not especially wealthy, families. Parents are usually attracted to the school because of the program and its approach. Sometimes their interest is due mainly to the fact that their children have learning or social problems that they feel are not or will not be properly handled in traditional classroom settings. By and large, however, the children in the school resemble children of any other school. There is a range of abilities and interests such that the composition of the student body could be considered average or typical.

Although the school is unusual in some respects, the single most important characteristic enabling it to be successful in doing theme studies is one that exists in many elementary schools and that can be brought into being in virtually any of them—flexibility. Two examples may serve to illustrate. A theme studies teacher does not have to worry about maintaining an absolute balance of activities on a daily basis because it sometimes happens that the demands of a theme study make it necessary to focus heavily on one area, say social studies, for a few weeks while doing little in another, say science. This is not problematic because the balance will shift at another time. A theme studies teacher is also alert to unexpected opportunities that may arise. One day, one of the teachers at D. U. E. S. happened upon some men working on the roof of a house two blocks away. As luck would have it, the children were studying housing construction and had just run into some perplexing problems about how to build a roof. The teacher hurried back to the school, assembled the children, who had just finished lunch, and relayed her news about the roofers. They hastily did a brainstorm so they would have questions for the roofers and then all quickly went to the construction site for a roadside interview.

That's flexibility. Flexibility demands that the organization and administration of a school program, of the use of time and space, and so on, be determined not by tradition, whim, or fiat but by the educational needs of the children. When those needs change or when someone comes up with a new idea for fulfilling them, everyday patterns and routines should bend and be rearranged to accommodate the changes. This can be done in all elementary schools and by all elementary school teachers.

This book is organized to take the reader on a guided tour of the theme study approach, both in theory and in practice. Chapter 2, as its title suggests, explains what the theme study approach is, how the teachers at D. U. E. S. go about planning and implementing a theme study, and what is gained by using this approach. The chapter also touches on the current teaching approaches incorporated by theme studies at the school—the whole language approach to reading, the process approach to writing, the problem-solving approach to math, and so on. More on this subject is left until Chapter 9.

Chapters 3 to 6 describe full-scale theme studies undertaken by the three groups in the school during one entire academic year. That year the overall theme was "People and Their Work." The specific studies pursued by the three groups all revolved around houses or other kinds of buildings and building construction. One advantage of looking at several theme studies on the same or related topics done by different age groups is that they demonstrate how varied in-depth studies can be. In the fall term, the oldest group and the middle group actually built a playhouse in the course of their theme study. However, because this was the most ambitious theme study undertaken and is therefore somewhat less representative than the others, it does not appear as the first example. It is preceded, instead, by descriptions of theme studies done in the second term. This makes no difference since the order is interchangeable.

Chapter 3 deals with the middle group's study of housing around the world ranging from northern igloos to African adobe houses—how the children decided what questions to pursue; how they gathered information to answer their questions; and how their study culminated in making models, books, posters, and games to illustrate and discuss what they had learned. While this was going on, the oldest group was studying housing from a different perspective. Chapter 4 takes us through their examination of the history of construction methods and tools beginning with the Stone Age and moving up through the Middle Ages, which, with its castles and cathedrals, caught the children's imagination and became their main focus of attention from then on. As part of this focus, they also studied the working lives and social relationships of the people of the day—the artisans, serfs, lords, and clergy.

In Chapter 5, we come to the construction of the playhouse. This chapter, which is laid out in a fashion that enables the reader to follow the work of either the middle group, or the older group, or both, tells how the children gathered enough information through reading, experiments, field trips, and interviews with workers to prepare blueprints and models, to secure a building permit, and to finally accomplish their grand objective. At the same time, the youngest group of children was also studying building construction. In Chapter 6 we see how they learned about various structures and the materials and tools needed to build them and how they applied their knowledge by building different kinds of structures using different kinds of materials. Their participation in assisting the other two groups with the finishing touches of the playhouse is also described in this chapter.

Like the four previous chapters, 7 and 8 are concrete, step-by-step descriptions of theme studies but on a smaller scale and of a more specialized nature. They are also examples of wider cross-age grouping because they involve all the children in the school in joint efforts. Chapter 7 describes how the children and the teachers work together to set up and operate a lunch business several times a year. We discover how "Chili Enterprise" works from the time the children select recipes to the time they clean up and do the bookkeeping after the meal is over. Chapter 8 takes us through all the steps involved in writing and producing a play with children—selecting a fictional children's book; adapting it to a script; making sets and props; rehearsing; and finally performing the play for an audience of parents, other family members, and anyone else who is interested.

Chapters 9, 10, and 11 address concerns that teachers and parents may have about any approach, particularly an unfamiliar one. Using a question-and-answer format, Chapter 9 provides responses to the questions most frequently asked about the theme study approach. This chapter deals with a broad range of issues such as how the children learn the three Rs, the advantages and problems of children working in groups, motivation, and teacher expectations, to mention only a few. Chapter 10 is about the evaluation process and why the theme study approach requires forms of evaluation that differ from the traditional ones. It describes what is evaluated, why, and how. Chapter 11 gives a view of discipline consistent with the philosophy underlying the theme study approach and a description of how this view is translated into practice.

The book concludes with a chapter that discusses the applicability of this approach to typical elementary school classrooms. This chapter also indirectly suggests how teachers might begin to implement the approach by giving a concrete account, drawn from our own experience, of some of the problems that arose at first and of some of the solutions that evolved over time.

Because this book chronicles the experiences and views of a group of three teachers, it is written in the first person plural. However, when the work of a single group of children is being described, only one teacher is involved. Thus, in Chapter 3 which is about the Middles, Chapter 4 the Olds, and Chapter 6 the Youngs, the singular form is used. "We," then, normally refers to "we teachers." There are times, however, when "we" refers to "we teacher(s) and children." Ordinarily, those referred to should be clear from the context. Otherwise, different words, such as "we teachers," are used.

Sometimes illustrations in the book contain writing by the children that is difficult to decipher. In such cases, "translations" are supplied; sometimes they are handwritten within the illustration and sometimes they are typeset underneath or to the side.

Theme Study: What It Is and How to Do It

There are piles of books, posters and diagrams. There are files, newspaper clippings, fishermen's journals and what have you to aid the children in their inquiry . . . Fishing tackle is in the middle of the room and a lobster trap entices one from under an array of crayons and colored pencils. The message is clear. This is a learning-investigating environment. Please talk, exchange ideas, voice your opinions. Please don't be quiet! The learners are center stage. This is their environment. They created it and roam around in it, with a couple of adults "standing by." These are their teachers or learning facilitators. . . .

Learning is a process here, not an end-product delivered to the children by a lecturing teacher declaiming from the front of the room. Absent are the traditional perimeters of the classroom. There are no rows of anonymous desks, but rather scattered round and square tables where groups of children sit and do their work. Everyone is working on something whether it be writing a thank-you letter to someone who showed them slides of "fishing in developed and underdeveloped countries" or finishing research on a given topic.

What the teachers do is prompt, advise, initiate the discussions which lead to new ideas and which stimulate heated debate. They organize the great wealth of resource materials which replace the traditional classroom texts. . . . They are there not to force their particular points of view on the children, but rather to point out to them the wealth of knowledge, the many different points of view out there from which they must choose—in school, as well as in life in general.[1]

Toward a Definition of Theme Study

What is the theme study approach? One teacher recently told us about the theme study she did with her second graders on the subject of Valentine's Day. The children read a story about it, had a discussion, learned a relevant song, wrote and illustrated poems and short stories on their experiences and feelings about Valentine's Day, pasted their math work on bright red valentines, and finally displayed their work for each other to admire. Viewed from a very limited perspective, this, indeed, is a kind of theme study—the focus was on a topic of interest and combined several school subjects (reading, writing, speaking, listening, math, music, and art).

However, if this is all that is meant by theme study, then virtually all elementary school teachers do it, and there is no need to say anything further about it. Such is not the case. Taken as an overall approach, a way of conceiving of and developing curriculum, theme study is much broader and more sophisticated.

Moving away from the Valentine's Day example to the ideas of theme study in this other, more developed sense, let us describe what it is. To begin with, as an approach to teaching and learning, theme study is not peripheral to the curriculum. Nor is it of brief, passing duration or interest. Theme study refers to the core of what children do in school. It is the core in that it defines what is to be the center of attention, incorporates many traditional subject areas within it, and develops over a long period of time. As our weekly timetable shows (see page 11), about half of the work time in class is spent on theme study. However, there are some areas that cannot be fully included in our theme study work. This is because theme studies do not always offer enough exposure to these areas. That, however, does not matter. Whatever fits naturally is incorporated into theme studies; whatever does not is dealt with separately.

The theme study approach to curriculum also has certain other important characteristics. First and foremost, it involves in-depth study. A theme or topic (not reading or math or science) is the focus of attention. For a theme to qualify as deserving of study, it must fulfill several criteria: it must be of interest to the children; it must be broad enough so that it can be divided into smaller subtopics also of interest to the children; the relationship of the subtopics to the wider context must remain clear; and the topic should not be geographically or historically limiting. Throughout the study, the topic should lend itself to comparing and contrasting ideas and permit extensive investigation of concrete situations, materials, and resources. The topic should be conducive to breaking down the walls within the school—those invisible barriers that artificially demarcate knowledge from itself and place it in categories called ''subjects''—so that a rich cross-disciplinary program is possible. The topic should lend itself also to breaking down the walls between the school and society that prevent children from using the surrounding world as a laboratory for their studies. It should encourage an understanding and appreciation of the community.

Thus, for example, a suitable theme for elementary school children, especially those living near the sea, would be oceans, which is one of the themes studied at D. U. E. S. A subtopic might be the fishing industry, which holds out a number of possibilities: historical and contemporary techniques of fishing; working conditions of fishermen; fish processing plants, both technical and organizational

WEEKLY TIMETABLE

	Monday	*Tuesday*	*Wednesday*	*Thursday*	*Friday*
9:00–10:30	Theme	Theme	Theme	Theme	Theme and Music
10:30–11:00	Recess				
11:00–12:15	Math and French / 11:45–12:15 Lunch	Math and Music	Theme	Math	Math and French
12:15–1:15 / 1:15–1:35	12:15–2:00 Swimming	Lunch			
		Meeting			
1:35–2:45	2:00–3:05 Math	French and Theme	French and Math	French and Theme	Gym
2:45–3:05		Silent Reading			Reading in pairs
3:05–3:15	Clean-up				

NOTES

This timetable applies to all the children in the school.

Wherever two activities are listed in one time slot, it indicates that while some children are engaged in one activity, e.g., French or music, others are doing the other activity listed; this rotates so that all children do both.

The children are divided into two groups for math (about five hours a week for each group), two groups for music (one hour a week for each group), and three groups for French (one hour and forty minutes a week for each group).

Meetings of the whole school are held most days after lunch to discuss problems or announcements. Items for discussion are initiated by both the children and the teachers. (See Chapter 11 for more information on school meetings.)

We do not adhere to this timetable rigidly. When we are preparing for an open house (see pp. 17 and 29), or getting ready to put on a play (see Chapter 8), or when some other aspect of our work requires more time, we make adjustments in the timetable.

aspects; conservation of fish stocks; fishing communities; and other such areas for exploration. As can be seen, even the subtopics are broad. This breadth is necessary if the work is, in fact, to be an in-depth study. Broad subtopics also permit the necessary flexibility in making decisions about which directions to take. So, for instance, children studying technical aspects of fishing (the equipment and methods used) might want to find out what happens once the fish are caught, and that would in turn lead to an investigation of the fish processing plants. It must be remembered that the first criterion for selecting a theme or a subtopic is student interest. Therefore, flexibility is essential. This is not to suggest that every whim must be catered to. Once a direction is established by the teacher and the children, it is pursued. Theme study is, after all, both a focused study and an in-depth study.

It can also be seen from the above example that in emphasizing the topic and not a subject or skill area, there would nonetheless be ample opportunity for activities involving the traditional subjects—reading, writing (including spelling), math, science, social studies, art, and music. These would be automatically incorporated in the course of such a theme study.

A healthy sign of the day is that growing attention is being paid to certain teaching and learning approaches that flow from current research. These pertain to particular subject areas: the whole language, or psycholinguistic, approach to reading in which meaning, rather than phonics or word recognition, is central; the process approach to writing, again with meaning, not the conventions of transcribing, coming first; the problem-solving approach to math through the use of concrete materials; and the discovery approach to science and social studies. All of these emphasize process rather than the traditional interest in accumulating factual knowledge and the almost exclusive concern with end-products. Rather than looking to see if the child ''got the right answer,'' the teacher who makes use of these approaches is interested in what the child is doing along the way—what thought processes are being marshaled.

The emphasis on process is a tremendous advance. Yet something still seems to be lacking. If we focus only on the process and ignore the substance, much is lost. Regardless of the approach used, there is always content; we always study about something. It is not just *how* we study that is important but also *what* because not all topics are equally deserving of our time and attention. The strength of the theme study approach is that neither content nor process is ignored. Theme study incorporates processes that involve focusing on meaning to make sense of the world and relying on one's intelligence to solve problems and discover relationships. Theme study draws on and combines all of the approaches discussed above— meaning as central, problem-solving, and discovery. It is impossible to imagine a theme study that at all resembles those described in the next several chapters that, for example, deals with reading in any but a whole language way. The latter is part and parcel of the former. (For more discussion of these processes, see Chapter 9.) At the same time, the theme study approach also centers on topics of relevance.

Another essential feature of theme study is that all learning is undertaken for a purpose, a purpose that relates to the content to be studied. The form in which the content is clothed is secondary. In other words, children study about oceans because it is important to know about them. The study is not just a thin excuse for teaching children to perfect their recognition of words, spelling, punctuation, and so forth. These skills are indeed learned but not through drill. They are learned because they are identified as necessary tools for achieving another purpose.

As is true of any other school program, theme study takes place within a larger classroom context. If a theme study program is to be successful, a certain kind of learning environment is necessary—one in which teachers recognize that learning is a social activity. People must work together and cooperate for the maximum progress of all concerned. This view is in sharp contrast to the isolation and competition common to so many classrooms.

At D. U. E. S., defining learning as a social activity suggests several things: an accepting learning environment must be provided; children work together and help each other both academically and socially, which means they have to talk and move about; parental involvement is welcomed and encouraged; and close links are maintained with the community, which is used extensively as a resource. In this environment, full efforts are expected on behalf of both oneself and one's classmates.

Guidelines for Planning a Theme Study

Perhaps the idea of theme study will become more vivid and seem more manageable if we now concretely describe the steps involved in planning a theme study, particularly if we root the process in a particular situation. Therefore, let us look at how a theme study is planned at Dalhousie University Elementary School, described in Chapter 1.

At D. U. E. S., theme study involves the entire school for the full academic year. Despite the fact that the particular focus from one age group to the next usually varies in order to meet the needs of different stages of learning development, all the children have numerous opportunities to see the similarities in each other's studies. As a result, children of all ages tend to share information about their theme work when outside on the playground and during lunch hour.

Selecting a Theme

The teacher's first step is to select a theme according to the criteria given in the discussion on definition above. Then we, the teachers, have to do a certain amount of preparation before the school year begins. Working together, we start off by brainstorming potential subtopics, activities, and resources. This is simply a vehicle for eliciting ideas. (More on this below.) Once we have a number of ideas before us, it becomes easier to decide which ones might be appropriate for each group of children. By this means, a tentative framework and schedule are developed.

Identifying Resources

Next, we investigate and organize as many appropriate resources as possible. We try to locate more than we will actually need in order to allow for flexibility during the year. Teachers using the theme study approach tend to become constant watchdogs for applicable teaching/learning materials. The resources generally fall into a number of main categories:

Print Materials

Children's nonfiction is, of course, an excellent source of information for practically any theme. The local public library usually has a good selection of such books written at different levels and offering a wide range of information. These books provide younger children with plenty of excellent illustrations along with short passages of text, which are often in large size print and clearly spaced, making independent reading possible even for beginners. Yet nonfiction is more difficult for children to read than fiction. A story has a definite format, usually pictures, and perhaps dialogue so that if children miss some words, chances are they can still understand the story line. With nonfiction, there aren't as many context cues to help readers, and when they miss a few words, those that follow may not make much sense. Consequently it takes children longer to read nonfiction than fiction.

Nevertheless, when we cannot find books that contain precisely the information needed at the children's reading levels, we turn to adult nonfiction to enable the children to continue their investigations. Such books can be invaluable resources for theme study because they contain so much information. The children can learn things from looking at pictures and diagrams in these books. The teacher can read relevant sections to the children or rewrite the information at a level they can handle by themselves. With such material, extensive discussion is often necessary, but the children can understand and assimilate difficult concepts if enough concrete examples are provided to make the ideas clear.

Including reading material that is somewhat advanced has a number of advantages. To begin with, children learn very quickly that books that are more intimidating, that is, those with denser texts and fewer pictures, actually yield more information. Put another way, children learn that the effort to extract the information may be greater than the effort a simple storybook would demand but that the reward is greater because more can be learned. They also begin to develop reading strategies to handle the more difficult material: they learn to ask pre-reading questions, to skim in order to locate information, and to recognize similar formats. Because theme inquiry necessitates reading for a purpose, it encourages the development of such active reading skills.

Children's fiction can also be a useful resource because such books often contain accurate factual information in addition to the story. Fiction also provides another dimension for the theme study.

Concrete Materials

The use of hands-on materials is absolutely essential when doing theme studies because there is no substitute for the impact that firsthand experience can provide. Thus, we make great use of concrete materials, including both those we can bring into the classroom (for example, to learn how pulleys work, the children experiment with pulleys, ropes, hooks, and weights) and those which require field trips (for example, in studying about living things, a group of children and their teacher might go to the beach, collect whatever living creatures they can find, and bring them back to school where they dissect them or put them in the school aquarium for observation). We think of activities that involve materials other than paper and pencil. We have found that we can teach quite complicated and sophisticated concepts as long as the ideas are applied to some understandable experience or model. Effective use of such materials involves recording the information obtained from the firsthand experience and is often heightened by combining it with reading.

The Community

Since the objective of theme study is to make the world relevant and accessible to children, the community plays an important part. We consult many people as sources of information. Everyone, from family and friends to experts in various fields, is consulted for information and for contacts leading to additional resources. By consulting others, we don't have to limit ourselves to only those topics that we know. Whenever possible, we draw upon the rich resources of the community by inviting people to come to the school and by having the children visit relevant people and places outside the school. If these experiences are to be purposeful, there must be careful preparation in the classroom before the visitor arrives or the visit takes place and plenty of follow-up work to consolidate what was learned. Other frequent community contacts that the children make are phone calls to gather information or to locate difficult-to-find materials and thank-you letters to show appreciation to people who have assisted their learning in some way. Occasionally, when appropriate, the children provide services to the community.

Films

Films provide a good way of making learning concrete. As with adult nonfiction books, we sometimes show films that are at a more difficult level than the children might ordinarily see. Such films, or the relevant parts of them, are thoroughly discussed and then, if necessary, shown a second or even third time to allow the children to become familiar with the concepts. During the showing of the film, or immediately thereafter, the children are expected to make notes about what they have seen.

The Children

The children, of course, are a major resource. Because learning is very much a social activity, we make an effort to discover each child's areas of experience and expertise and to encourage the other children to explore these areas by exchanging information and experiences and by asking each other relevant questions. To supplement their own and each other's ideas, the children also bring in books and concrete materials from home.

The Parents

Active involvement by the parents facilitates the children's learning because when theme topics are discussed at home, the children become even more motivated in their school work. To stimulate such involvement right from the start, we hold a meeting at the beginning of the school year to inform the parents about the theme to be studied and to ask for their help in generating ideas for field trips, books, films, and other interesting resources.

Obviously, finding applicable resources will vary for each theme. For some themes, field trips may provide the best opportunity for learning, supplemented by books, films, and other resources for classroom study. Other themes may rely more heavily on another resource as the primary source of information. Since we repeat themes every four years, the search for useful resources becomes an ongoing activity with films, books, and field trip ideas being added to growing files of references and materials. If these files are kept up, preparing for a theme study becomes less time consuming and more effective.

Finishing Touches

After identifying relevant resources, we continue our advance preparations by doing a bit of studying to familiarize ourselves with the content of the theme and the subtopics to be studied with the children. During the year, of course, we are bound to increase our knowledge along with the children, which has the added benefit of providing an opportunity for the children to see adults as learners and not just dispensers of knowledge.

By this time, we have integrated the information we have gathered and have narrowed down our planning. We have a good idea of the reading materials available; we have a list of possible field trips we can take; and we have some ideas for classroom activities. Now we can plan a tentative lesson sequence and the first day of school.

The beginning activities are crucial. We don't want to overwhelm the children with too much at once. On the other hand, we want to use introductory activities that will be broad enough in scope to give us a good idea of the children's interests and present knowledge about the topic. This initial assessment is important, not only because we are concerned that the curriculum be relevant to the children, but also because it gives us indications of how and where they can contribute to the curriculum. Children come to school at age five with efficient learning strategies, and therefore they can and should share in decision making about their learning.

This is not to say that our classes are free-for-alls with children doing whatever they want. On the contrary, our days are structured, and the children are expected to complete their work on time. If they have wasted class time, they must use part of the recess or lunch period for work. However, we don't plan our days to the "nth" degree because it is important that the children influence what happens. Their suggestions for activities are not only acknowledged as valid; they are acted upon.

The final step in the preparations is to consider and plan ahead for children with special needs.

The steps in teacher preparation outlined above can actually be described as the steps that anybody takes when solving a problem. First one thinks of a number of ideas. Then one begins researching the ideas to see which ones hold water and whether new ideas emerge. One then consolidates what one has learned and, depending on how satisfactory that is, one may consider the problem solved or may choose to go back to do more research.

This sequence also describes the learning process that the children will go through as they work on the theme. They, too, with the guidance of their teachers, will consider various ways to research a topic. Then they will proceed to gather information through activities, reading, and writing. Assembling what they have learned into coherent patterns and applying this knowledge to some specific purpose will follow next. At this point, they go beyond what we do in our preparation. The final step, presenting the results of their inquiry, will take place at an open house at which time the children will display, explain, and demonstrate the fruits of their labor to parents, brothers and sisters, friends, and other guests.

These four steps—planning, gathering information, integrating and applying what has been learned, and presenting—constitute the pattern we follow for all theme studies.

Guidelines for Implementing a Theme Study

Brainstorming

Like the teachers, the children initially become involved with the theme study through brainstorms, which are basically recorded discussions about a certain topic. These discussions have a particularly important feature, namely, no ideas or suggestions are rejected. One purpose of brainstorming is to help focus thinking on the topic, highlighting as many details as possible. Brainstorms serve a number of other useful purposes as well. They are good indicators of the children's knowledge of a topic. Teachers need to be aware of this if the new learning is to be rooted in the children's previous knowledge. Brainstorms can also help teachers identify the areas of greatest interest both to individuals and to the group, and this, in turn, helps teachers make maximum use of the children's motivation.

There are social benefits to brainstorms as well. Because participation is encouraged from everyone, no one need fear that his or her ideas will be considered wrong or of no value. All the children come to realize that they can contribute and are expected to do so. They also learn that their classmates have an equally important voice. Of course, respect for other people's opinions has to be encouraged from the beginning, but once children feel the respect of their peers, they recognize the value of returning that respect. We help them to understand, through direct experience, that working in a group or with a partner is a productive way to learn, that cooperative efforts produce many positive results. The finished brainstorm, with all contributions from the group recorded, is visible proof that cooperation is efficient and worthwhile.

Used at the beginning of a theme study, brainstorming helps the teachers and the children decide the direction for immediate study. Once this direction has been determined, the teachers can choose from among the resources they have already gathered, and the theme study can begin. However, brainstorms are used not only at the beginning of a theme study. As will soon be evident, the children brainstorm whenever there is a need to generate and categorize a broad range of ideas. Brainstorming is also an effective means of summarizing at the end of a theme study because it provides a review of the information and ideas as well as how they are organized, and it demonstrates in graphic form the growth of the children's knowledge and overall progress.

Brainstorming can be approached through a discussion in which children explore as many dimensions of a topic as possible by contributing all ideas and information they think relevant. The initial form of the brainstorm is a free-flowing diagram. This diagram is simply a matter of expediency—when ideas are coming fast and furiously, there isn't time to list them in neat columns. Remember, at this point, the purpose is to record all ideas and suggestions without question. When necessary, the teacher acts as secretary for these discussions, writing everyone's suggestions on the board. A brainstorm can be recorded using a simple wheel format with the topic in the middle and the information around it like the spokes of a wheel. This wheel-shaped brainstorm can become more complex by grouping related ideas together around the circle and labeling or categorizing them under headings.

During brainstorming sessions, the children always work either in a large group,

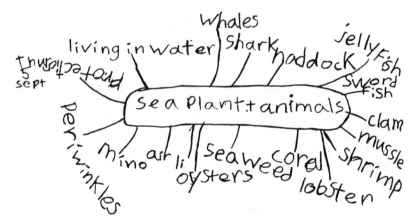

Example of a Simple Brainstorm
Age 8

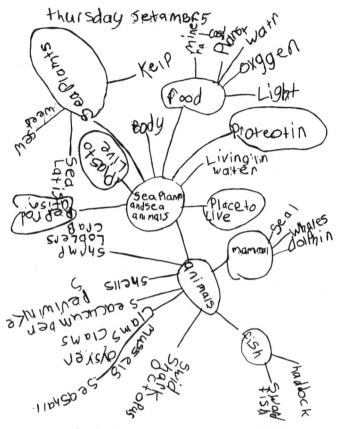

Example of a Brainstorm Grouping Related Ideas
Age 8

a small group, or with a partner. The older children, who have considerable experience with this activity, can record while information is being generated. Sometimes children work together in pairs and then bring the results of their brainstorms to the whole group where a large, composite brainstorm is then made. At other times, they work in pairs after a group brainstorm to further elaborate and record the ideas.

Whenever children do brainstorms, it is most important that they realize that their only concerns should be generating and recording ideas. By necessity, this means that neatness and accurate spelling are not priorities. When children don't know how to spell words, they are encouraged to write them down as best they can by sounding them out and by trying to remember whatever spelling rules they may have learned. However, they are responsible for being able to read their own work, because they will need their notes for other related tasks. Editing for spelling will occur at later points in the theme study.

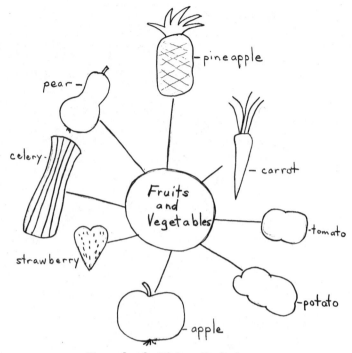

Example of a Picture Brainstorm

Another way to record brainstorm ideas with young children is to use pictures rather than words. This makes the record more accessible. Sometimes it is more appropriate to use pictures even with older children. For example, during a theme study on anatomy, a brainstorm about bones was best recorded by having each child draw a lifesize outline of the body and diagrams of all the bones in the body as each child visualized them.

Once the first set of brainstorms has been completed, the theme study is under way. The teachers, having chosen the initial directions their groups will travel, select from among the resources gathered (the books, films, concrete materials, field trips, etc.), and the whole school sets out to explore their topics. This exploration involves an approach to study that all the children are expected to learn and that consists of two main features, namely, working together with others, and organizing and recording information.

Grouping the Children

Recognizing that intellectual growth is fostered when the social, interdependent nature of learning is integral to the learning milieu, we structure learning activities to encourage optimal interaction. Because most work is done with a partner or in a small group and because learning requires that students articulate their thoughts, it is necessary for children to talk a great deal about what they are learning. It takes time and support for children to develop the social skills necessary to work efficiently with others. This means that some school time must be allotted to promoting successful working relationships. Such a process is facilitated through discussions and demonstrations and by working through each step with socially unskilled children.

After some experience and discussion about choosing partners, children can usually make appropriate choices themselves. However, with some children, it is necessary for the teacher to designate a partner and provide additional support. Sometimes this is due to academic difficulties in which case the teacher will pair up a fluent reader and writer with a less fluent one. In this way, the fluent child will provide continual support and reinforcement of fluent reading and writing strategies. There may also be difficulties with socially unskilled or unmotivated children that again require a careful choice of partners. Developing productive relationships is possible only in a noncompetitive environment in which the children encourage each other's efforts.

Organizing and Recording Information

The children must be able to actively make the information they encounter meaningful to themselves. The availability of resources does not guarantee that learning will automatically take place. Nor does it suffice for a teacher simply to present information or resources to children. They must learn to find, organize, and record information themselves. At the Dalhousie University Elementary School, the children regularly use several methods such as the following for just that purpose.

Brainstorms

New ideas must be integrated into a person's previous knowledge. Children need to develop a broad understanding of the world around them. They need to get a sense of the whole rather than being limited to the smaller pieces. While at the earlier stages, brainstorms serve to get out as many ideas as possible and give children a starting place to categorize them, at this point, they provide an overall picture of the whole as well as the parts and how the parts relate to the whole and to each other. As graphic representations, brainstorms make it relatively easy for children to grasp these relationships. As was mentioned earlier, the brainstorm format is flexible in that it can be used at any point in the theme study to help children develop a broader perspective.

Questions

In conjunction with brainstorms, during which children identify what they know, it is useful to develop lists of questions of things they do not know. Asking good questions is a skill that improves with experience and knowledge. At first, when children try to think of questions about an unfamiliar topic, their questions are very superficial, but as their knowledge of the topic increases, the quality and depth of the questions also improve. When children are encouraged to ask questions continually, their questions become more detailed and more focused.

Since ideas generate ideas, formulating questions with a partner is an effective activity. The constant exchange of ideas helps not only to generate an increasing number of questions, but also to model good questioning for those children who tend to ask superficial or irrelevant questions. While the older children can work with their partners in this activity, the five and six-year-olds need to work as a whole group with their teacher. They identify information that pertains to one of the questions and discuss the answers while the teacher does the recording. As they become more capable, they gradually develop a measure of independence in using the methods that have become familiar through the modeling of their teacher.

Once a list of questions has been created, the teacher can introduce resources that might answer some of them. However, not all questions need to be answered. Some are not important enough to merit a lot of time while others are too difficult to answer for any number of reasons. If children are used to being given an answer for every question that is asked, they may find it a little unnerving when some questions go unanswered. In time, however, they learn to accept the fact that not all questions are of equal importance, that good questions are not always easily answered, and that some questions have no known answer while others have more than one. If children at an early age learn to view the world as a fascinating but complicated place, they are capable of studying topics of great depth and complexity.

Charts

As they add to their knowledge, children need to be able to identify important points and ignore less relevant ones, to discriminate. They also need to know how to organize their ideas so that they are usable. One effective method of accomplishing these two objectives is to make charts.

Before trying to make and use charts by themselves, children need to see demonstrations of the process. While the group supplies ideas, the teacher writes them in a chart. The children must think about what is relevant to add and where in the chart it should be placed. Some excellent discussions and problem solving occur when certain information can be put in more than one spot or is important but cannot be placed in the chart as it stands. Perhaps a new category or question must be added. As the children gain experience with charts, they begin to do this work with their partners. This activity helps to keep the thinking focused on the information and ideas and provides support when dealing with difficult concepts.

A simple chart may be organized by listing children's questions about a topic down the left side of a page and by leaving enough space on the right for answers.

This type of chart may look like the example below. In this particular case, the children were also asked to record the titles of the books in which they found the answers. A variety of nonfiction materials with a wide range of reading levels had been made available, and by noting the titles, the children would have a record of their sources for possible future reference. They could also compare which books gave the best information for certain kinds of questions as well as which ones were easiest for them to read. Through this type of activity, children not only learn about the topic but also about how and where to find information independently.

When the children have become more adept at working with charts, a more sophisticated type of chart using categories can be introduced. Since the children

Question	Answer	Book
1) What makes the back move?	CRKDLiG (cartilage)	
2) What do the bones in the feet look like?	iT* LöKSi LiK a had (It looks like a hand)	
3) How many bones are in a finger?	4	
4) How many bones are in your body?	260	Granada Guides Human body
5) Do bones bend?	yes	the skeletal and Movement
6) How do bones break? Can they mend? How?	tnaps dld (traps blood)	
7) How do bones stay together?	BY liGAmenTz (by ligaments)	the Skeleton and Movent
8) How many parts are in your head?	8	Thi2 12 Your Body
9) Is there a bone in the nose?	Yes	0
10) Can bones grow? How do they grow?	NO	0
11) What is a bone made of?	MaCo an bcinjd (marrow and calcium)	
12) What do bones do?	TheA CeP YOU CADING-UP	secrers of the human body

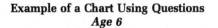
(They keep you standing up)

Example of a Chart Using Questions
Age 6

have been learning how to categorize and group ideas during the brainstorms, the same categories can be used to provide an excellent starting place for further study of the topic. An example of a chart using categories derived from a brainstorm is shown below. As in the question chart, the categories are listed down the left side of the page, leaving room for information to be written beside them.

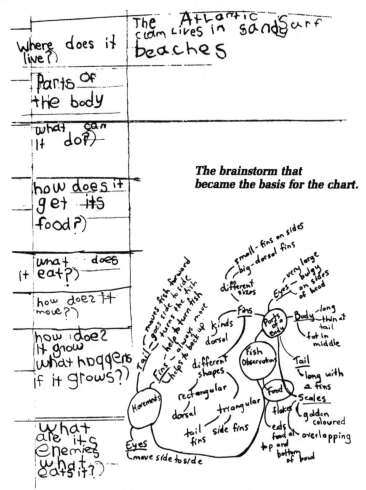

The Atlantic clam lives in sandy surf beaches

Where does it live?)

Parts of the body

what can it do?)

The brainstorm that became the basis for the chart.

how does it get its food?)

what does it eat?)

how does it move?)

how does it grow what happens if it grows?)

what are its enemies what eats it?)

Example of a Chart Using Categories Derived from a Brainstorm
Age 6

Eventually, when they have gained enough experience, children can create charts that compare sources of information. This is done by finding information about the same categories using different sources. Such a chart helps children compare the merits of certain sources of information. It can also present some interesting situations when contradictory facts have been uncovered.

(The rafter is solid and holds, the ridge pole. The ridge pole is attached to the wood.)

	Book 1	Book 2	
sofety (safety)	The rafter a salD anD hlaD. anD The ridgepole is dltchd To The wood	If Thir are lit cracks They stu fed with mud	(If there are little cracks, they are stuffed with mud.)
whaT is spacies (What is special?)	The house is worm (The house is warm.)	They stack rock up Jesias The walls, so it will be w	(They stack rocks up beside the walls so it will be warm.)
wdomnis (Warmness)	They piant flowers on The roof and it mikes it warm (They paint flowers on the roof and it makes it warm.)	if Thir are liTl crack worm They stuffed with w	(If there are little cracks, they stuffed it to be warm.)
NhaT is The house maDe of?	saiins pesis of erra anD Gno flawrs bricks woDd srone (Solid pieces of earth and ground, flowers, bricks, wood, store.)	wood – earTh flowers bricks - stones Sod weeds vine	(Wood, earth, flowers, bricks, stones, mud, sod, weeds, vines)
is it harD To DiiD (Is it hard to build?)	yes Becas you have to make up so mrxie blks (Yes, because you have to make up so many blocks)	no becaUse ail you have to Db is stack The bloog up.	(No, because all you have to do is stack the blocks up.)
how is The house maDe	Logs are spit to made for the loof and if lhir ore not Tres Then sos (Logs are split to make for the roof, and if there are no trees, then sod.)	They stack The wood up anD cut aslant and so iTD will fitt To GaThr	(They stack the wood up and cut a slant and so it will fit together.)
whele is The house	Ireland	Woods	
whaT Are The problems	Gross is hot cood for a fouse	There isent much Trees	(There isn't much trees.)
benifats (Benefits)	Grass anD rooTas make a Good tous if you use it (Grass and roots make a good house if you use it.)	Grass us. To male Good siDing mitrd ouT aT saw in	(Grass used to make good building material, but put straw in.)

Example of a Chart on Sod Houses That Compares Sources of Information
Age 6

No matter what kind of chart is used, children should be encouraged and helped to turn to any resource that will assist them in completing the chart. All of the resources mentioned earlier qualify: books, films, concrete materials, and field trips. All are legitimate and useful sources of information. If the reading level of a print resource is too difficult, it can always be read chorally with a teacher or another child who is a more fluent reader.

Whenever a chart is developed, room should be left at the end for any additional categories that might emerge later. Other than that, there are no set rules for developing charts. Variations, both in organization and use, emerge depending upon the theme and the children who are studying it. Regardless of the forms they take, one of the greatest benefits of using charts is that children can see at a glance which areas have been researched and which remain to be done.

Drawings

Many themes provide ample opportunity for using concrete materials as resources either in the classroom or on field trips. Sometimes the simplest and most complete way of recording information gleaned from concrete materials is through labeled drawings and other illustrations. With young children who are not yet writing fluently, these are a particularly effective means of recording information. Attempting to draw something as realistically as possible helps children of all ages pay attention to the details of what they see, and helps them learn to be thorough and precise. Careful labeling reinforces these habits while increasing the amount of information in the drawing.

Synthesizing and Presenting What Was Learned

This pattern of using brainstorming and questioning as techniques for identifying what to explore, then turning to a range of resources for information and ideas, and finally organizing and recording the information using the formats described is repeated over and over again. But a theme study does not end by simply stopping. The final stage of a theme study at D. U. E. S. consists of synthesizing and presenting what was learned.

Children are curious and motivated to learn if they see a purpose for the learning. Of course, the most fundamental motivator is interest in the topic under consideration. In addition to this intrinsic goal, our children have another goal in the form of open houses or fairs which are open to the public. Twice a year, the children display and present the results of their theme work at these open houses. In preparation for an open house, the children's work proceeds through the following steps.

Review and Synthesis

The information and ideas that the children have been gathering, developing, and organizing from a variety of sources throughout the term need to be reviewed to be sure that everyone understands them and knows why we did what we did. This will not be accomplished by the mere repetition of work already studied. At this stage, information and ideas must be pulled together into a coherent form; synthesis is called for. Accordingly, what was studied must appear in forms that are different from the ways in which the children have already recorded it. So, for example, charts may be rewritten as books or posters. In order to rewrite information and ideas in another way, children need to really understand what they have learned.

An excellent catalyst for synthesizing is, again, the brainstorm. Because children have been investigating smaller areas within the theme study, they now need to discuss the topic as a whole in order to understand how the smaller pieces fit into the overall framework of the theme. It is extremely helpful for children to brainstorm at this point because it consolidates their understanding of the relationships between ideas, and at the same time, shows the children how much they have learned.

Once they have gained a larger idea of the topic, the children can begin to rewrite the information and ideas from the charts into the format they think best conveys to others what they have learned. With the help of the teacher, the group chooses a way of presenting the information from a range of possibilities (books, audio cassettes, posters, games, models). Using the new format, the children need to consider the most sensible order of presenting the categories, which often conveniently lend themselves to rewriting as chapters of a book, paragraphs of a report, parts of a poster, or sets of game cards.

Preparing Written Work

Rough draft.   The children write all the time. Previously, they always recorded their findings, whether from field trips, experiments, readings, or other activities. Now they must rework the material into new formats. In both cases, when they first set pencil to paper, they know that neatness and accuracy in spelling and punctuation are not expected right away. They begin with a rough draft; the objective is simply to get ideas on paper.

Revising and rewriting.   Once the children have established what it is they are trying to say, they go back and check to see how successful they have been by reading it to a partner or a teacher. Does it make sense? Is it clear? Is it complete, or are there gaps? These are the main concerns at this stage. Not only must the writers be willing to accept the ideas of others, but the others must learn to provide helpful comments that are not overly critical. These skills are frequently used by the partners in their theme work, but the children still need time and teacher support to refine them.

The rough draft will probably be revised more than once as the work progresses. Learning to revise involves a number of developments. At first, the children are reluctant to change anything except to add something at the end. Then they move on to the insertion of words and sentences and then deletions. Next, they learn to reorganize what they have written. These developments come with experience and needless to say, do not happen all at once; they develop gradually over time.

Editing.   Once the ideas are clear, the children go back over their rough copies to correct their spelling and punctuation. We consider these corrections to be the finishing details in the writing process. To do this work, the children themselves determine which words they think are incorrectly spelled and what punctuation marks are required and where they are to be placed. The children are then guided in the use of appropriate resources for making the necessary changes. For example, to correct their spelling they may use their original sources of information, ask a friend, ask the teacher, or use a dictionary. By being responsible for identifying the problems and making the changes themselves, the children learn about

> If a storm cumes [comes] the raf [rough]
> wahs will take bits off the
> islind . and The wavs keep
> braking off the coast and after
> yers it makes a hole.and
>   The hole makes a
> crak all the way   to the
> top of the rock. and The top falls off and
> in the waves the rocks rub toger
>   thanks to
> and the rock gets smoother and smaller
> see erosion. There are dunes.
> hanging is called) because we have erosion
> we have sand and dunes.

Example of Revised and Edited Rough Copy
Age 7

correct language usage through application rather than merely imitating the teacher's examples or drilling on words and rules isolated from applied language.

With this process, the final result is usually not perfect; errors are often overlooked by the children. The teacher must use discretion in striking a balance between bringing these oversights to the children's attention and waiting until a later stage in their writing development.

Neat copy.   Now the written work is ready to be made into a neat copy. At this point, attention is paid to letter formation, word spacing, and general neatness. The fact that the work will be on public display provides great motivation for the children to put forth their best efforts.

> If a storm comes The rough waves
> will Take bits off The island. The waves
> keep braking off The coast. After years
> it makes a   hole. The hole makes a
> crak all the way To The top of The
> rock. The top falls of into The
> water and in The waves The Rocks
> rub Together and The rock gets
> smoother and smaller. All This changing
> is called erosion because we have
> erosion we have sand and dunes.

Example of Neat Copy Ready for Presentation

Preparing Displays

A similar process to that for written work takes place in the production of art work for the final presentation of the theme study. First ideas are generated and discussed. Then the most appropriate ones are tried out in rough draft form. The children are encouraged to exchange their knowledge of art techniques. After hearing each other's opinions and the opinions of the teacher, the children make changes and produce the final copy. As with writing, the final product may have to be done more than once before a quality commensurate with the children's abilities is achieved. In the end, the children are proud of their accomplishments.

The Fair—Speeches, Demonstrations, and Guided Tours

Along with the finished displays at the fair, the children bring their study to life by giving speeches and demonstrations, and making short presentations to the visitors. By such means, the children serve as guides indicating the important points about their displays. Because of the children's involvement in producing the displays and their knowledge of the information underlying the displays, even those who are very shy are able to take part in these activities, at least on a small scale. The presentations are carefully planned and rehearsed in advance with everyone helping by providing suggestions for improvements in content, diction, and volume.

By the time everything is ready, the children are eager to publicly present their knowledge about the theme. It has been a long process from the first brainstorms to the completion of the final displays and presentations, and the children can be counted on to give it their all.

What Is Accomplished?

Essentially, the theme study approach is guided research. The children learn how to research topics of interest. In the process of doing so, they are also learning a host of skills. They are not only learning how to read and write but, in addition, are discovering that reading and writing are useful, rewarding, and enjoyable. They are learning a great deal about social studies, science, and math. They are improving their skills as artists. They are becoming more attentive and discerning listeners and more articulate in expressing themselves as speakers and writers. They are learning to use what they know as a foundation upon which to build new learning.

To a considerable extent, the children control their own learning. Through the theme study approach, children learn not only a great deal about the theme itself, but also how to be active participants in their learning, how to plan and organize their study, how to collect and record information and ideas, how to compare them and find relationships among them, and how to synthesize and present new learnings and insights. But none of this happens without extensive and varied practice in analyzing and questioning—in other words, *thinking*. This is the single most important outcome of the theme study approach. The children are engaged in what they are doing in a thoughtful way. They are not passively following someone else's instructions. Instead, they are required to consider alternatives and make their own decisions based on reasons they can explain and justify. They are learning to become independent and critical thinkers.

Yet another set of learnings can be identified. The theme studies teacher is removed from the center stage and replaced by the children, but not in a way that fosters mere whimsy and self-indulgence. Everyone is expected to behave responsibly and cooperatively. These expectations are recognized by the children as valuable and necessary. Consequently, the class functions as a collectivity whose members, individually and as a group, have academic and social needs that are to be acknowledged and respected. The program is geared to channeling and fulfilling these needs. When, in the process of doing this, there is a conflict with administrative convenience, it is the latter that yields. By functioning as a collectivity with common problems to solve, the children learn to cooperate with each other and their teachers. The children learn that they can be useful and contributing members of a group; this, in turn, helps them develop confidence in themselves as learners and decision makers. Armed with self-confidence, a sense of responsibility, and the ability to cooperate, they have the prerequisites to expand their interests and embrace learning.

Lastly, we have discovered a special bonus that goes with using the theme study approach. As teachers who do theme studies, we cannot shy away from the unfamiliar but, instead, must plunge in and explore the unknown. In so doing, we study themes *with* the children. As a result, we too learn far more than we would if we were searching for "right answers" in stilted and contrived textbooks.

III

LARGE-SCALE
THEME STUDIES

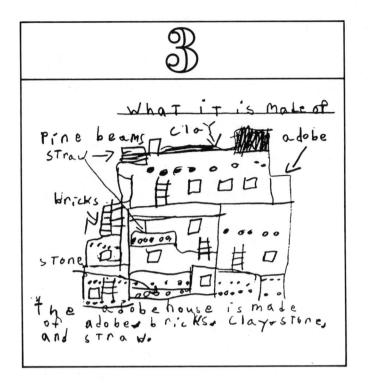

Around the World in Sixty Days: A Theme Study about Houses with the Middles (Ages Six to Eight)

As visitors entered the room on this open house occasion, they saw tables displaying models of different kinds of houses. Sod blocks were carefully balanced against a drinking-straw frame to represent a sod house, plasticene blocks were fitted snugly to form a pueblo adobe house, and there were igloos and African adobe houses also made of neatly formed plasticene blocks. These carefully displayed houses were surrounded by posters, books, and games offering explanations about each of them—the construction methods used; materials required; difficulties of construction; and information about the land and the people who build and use them.

What the visitors noticed most were the enthusiastic guides proudly and knowledgeably displaying their work and expertise, for these guides were only six, seven, and eight years old. The tables they staffed were hubs of activity—books being read, games being played, and countless questions being asked and answered.

How do children of this age gain the skills and confidence required to read, write, build models, design games, display their work, and publicly answer questions? Let us take a look at the theme study that generated so much constructive activity.

Choosing the Theme

In the fall term, the children had been involved in learning how to construct a building as well as actually building a seven-by-five-foot playhouse for the playground. (For an account of this theme study, see Chapter 5.) When thinking about the possibilities of developing this theme further during the second term, I considered a number of factors. The theme should build on the knowledge and experience gained from constructing the playhouse. It should be of real interest to children of this age, and it should be of importance in the real world. In addition, because time to find information from print had been somewhat limited during the fall, the next part of the theme study should provide plenty of opportunity for the group to read about the topic independently. Consequently, finding resources at appropriate reading levels would be essential. Taking all of these factors into consideration, I chose "Houses Around the World" as the topic.

Teacher Planning

As soon as I had chosen the topic, I searched through two of the most reliable teacher resources, the library and the film catalog. Since we obviously could not travel to see housing in other parts of the world, and there was no museum nearby that dealt with this topic, I concluded that the library and the film catalog would contain the most concrete and interesting resources to spark the children's curiosity.

I found that both the children's and the adults' nonfiction sections of the library, as usual, contained a gold mine of information at a wide range of reading levels and with plenty of big, beautiful, color pictures. Finding good films was more problematic. Many of them were about aspects of life other than housing, and most were on a relatively mature level. I chose a few of the more accessible and direct films and made note of some of the others. If the children were really interested, I could use some of the more difficult films and make them understandable by showing them repeatedly with lots of discussion, or by showing only certain selected parts. In any event, the children's interests would eventually determine which films were most appropriate.

With some idea about the direction that the theme might take (after all, by now I knew the children well and had some idea about what kinds of subtopics would likely interest them), I did brainstorms by myself about a number of questions. What other resources might be available? Whom did I know who had some expertise or experience that the children or I could use? How could the theme be introduced so that it would make the most sense and be of real interest? What kinds of activities might we undertake in the course of the theme study? With some ideas in mind, I now felt prepared and enthusiastic. Nevertheless, I would still need to be flexible in order to adapt to the actual shape the theme would eventually take.

The Children Get Started: Brainstorming and Categorizing

The children had not done much systematic comparison of ideas when we were building the playhouse. I needed to give this sort of activity immediate attention because it is a necessary tool for understanding and organizing new information. Discovering how to compare and organize ideas about housing around the world seemed like an obvious place for the group to begin.

To do this, the children first had to generate what they already knew about housing. Working as a group, they brainstormed everything they knew about houses around the world. As the ideas were given, I wrote them down using a circle brainstorm. At the same time, we organized the ideas as I asked the group questions such as, "Where should we put this new idea? Does it belong with any others we already have? Can we give this group of ideas a label or category name?" To help the children see the difference between the categories, I wrote each one down with a different-colored marker. It took a great deal of discussion before each group of ideas was categorized and labeled, but patience proved to be worthwhile because the activity demonstrated the usefulness and process of organizing. The resultant brainstorm is shown below.

If a teacher is genuinely interested and the topic is of real importance, it is usually easy to motivate young children, especially if they are encouraged to contribute what they know right from the start. The children's early interest in the topic was spurred by the shelves of library books with their gorgeous pictures of faraway places and exotic-looking houses and by the films about very different kinds of houses.

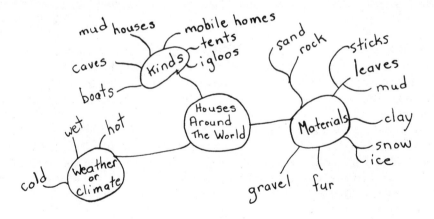

Brainstorm about Houses Around the World

The first film was *Dahomey* (Children of the World Series. Directed by Denis Hargrave. 28 min. 13 sec., color, available through the National Film Board of Canada). It shows life in a small community in an African country where people live in houses built on stilts high above a lagoon. To aid subsequent recall for our later discussion, the children wrote down a few words about the things that impressed them as they watched the film.* Because many of the children had never considered the possibility of such houses, this film aroused their curiosity. The discussion that followed attested to the amount the children had learned about construction during the fall term. They wanted to know how the foundation could consist of only stilts and how the poles were attached to the frame. The film also stimulated interesting discussions about the Third World and about living conditions different from their own. I recorded all comments and ideas, again using a circle brainstorm and colored markers to differentiate categories. Although the children still found it difficult to determine categories, the activity was becoming a challenge to them. How many categories and different colors of markers could they use? Could they think of a category name?

The next film they saw was *Sami Herders* (Directed by Hubert Schuurman. 27 min. 50 sec., color, available from the National Film Board of Canada), which documents the life of a nomadic family that herds reindeer on the northern coast of Norway. The children again wrote notes during the film, and used a circle brainstorm to record the ideas from the discussion that followed. The children became even more interested when they began to see how vastly different the housing needs of people in different parts of the world were.

With these film experiences to draw upon, we began to compare ideas about the two types of houses they had depicted in the circle brainstorms. Using a chart, I asked the children what was the same about the types of houses and what was different about them. As the children offered their ideas, I encouraged them to consider what a suitable category might be and recorded all their suggestions in the appropriate places. By the end of the discussion, the chart looked like the one on page 37.

Next we developed an expanded chart incorporating these categories and adding others. The purpose was to enable us to compare many kinds of houses around the world. Although it took almost two weeks of discussions to generate the categories, the result was a usable format, which the children felt proud of and understood.

Thus, from our simple brainstorm, we had successfully transferred our ideas to an easy-to-use chart. This working out of ideas in two different formats was an important step in developing the children's thinking because ideas are not useful unless they are clearly organized and lend themselves to comparison. We were now ready to gather more information about different types of housing.

---

* This early practice in note taking is further developed by the older children. See pages 58–59 for more on this.

	Same	Different
How the house is made	The houses have wooden frames.	Vines are used as nails to keep the wood for the houses together in Dahomey.
Weather Conditions		In Dahomey they dress in shorts and shirts because it is so hot there. The Samis have heavy clothes because it is so cold.
What the house is made of (materials)	They both use materials which are easy for them to get.	The Sami make their tents out of skins. In Dahomey they use poles and hay.
Good things about the house (benefits)	Both houses kept the people dry and comfortable.	The tents were easy to move and the stilts kept the houses from getting wet.
Where the house is		The tents were in Norway and the stilt houses in Dahomey.

Gathering and Recording Information

To begin this next phase of our work, the children, as a group, were to read information from a text, which we would then record on the large chart we had prepared. Because this activity was difficult, I assisted them. I chose part of a book called *Simple Shelters*, by Lee Pennock Huntington (New York: Coward, McCann and Geoghegan, 1979) that described some stilt houses in New Guinea that were similar to the stilt houses of Dahomey. Being able to bring some of their previously acquired knowledge to the new book helped the children focus on the meaning. Because of the difficulty of the reading level, we read it together, slowly and aloud in choral fashion, stopping frequently to discuss and clarify the meaning.

Because it is crucial that children take an active part in their own learning, they are expected, right from the start, to help supply sources of information (books, films, articles, pictures, and artifacts) and to discuss what we are studying. Because children should be thinking all the time, I repeatedly asked questions such as, "What do you think that means?" "Does it make sense?" and "Do you agree with these ideas?"

In this way, we read through the whole text together. Then we reread it slowly and stopped whenever someone thought that something we had read could be included in one of the categories on our chart. When this happened, I recorded the information on the chart and asked the children how it might be worded and how to print it so that it would fit into the box on the chart. I also mentioned letter size and formation and word spacing.

After a few examples, I paired off the children to continue this work in their own books. Whenever the reading and writing were difficult, I chose the partners to ensure that problem readers were paired with more fluent readers so that the children's experiences with reading factual text for information would be focused and successful.

Teamwork*

The children almost always work in pairs or small groups rather than alone. Teamwork emphasizes that learning is a social activity and that two or three working well together can produce more satisfying results than one working alone. What one doesn't know, the others may be able to supply. By working together, the children demonstrate skills for each other. It is a more secure way to learn. Working with the support of another, children are more likely to take risks and to try something when they are not sure what the result will be.

Initially, the teachers decide on the teams. We may group children in order to balance strengths and weaknesses or for social reasons. Eventually the children choose their own partners. They soon learn whom they can work with and whom they can't. At the same time, we talk about what it means to be a good partner and how to cooperate with each other so that all benefit. When there are problems, the children usually work it out for themselves. Living up to the expectations of peers can be strong motivation for children to change their behavior. We intervene only when a quarrel erupts or if someone is wasting too much time.

The children copied the chart and then began to read the text with their partners, inserting further information into the chart. For those whose reading levels were significantly lower than the text, I had rewritten and typed the main ideas into simpler language and had duplicated the sheets. These rewritten materials, however, did not have the pictures attached. The lack of pictures, surprisingly, boosted their popularity because the children who were using these materials thought them significantly harder than the ones with pictures! When reading difficulties, with either version of the text, occurred and could not be overcome by asking a partner or other children, I assisted by chorally reading the difficult section with the child having the difficulty.

The results of this work, which took two days to complete, were varied. Some children understood the idea of using a chart right away, while others were bogged down by all the decisions that had to be made concerning reading, writing, thinking, and getting along with a partner. I accepted the results positively no matter

---

* Descriptions of procedures of general relevance for conducting theme studies are set apart as shown here so as not to interfere with the chronology.

what is special about This house ?	New Guinea stilt house It rains hile avre Day Thay nevr ran out of waor (It rains here every day. They never run out of water.)
whaT is This house made of	Stiks LOgs BaBo stra rats (sticks. logs, bamboo, straw. rafters)
where is The hoys	new Guineg is a laind norTH of asralya (New Guinea is an island north of -Australia.
Problems with The house	Thir IS LOS OF in Saks (There is lots of insects.)
Benefits of This house. (They live near a stream so tney can go fishing every day. They have string baas. (to keep out insects))	They LiVe nir a strem so.They can Go fishing evry Day Thoy have sfing Bags

Chart Using Categories
Age 6

how little work had actually been accomplished providing that effort had been applied.

The children and I discussed the two days of activities. What had caused problems? How had solutions been worked out? Had any new categories been added? Did some information belong in more than one category? What had the children done in such a situation? Who wanted to show and read their charts?

Since the school is noncompetitive and no marks or grades rank children against each other, it is possible for them to show and discuss their work with very little putting down of each other. Nevertheless, even under these favorable circumstances, it sometimes takes much discussion to reduce some children's desires to negate the efforts of others. By and large, however, the children were proud of their accomplishments and interested in what the others had done.

The activities described above were only the beginning of the children's experience using charts. Because the children had been fascinated with the nomadic reindeer-herders they had seen in the film, *Sami Herders*, a reading selection was chosen that built on their interest and the knowledge gained from the film. It was about the shelters (in this case tents) of another nomadic people, the Bedouin, from a book called *Houses and Homes*, by Carol Bowyer (London: Usborne, 1978). We chorally read the passage and then slowly reread and discussed it. Meanwhile I recorded the children's ideas on the chart, which contained the same categories as before, and then asked them to continue this activity with a partner. I had again prepared a simplified version of the text without pictures that I distributed to those who needed one.

Once again the children copied the chart, but this time I asked that they do it on a left-hand page so that it could be extended to cover two pages later. As they worked, I commented on their improvements in using this process. The class discussion that followed showed that, indeed, both their competence and their confidence were growing.

The children were ready for the next, slightly more difficult step—comparing sources of information. I gave them a second article to read about the Bedouins. "Houses of Hair," taken from *Bedouins*, by Fidelity Lancaster (New York: Gloucester, 1978) was written at an even more difficult level and contained more detailed information. We read it together slowly, and after the rereading, discussed it. This time I demonstrated how the new information could be fit into the chart we had already completed about the Bedouins by extending the lines and, using the existing categories on the left, by placing the new information next to the information already recorded. In this way, we could compare information in the same category from two different books.

Due to the difficulty of the reading level of this text, we worked in one large group, with tables pushed together, rereading bits of the text and writing down the ideas. Although this work went slowly, the children still noticed the differences between this text and the one they had already finished. They made comments about how much harder this book was but also about how much more informative and interesting it was. From their playhouse construction days, the children had learned to appreciate the value of detailed information.

Independent Projects

The children were buoyed by their success with what to them were very sophisticated charts. To encourage this enthusiasm, I introduced the idea of individual projects. I explained that each group of two children would select a housing structure that appealed to them and investigate it on their own. The idea of choosing an independent project topic gave another shot of adrenalin to the work efforts at hand.

Houses and Homes

		The Bedouins
WhaT is speciəl about this house	It can come abart so they can move it.	in samr tent siDs can rise and wintr The siDs are Dwn (In summer the tent sides can rise and winter the sides are down)
whoT is The house made of	Clorh and anaml skins . (cloth and animal skins)	It is made of Gots har onD Gots har. onD wovin in to strips (It is made of goat's hair and (camel) hair and woven into strips)
how is The house maDe	Well frst you Ty The cloth To Gothr with vines ano Then you Tly The cloths ano ano stis to Gothr To The Poles	They weu anD sow log strips anD 8 ar 10 strips arewivin in To The rof (They weave and sew long strips and 8 or 10 strips are woven into the roof.)
wiere is The house	in all cihds of Disers (In all kinds of deserts)	
house safeTy	Thir are las of Poles To make it steaDy. (There are all kinds of poles to make it sturdy)	The Gots hir is Baor Be cas camol har is not waor Prof anD Gots har is (The goat's hair is better because camel hair is not waterproof and gots hair is.)
are There any Probiems with This hous	Thir are all cins of Bugs (There are all kinds of bugs.)	
what are the bebafits of This hous	its cin of cool anD PriviT (Its kind of cool and private)	

Chart Comparing Information from Two Books
Age 7

Projects

All projects include the following steps: brainstorming, categorizing, and making a chart (as the older children gain experience and confidence in doing projects, they tend to combine these three steps); gathering information (reading, interviewing, and so forth) and putting it into the chart along with the sources of information; writing up the information in a rough copy; revising and editing it—alone, with a partner, or with the teacher; and writing a neat copy with appropriate illustrations. Although the write-up usually takes the form of a "book" on a topic, variations in presentation are encouraged.

In the information-gathering stage, the children are given different readings with somewhat different information on the same topic. They should read most, but not all, of the materials. They may do this with a partner if they wish. Usually children want to read what others read and, consequently, often end up reading everything that is distributed.

Because they have been prepared for reading by the general discussions and by doing a brainstorm for the project, they know what to look for and, after a while, the more experienced readers learn to skim a text to extract what they need. Being exposed to so many sources helps the children become aware that not all printed text is well written, that there are many different ways of writing, and that different people emphasize different aspects of the same topic. Using a variety of sources offers opportunities for the teacher to help the children learn to identify these differences. This awareness develops over time as a result of brief and casual hints from the teacher.

On occasion (if it can be arranged), the children come across conflicting views and information, which makes clear to them the importance of using more than one source of information. As soon as they realize this, they make comments such as, "But you read only one article! How do you know it's all true if you don't even know what the others wrote?" or, while reading a text, "I don't believe this. It can't be true. Do you believe what this says?"

Although the children are encouraged to work with a partner at every stage, each child has to write up the project independently. Before writing, discussions (with or without the teacher) are necessary to help the children learn to articulate the ideas and information they have gathered.

In preparation for the projects, I had made a file box and collected articles, books, and portions of books that provided information about houses around the world.[1] The reading level of these texts varied to meet the diverse reading levels of the group. I placed the texts in alphabetically arranged files in the box so that filing could also be introduced in a purposeful way. Each file also contained at least one typed page that I had rewritten from the original text in easier language and simpler form. The box contained a file for each of the following: African adobe houses, Amazon River houses, Bali community housing, Bemba mud huts, early earth lodges, general information, houses in hot places, houses in wet places, Inuit igloos, Masai huts, New Guinea stilt houses, North American native people's houses, pueblo houses, stone houses, tents, and yurts.

I introduced the project box with the understanding that if a topic came up that had not been included in the box, I would make every effort to find appropriate materials and add them to our collection. None of the children mentioned any topic that they particularly wanted to have included. The topics were probably still too unfamiliar to the children to elicit any strong feelings or interests.

Discussion about the project box raised questions and concerns about its use. I explained that each pair of children could choose only one topic and that the children would have to select this topic very carefully because once they started working on a topic, they would have to complete it. In the same way, their choice of partners would have to last for the duration of the project. I made these stipulations to discourage frivolous or hasty choices and to stress responsible decision making.

The children and I also discussed the nature of the project. I explained that each set of partners would work together but that all the children would do their own writing individually in their own notebooks. I told the children that each project would include a brainstorm about the topic, questions the partners would like to answer, a chart of categories to help answer these questions, information from at least three sources written into the chart, a model of the house, and finally a rewritten version of the findings that would best tell others what they had learned. The children knew that their work would be put on display at the spring fair. We discussed the amount of time all of this would take and allotted almost two months for these projects. To help get the children organized, I marked the pages to be used for brainstorms, questions, and charts in their notebooks.

Despite the vast quantity of work that lay ahead, the children were eager to choose topics and begin work. I gave them plenty of time to peruse the files and to choose a topic and a partner. There was a great deal of excitement as they browsed through the files. After almost an hour, there were two boys who had still not chosen a topic. Finally, they came running over to tell me that they had made up their minds. They would do "General Information"!

The Early Stages: Brainstorms, Questions, and Charts

The work got under way. Each pair began trying to do work independently that had, up to this point, been done with the whole group. However, they had repeated the process enough so that most of the children felt confident with their own and their partner's efforts. When difficulties arose, there was now a number of people in the group available to give assistance. This cooperation not only provided a great deal of reinforcement, but also showed the children that learning can result from anyone around them.

Working in pairs, the children did brainstorms. One person would give an idea about the topic, and then both would write it into their own notebooks. They usually took turns except in those instances where one partner was more knowledgeable than the other. Some pairs were able to categorize information right from the start; others needed more time for this activity; while still others did not ever categorize but simply listed all their ideas around the circle. Each of the resulting brainstorms looked unique, as the two examples on pages 44 and 45 illustrate.

Despite the differences, I accepted the work if it represented effort at a level appropriate to the particular child. Although the teachers in our school try to discourage children from working only to please the teacher, we still need to maintain standards of acceptability. These are often discussed with a child and established as goals toward which the child should work.

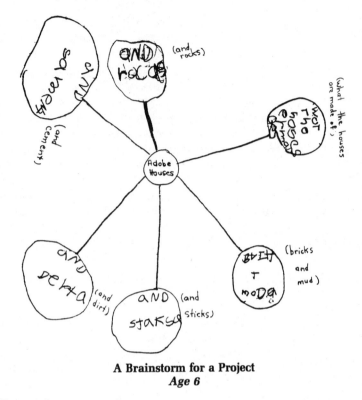

A Brainstorm for a Project
Age 6

   Once they had brainstormed, each pair of children thought of and recorded questions about their particular kind of house. Again the results varied greatly from group to group. Each pair brought their lists of questions to the whole group along with reports telling what topic they would be researching. The children suggested other kinds of questions that might be asked and exchanged ideas about additional sources of information other than those found in the files. For example, one child in a pair that had chosen to investigate pueblo houses had a good friend who lived in New Mexico and could possibly send them relevant information. They decided to write a letter to this friend. This gave some of the other children the idea of writing letters to get information for their projects as well. Two groups were working on igloos and, after talking it over and with a little help from me, decided that they would write to the Department of Inuit and Northern Affairs for information. The discussion ended with everyone promising to think about and inform the others about additional sources of information for any of the project topics.

   Whenever the children came up with a new question, it was added to the others. From time to time throughout the duration of the project, I suggested that they try to add more questions to the list. After a while, it became clear to the children that the more information they gathered, the better their questions were.

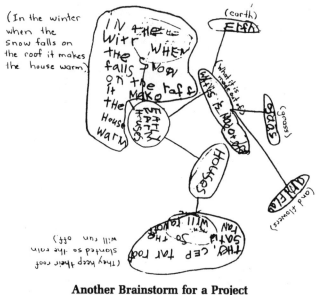

Another Brainstorm for a Project
Age 6

The next task for each group was to generate their own set of categories to use in a chart. This was not much of a problem because the children had by now become used to trying to think in categories. Although not everyone found it easy and not all categories were equally useful, every child had some idea about where to start. Most groups referred back to the charts we had done together and used some of these categories. The more inventive thinkers made up their own categories. In general, I kept a close eye out to ensure that each set of partners would have a workable chart with enough broad categories about important areas to experience success when trying to fill in the chart. In addition, I made suggestions to each group about including the problems and benefits of the particular kind of house in order to encourage the children to think about the social conditions under which the house was built.

The resultant charts were very different, which particularly pleased me. Obviously, the children felt confident enough with the idea of looking for chunks of connected ideas to do this activity themselves.

Research

Next came the laborious task of gathering information about the categories. Each pair was already working at its own pace and so the activities being carried out around the room looked very different. I made sure that all the children were doing a thorough job, exerting their best effort, and not just rushing through. I had to prod the dawdlers so they would not get too far behind.

Each set of partners read a piece from the file and then reread it slowly to find information to put in the chart. They repeated these activities until they had read three selections. The process was difficult and time-consuming, and I spent much of my time helping the partners read through the information and discuss it until they felt confident enough to write something in their charts. However, because of the previous group work, some of the children could also help their classmates when they ran into difficulty. The built-in repetition of the task helped the children,

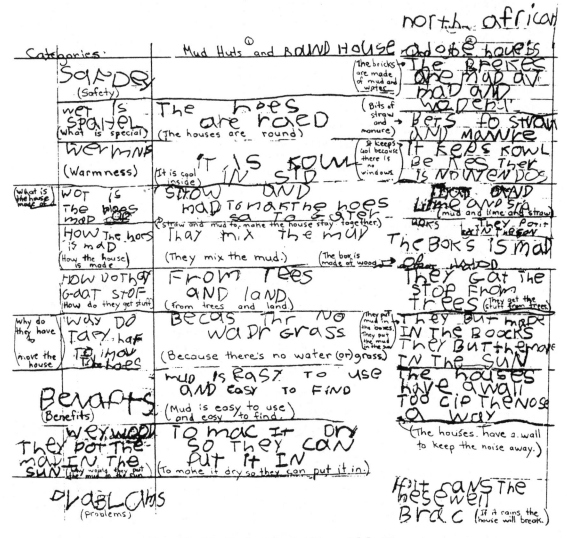

Chart Used for Project about African Adobe Houses
Age 6

even the more hesitant readers, increase their sight vocabularies, improve their reading strategies, and gain greater self-confidence. By the third selection, most groups decided to try what seemed to them to be a really hard piece. They succeeded in being able to understand some of the information and record it in their charts.

While this was going on, some of the children were also busy writing letters to get information. These letters had to be written first in rough form, then revised and edited, and finally copied in neat form. This process enabled the children to concentrate on one thing at a time. First the ideas were considered. If, for example, a child did not know the spelling of a word, the child would either sound out the word or write it down as it might look, but without spending too much time on spelling at this stage.

When the rough draft of a letter was finished, the author would read it to another child and then to me. At each reading, the other child or I would point out the parts that were not clear or complete, and the author would make the necessary changes. Once revised, the child would circle the words that might be incorrectly spelled. Correct spelling could be discovered in the dictionary, from a friend, or from the teacher. Finally the child would rewrite the letter using as careful letter formation, spacing, capitalization, and spelling as possible. The child would also address the envelope, affix the stamp, and then wait for an answer. Luckily everyone received replies to their letters.

By now the children were involved in comparing information from different sources. The children who were studying igloos had received an article through the mail from the Department of Inuit and Northern Affairs that provided some interesting discussion along this line since the information in this article about finishing the roof conflicted with the information they had read elsewhere. Even

Letter Asking for Information about Igloos: Revised Rough Copy
Age 6

at this tender age, the children recognized that they had two opposing set of "facts," both from seemingly reputable sources. Some decided that the information from the Department must be more accurate while others thought that maybe there was more than one way to finish the roof. The children incorporated this new information into the project by adding it to the chart and using it in making the model.

In the meantime, now that I knew what types of housing the projects involved, I had booked more films. I showed these films to the whole class even though most children were not working on the topic dealt with by a particular film because all the children would benefit by viewing and discussing all the films. The most informative one was *How to Build an Igloo* (Directed by Douglas Wilkinson. 10 min. 27 sec., color, available through the National Film Board of Canada). I showed this short film three times while the children took notes. After each viewing, they discussed what they had noticed and recorded. They picked up more details of interest with each viewing.

I showed another film, *Not Far from Bolgatanga* (Directed by Michael Rubbo and Barrie Howells. 28 min. 25 sec., color, available through the National Film Board of Canada), to give those making the adobe houses some idea about what these houses look like. Because most of the film was not applicable, we watched only some fleeting pictures of the adobe houses in Africa. Unperturbed by this, those making the adobe models were thrilled with this opportunity. We also viewed the part of *The Gabra* (Directed by Nancy Archibald. 56 mi. 45 sec., color, available through the National Film Board of Canada) that showed a type of nomadic tent used in a hot climate. Unfortunately, I could not find any other pertinent films.

In addition to watching the film that showed African adobe houses, the two children researching this subject had a chance to interview an African exchange student at the university. They prepared questions that I photocopied, and they then cut the questions apart and pasted them onto a large sheet, leaving enough room to write in the answers. Now they were ready for the interview. They spent almost an hour asking the African student questions and taking notes on his responses. What a successful experience this turned out to be! Not only did the children learn more about constructing adobe houses, they also learned to appreciate someone from a culture very different from theirs. Afterward, they wrote thank-you letters (following the usual procedure of writing a rough draft, revising, editing, and finally preparing a neat copy) and proudly delivered them in person.

Making the Models

When a set of partners had finished gathering information from the file and other sources and recording the information in their charts, they were ready to plan how to make their model as accurately as possible. The ideas varied considerably among the pairs depending upon their experience with such kinds of construction projects. The members of each pair discussed their ideas with each other and with

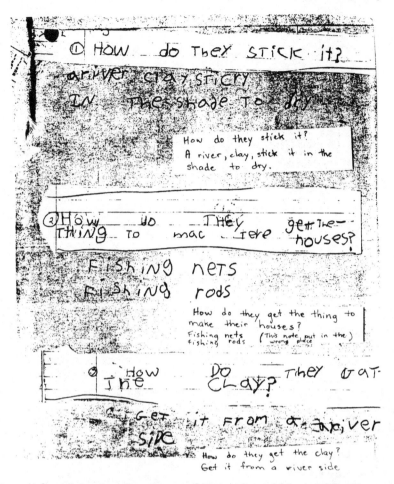

Excerpt from Interview Questions and Notes about African Adobe Houses
Age 6

me and then wrote down their plans. When the plans seemed clear, and when the children had figured out the construction methods they would use and had gathered the necessary building materials, the next phase of work began.

At first, one of the igloo groups tried to use sugar cubes for snow blocks. However, as cube after cube broke (and consequently, a few just had to be eaten), these children realized that sugar cubes would not be a feasible material. Seeing the adobe house group using plasticene, the igloo groups got the idea of using plasticene snow blocks. This turned out to be a terrific idea. The children were now able to follow more closely the methods used by the Inuit and to build their models slowly, taking them apart when there were structural problems and then rebuilding them. Finally the igloos were finished. They didn't really look the right

Plans for model
1. carbord for Platfourm
2. make a circle of mud
3. Put some earth on the mud
4. Put wood chips on the earth
5. Put stones on the wood chips
6. Put little pces of brick on the stones
7. and start all over again
8. Put some little boards on the top
9. Put flowers on the boards
10. Put some grass on the flowers

Plans for a Model Sod House
Age 7

color, of course, but this led to another inventive solution—flour. With a light coating of flour, the igloos looked authentic.

Other groups had also been busy solving similar types of problems. The African adobe house group made its house of plasticene bricks prepared in a miniature cardboard mold designed to resemble the wooden molds actually used by Africans to form the bricks. The sod house group constructed a "wood frame" made out of straws ingeniously held together by pins. The children used sod blocks, dug out of half-frozen backyards and carefully brought to school, cut into small pieces and gently stacked up against the frame to build their houses. For the thatched roof, the children used loosely interwoven grass pieces. The result was a very convincing-looking sod house.

Making models brought to life the conditions and difficulties involved in the construction of each type of house. It also increased the children's enthusiasm for the topic, because now they felt like real experts. With the models carefully placed on a shelf to await the quickly approaching fair the children turned their attention to the final stage of their projects.

Preparing for the Fair

Having experienced the fall fair, the children had some thoughts about how to display their work. With these thoughts in mind, they brainstormed interesting ways to display their projects so that others could learn from them. They had many ideas. Projects could be written up as books with a cassette for those too young to read them. Books might also have a quiz attached so that readers could test themselves on what they had learned. Posters might give colorful pictures as well as information. Games might be a fun way to teach people about a particular kind of house. Because all of these would involve a more or less equal amount of synthesizing of ideas and writing, I allowed each pair to choose the display format that was most appealing. The teamwork that had gradually grown throughout the project would be put to the test as the jobs of designing, writing, and drawing were planned and executed, because each person's finished work had to be accepted by the partner since the contributions of both would be displayed together.

We began. The children composed the written work from the charts as well as all other sources of information that had been used since the charts had been completed (films, interviews, and replies to letters). They wrote their pieces first as rough drafts with effort being concentrated on the thorough synthesis of information and ideas. The charts provided an easy way for them to organize and transfer their ideas; each category on the chart could be rewritten as a separate chapter of a book, part of a poster, or a set of information cards for a game.

Those children who were planning to write books needed to decide how to arrange their categories so that people reading the books could understand them without difficulty. Through discussion, they decided that a suitable order of categories might be: where the house is located; what it looks like; how it is built; problems connected with the house; and finally, benefits of the house. Some children decided upon other patterns of categories. Posters were organized in the

These numbers show the order in which the categories were used as chapters in the finished book about sod houses.

Chart Used for Project about Sod Houses
Age 6

same way so that viewers could easily understand the information. Even the games were tried out in rough form first to make sure that all the writing, including the rules of the game, was legible and easy to follow.

Following our standard practice, the children read their rough copies to each other and to me. We made suggestions for additions, deletions, and rearrangement of ideas to help clarify the writing. Sometimes, a child had to revise by rewriting parts of the work. This was painstaking and at times frustrating. However, since the children knew that their families and many other people would visit the fair, each child realized the need for high standards for all the work on display. When the children had finished revising their work, they edited the game cards and rules, the books, and the posters for spelling and punctuation in the same way as they had done with the letters. Then they rewrote their final copies carefully, using their neatest printing.

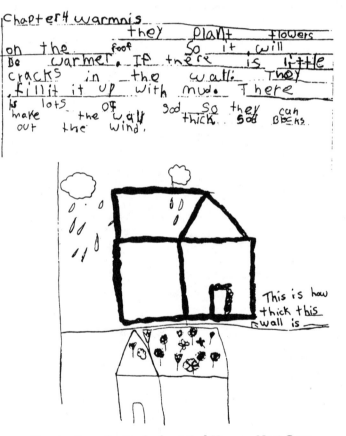

Chapter from the Book about Sod Houses: Neat Copy
Age 6

Despite the fact that I carefully monitored everyone's progress to make sure that each group was scheduling its work according to the time available, some groups were slow to complete their projects. Completion was essential so that all the children could feel a sense of pride and accomplishment after working so long and hard on these projects. Therefore, some children had to work extra time during play and after school to get their displays ready for the fair, an experience that taught them some important lessons about managing their time.

After so much hard work and so much thinking, reading, writing, designing, building, and working together, the projects were finally ready for the fair. These six-, seven-, and eight-year-olds were bursting to show the visitors what they had made and learned. When the visitors finally flooded in, the children showed and explained the models, books, games, and posters they had prepared, eagerly answering all questions. Whenever there was a lull, they quickly looked for yet some more "customers." Looking around that exciting room, I realized that the effectiveness of this theme study was being demonstrated before my eyes by the children's self-confidence and their eagerness to share their newly found knowledge.

The History of Buildings:
A Theme Study with the Olds
(Ages Eight to Ten)

Because the general theme for the year was "People and Their Work," I thought it would be interesting to study the history of buildings. This study would include the development of technology and the social forces behind these developments. Knowing that this was a great deal for eight- to ten-year-old children, I planned to focus on the general thrust of history, elaborating where necessary and where the children showed greatest interest.

What follows is a description of how a teacher might prepare for this theme study. Included are my own actual preparations as well as other possibilities. It is useful to begin with brainstorms on topics such as the following: major stages in the development of technology, technical aspects of structures, functions of buildings, major social and economic reasons for changes in the functions of buildings, and historical and geographical variations in buildings.

Brainstorming should be followed by such activities as trips to the children's and adults' sections of the public library to find information for the children as well as the teacher; a check of the audio-visual resources available (audio-visual libraries, National Film Board, TV stations, and museums); a visit to an architect; the purchase of some issues of journals on architecture; a trip around the city to become familiar with the variety of buildings and building styles that can be studied with the children; and a check of the resources in one's own school.

The next stage of preparation consists of designing hands-on activities, field trips and projects, and selecting appropriate reading material at different reading levels. Not knowing in advance what aspect of the building theme the children will want to study in depth, it is impossible to plan in great detail ahead of time. However, some general preparation on the main theme and some subtopics is necessary. In addition, a teacher should make notes of all ideas and sources of information as well as their location, because they might be of use later.

Finally the teacher should think about a specific goal that the children can work toward to make their learning activities purposeful rather than busy work, something that they will find worthwhile studying and that will be interesting to display and explain to an audience at an open house or some such event. I decided that we would try to make models to scale and write about them. These would be displayed and presentations would be given on the history of buildings.

As I went through these stages of preparation, I became quite fascinated with the topic. As a result, the list of subtopics and activities I planned to tempt the children with was long. Because I did not know in advance what would intrigue them most, because I needed a good overview of the history of building, and because I had become so interested in the topic myself, my preparations turned out to be rather extensive.

Introducing the Theme

We started off brainstorming about human needs. To give the children a chance to discuss the issue with each other, I asked them to brainstorm in their notebooks for about five minutes. Then they told me what to write on the blackboard while I repeatedly asked where I should put the information, thus forcing them to classify it.

When I asked the children where all these needs were fulfilled, they decided to do another brainstorm listing buildings and categorizing them according to purpose. Some children, however, soon noticed that certain buildings have overlapping functions or serve different purposes for different people. Others noticed that the size of buildings is related to the number of people who use the buildings or to differences in the wealth of the people using them. The categories were varied, reflecting not only these issues but also differences in the children's social, geographical, and historical awareness.

When I asked the group what they imagined cave people would have thought of their categories, the children guessed that the purposes of buildings depend on how developed a society is, its population density, and its geographic area. These new ideas were confirmed as we perused numerous issues of *National Geographic* magazine in a quick survey of housing. This in turn led the children to raise new concerns such as building materials and technology.

At this point, we tried to think of some things we would have to learn about in order to understand the present variety of buildings and their functions. We again brainstormed and categorized our ideas. I tried to guide the children's thinking by asking why there were so many different kinds of buildings. However, given the difficulty of this task, I had to ask more questions and refer to the previous brainstorm as well as the children's earlier comments to draw out specific structural, technological, geographical, social, and historical aspects of buildings.

After much discussion, the children thought that the sensible thing to do next would be to study: (1) structures (because the size, shape, and building materials of structures vary greatly and the children wanted to find out how these factors relate to the quality and durability of the buildings); (2) housing around the world (houses were chosen because they seemed to be the kinds of buildings needed by almost all people; therefore we would consider the size and shape of different kinds of houses as well as locally available building materials and local construction methods); and (3) the social history of building (people obviously change their way of living when they invent better tools, and there must be reasons for these developments; therefore, these aspects would also be studied).

Although the children arrived at these decisions in half a week and had made a good start, they were, at this time, totally unaware of how much work this study involved. So far they were enthusiastic about the topic in general. Because what we would concentrate on was not exactly clear, I would have to play it by ear and remember that my own enthusiasm would carry some weight as well.

Gathering and Recording Information

For two months, during January and February, the children and I engaged in the following activities almost every day.

Studying the History of Technology and Construction

To get some general overview of the development of technology and its relation to social organization, I read sections to the children from:

Tools in Your Life, by Irving Adler. John Day Co., New York, 1956.[1]

We discussed what was read, looked at pictures, and made notes. The central questions of our study were always considered by having the children predict and then read for confirmation. So, for example, when we studied the tools in the Stone Age, we focused on the history of building of that period, and I encouraged the children to predict what tasks might have been necessary for survival, how the tools might have been made, what kind of lifestyle would have been most suitable

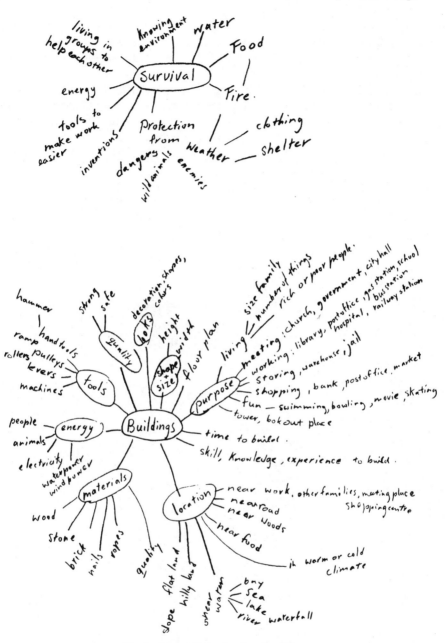

Brainstorms Introducing the Theme

at that time under those conditions, what kinds of buildings might have suited people, what structures might they have built, and how much work and how many workers such a building may have required. The children then read texts to see if their predictions were correct.

This approach prepared the children for the reading materials and the ideas contained in them, and for taking their own notes. However, I do not use this approach when the children have insufficient background knowledge of a topic, as it can otherwise easily deteriorate into underestimating the children and, therefore, talking down to them, boring them, and wasting valuable learning time.

When the girl who made these notes had to write about the topic, she discovered that her notes were incomplete and that she should have included her sources to facilitate finding the information again.

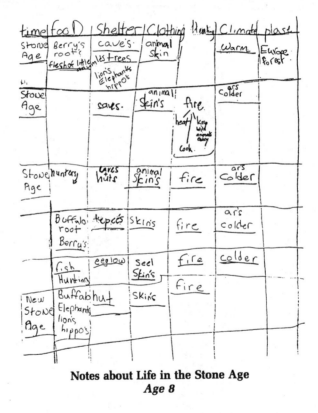

Notes about Life in the Stone Age
Age 8

Note Taking

Most of the time the children must have their notebooks and pencils ready to take notes. Whether the teacher reads to them or all read together (depending on the available number of copies and the difficulty of the text), the children and the teacher go through the reading section by section, the length varying from a paragraph to a page. They discuss what they read as well as the illustrations, if there are any. Next, the children decide what the main points of information are, and when all agree, they write about these points in their notebooks. If they do not know what to write, it is because they have not understood the main points and the group must continue to discuss the information.

Correct spelling is not necessary when taking notes as long as the children can read their own writing. The emphasis in such a reading and writing session is on the information and ideas, not on the spelling. Therefore, when children don't know how to spell a word they either ask a partner, use invented spelling, or look it up in the text they are using. If there is only one copy of the book and they cannot look up the spelling, the teacher writes it on the board.

Not all parts of a text contain information worth noting. Consequently, this reading/writing activity offers an excellent opportunity to help children learn to distinguish between main points and details and between new information and repetition, and to notice the sequence of presentation as well as the similarities and differences in the information.

Taking notes, especially when doing a project, is quite a difficult task at first. In the beginning, for example, the children tend to write too much or too little or do not see the need to make note of a point if they think they can remember it or if they think they know it already. In addition, sometimes the children do not recognize that they need help. However, the moment the notes have to be used, such problems surface. This experience, although time-consuming, is worthwhile because only the need for good notes demonstrates what kind of notes are useful.

Experimenting with Structures

To learn about the structure of buildings, the children experimented with structures made of blocks, strips of paper, and cardboard as well as three-dimensional shapes (such as bridges, arches, and towers) made with their bodies to discover stress points and the degree and direction of pressure. From these experiments, the children learned about bracing and balancing, about how and where to provide support, about the function of basic shapes in larger structures, and about the distribution of weight. The children found several books helpful in providing ideas for experiments on construction.[2]

After a few days, the structures made out of strips of paper became weak. The children suggested reasons for the weaknesses, and when they reached agreement, they prepared the list shown on page 60. Such writing usually does not get edited.

Why
Our Structures Collapse

(1) Not thick enough
(2) Glue melted
(3) Not balanced
(4) Large shapes
(5) Ynuppropeite shapes
(6) Had shapes that tip
            over
(7) To tall and thin
(8) Not enough support.

Example of Results of Experiment with Structures

Experimentation

The teacher usually presents experiments to the children in the form of an activity card that they read with a partner. The content of the cards tells the children what they are to do or find out. Occasionally, the teacher gives the instructions orally. Open-ended questions are asked as the children do the activity. To help them learn how to think about experiments, the teacher often asks the following questions:

- What do you have to figure out?
- What do you need to carry out the activity?
- What things or situations can you change?
- List the many ways in which you might try to figure it out.
- Which way(s) obtained the best results and why?

The children have to write up their experiments and add some labeled drawings. After they have written about their first experiment, they listen to each other read their work. Invariably they notice that the organization of their writing needs to be improved. The teacher helps them with this task by asking questions that will generate headings and the kind of information that should be included under them. The teacher and children list the headings and put them in an appropriate order. Once we have this format, it is tacked on the wall as a reminder. Note taking facilitates the whole process. Note taking has become a habit for the children because they know that the activities are done for a purpose and that they might well need the information later.

Throughout this procedure, the children are encouraged to try new things themselves, to take risks, and to learn from their mistakes by examining their work with others. All this helps them notice their shortcomings and design other formats until they find the ones that work best. This process of improving their work requires the children to become more informed and articulate about the topic they are studying and more analytical about their own and each other's work. It also means that they must develop some sense of the relationship between content and form of presentation.

The children and I also learned about the characteristics of various building materials. We collected and discussed some pictures of buildings, went on a walk to discover the common features of most buildings, and visited an architect. All of these activities, along with the reading, provided a good background for our study and many opportunities to learn and use new terminology.[3]

Studying the Social History of Building and the Development of Communities

After a couple of days of reading about the Stone Age, I asked the children what they had noticed about how people lived and acquired food. Some answered that group work was important for survival. This insight led the children to discuss the various reasons for a division of labor, using examples from their own family lives, the school, and the community. We also discussed how and why particular work is often assigned to people of a certain age and gender. This discussion encouraged the children to look for specific forms of social organization in the history they were reading.[4]

Before long it was clear that we would study several different periods in the history of building. The children wondered how they would display all this information. Because what would interest them most was not yet clear, we decided to think of displays later. In the meantime, the children did small-scale projects on the various periods of history we studied. Each child kept these projects in a large, thick scrapbook so that everyone would have a history book to take home at the end of the school year.

The Stone, Bronze, and Iron ages saw the beginnings of math as people needed to measure time, count their goods, develop agriculture and trade, measure land, erect buildings, build bridges, and so on. Therefore, I tried in passing to interest the children in this side-topic by reading sections to them from:

The Wonderful World of Mathematics, by Lancelot Hogbin. Doubleday & Co. Inc., Garden City, N.Y., 1955.
(There are several editions of this book, and the older ones are more attractive than the more recent ones.)

Some children decided to read more of the book and write about the subject but most were not interested in pursuing it.

Keeping Track

In a setting in which children study the same theme but at times different subtopics and in which their stages of learning vary significantly with resulting differences in the thoroughness and depth of their work, it is necessary to keep track of all work done by each child. Keeping track is important not only for the teacher but also for the children, who fully accept differences among each other but expect everyone to do the same number and variety of assignments as evidence of being treated fairly.

As soon as each child has clearly defined assignments to do, the teacher writes them beside the child's name on a large sheet of squared paper posted in the classroom. These assignments are checked off as each aspect of the work is done—reading/experiment, notes, rough draft, revised and edited draft, and finally neat draft. The date is added when the assignment is completed. In this manner, it is possible to keep track of the work of all the children in spite of differences in levels and topics. The teacher and the children can see at a glance who has finished which assignments and what still remains to be done. The children hardly ever forget to ask the teacher to check off their work on the sheet. It is important to note that this posted chart of assignments does *not* show marks or any other form of evaluation. Display of such information is not the purpose of the chart.

At the end of January, the children were still showing their interest in housing around the world by leafing through the *National Geographic* magazines during spare moments. To accommodate this interest, I collected information on a great number of countries and geographic areas and marked them on a world map. The children guessed my intent, and each one selected a place on the map to study with the aim of finding out about the housing.

We brainstormed about what aspects of the natural environment would be important to people in deciding on building materials and the size and shape of their houses. This activity became the basis of an assignment. The tasks were to describe the location of the chosen area and show it on a map; to find out about the natural physical features of the area (elevation, climate, soil, and vegetation) in an atlas; and to use this information to predict the area's housing structure and building materials. The assignment would culminate in the children "traveling" to that country by reading about the topic, by writing their findings in the form of a letter to parents, and by making a model of the housing to "take home as a souvenir."

Since climate and description of location were new topics for the children, they had to learn some basic geography. First they had to find out where the very hot and very cold regions are and why these regions are hot or cold. We looked at a globe, made it spin on its axis, learned that the earth travels around the sun, and discussed why there are different climates.

To describe location, we did several things. First the children tried to describe each other's place in the classroom. After many efforts, they noticed that the most accurate descriptions of location in the room were those that referred to constants; so they used two adjacent walls of the room to describe each other's location. Next they tried to find constants on the globe. The equator was one, but the second was difficult to find because so many half circles could be drawn through the North and South poles. My suggestion to just agree that the meridian that passes through the town of Greenwich in the United Kingdom be called the 0° meridian was opposed because Halifax would be a better choice. For a moment, the children were speechless trying to reconcile the idea of "constant" with such an arbitrary decision. In addition, to make matters worse, the arbitrary decision was not even Halifax!

Naming meridians and parallels in degrees was very difficult for the children, but using an orange and drawing a few parallels and meridians on it and then cutting across its fruit sections helped solve the problem. The orange sections demonstrated how the angles describe degrees north and south, and east and west. Next we discussed and practiced how to determine location on a map, and how to read maps and use the key.

After a few days, the children started on their assignments, helping each other use an atlas and doing the other tasks.[5] There was a lively exchange of information because no two children had been allowed to choose the same area. In five to seven days, the children had finished their projects except for building the models, but we, in fact, dropped this idea because there was not much interest in models at this point.

Excitement about Buildings in the Middle Ages

When the children noticed references to pottery in their readings about the Stone and Bronze ages, they suggested that we make some pottery or, better yet, visit a potter, and so we did. This visit demonstrated very clearly why pottery was one of the earliest inventions as it required only a few relatively simple tools.

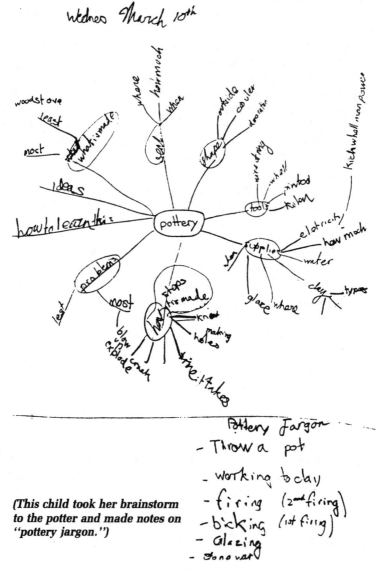

(This child took her brainstorm to the potter and made notes on "pottery jargon.")

Pottery Jargon
- Throw a pot
- working to clay
- firing (2nd firing)
- bicking (1st firing)
- Glazing
- stonevar

Brainstorm in Preparation for the Trip to See a Potter at Work
Age 9

On Thursday March 11th
our class went to Mrs Ravindra house.
Mrs Ravindra is a potter, she gave us a tour
of her workshop. I had to get information on
the tools. There are lots of tools in which
she uses like a kiln. A kiln is used
for hadening the clay

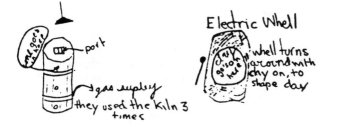

Electric Whell

whell turns around with clay on, to shape clay

grind here

whell goes arand to grind bits of clay

port

gas suplry
they used the kiln 3 times

The also was the whell witich was used for shaping the clay. Potters use a grinder for when 2 pots are stuck together in the kiln (it is called my pots are kissing) the grinder takes the extra clay of. There was on tool called a cone for seeing how hot the kiln is, if its hot enought the cone will bent down and melt, the higher the number on the side of the side is the hotter it has to be for it to melt. If a number 11 melted the kiln is too hot. You put 3 cones in a peice of clay and stick it in the holes in the kiln so you can just she it through the kiln

peice of clay

Excerpt from Write-Up of Field Trip to Potter: Neat Copy
Age 9

Field Trips

The purpose of a field trip is to gather information and to provide concrete experience not available from books, films, pictures, or other resources that can be brought into the classroom. A field trip serves to supplement these resources. Given its importance, the children need to be well prepared and to know what to look for. Therefore, the teacher and children brainstorm to generate appropriate categories. Then the children form as many small groups as there are categories, and each group writes questions about one of the categories. On the day of the field trip, just before they leave, the children, working in pairs, take a list of questions from either the category they worked on previously or another one. They may choose, as long as all the categories are covered.

The children should know what they are expected to do during the visit: listen and watch, ask all questions from the chosen list and any new ones that come to mind, and make note of the answers. At the end of the visit, one child who has been previously selected gives a thank-you speech (preparation consists of learning what kinds of things should be said and why). Back in school, the children compare notes and then each child writes out the information in rough form, edits it, and then writes a neat copy. In addition, everyone writes a thank-you letter again using the sequence of rough copy, edited copy, and neat copy. If there is not enough time for individual letters, a few children write the letter and others co-sign it.

The children seemed to enjoy the Stone, Bronze, and Iron ages. Their interest, however, immediately receded into the background once they discovered that the next period would be the Middle Ages and that it would concern castles and knights. There was no stopping them. And that is why we studied buildings and construction methods of the Middle Ages during March, April, and May.

Now, the daily work in school changed. First we spent more than a week on the following fascinating book:

Cathedral: The Story of Its Construction, by David MacAulay. Houghton Mifflin & Co., New York, 1979.

Because there was only one copy available, I read the book to the children and showed them the many beautiful illustrations, photocopies of which were put up on the wall afterward. The illustrations were excellent for highlighting perspective, proportion, and direction of light rays; and the text provided a good basis for discussing many aspects of work in the Middle Ages.

Throughout the reading of this book, the children took notes. We decided that it was best to have two kinds of notes: one a chronology of the story of the construction of the cathedral; and the other a glossary of terms about social groups and occupations, and terms related to construction. Some of the latter required labeled illustrations as well.

I gave each child a photocopy of the drawing of a cross section of the cathedral provided in the book. The children and I labeled the various parts, added measurements whenever they were given in the text, and, using these, estimated the lengths of several other parts of the cathedral shown in the cross section. In addition, we drew and labeled the floor plan and the side walls. Drawing to visual scale was done by looking at the proportions in MacAulay's illustrations. For example, I pointed to a major section of the floor plan, went to the chalkboard, and said, "This part of the wall seems to be about one-third of the total wall. So let's

In the floor of the cathedral there was a maze. then on every Sunday they had to try and get through it.

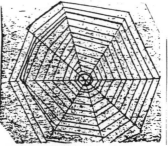

they built a maze on the floor of the cathedral inbetween the North and South Transept. every sunday morning the people of the town came to see if they could get through it. Getting through it was considered as worthy of Gods blessing as making a long trip through the countryside.

THE MAZE

Drawings and Information about the Maze,
a Fascinating Aspect of the Cathedral Floor
Age 9

(Voussiors are curved stones for the arches so that the arches can curve.)

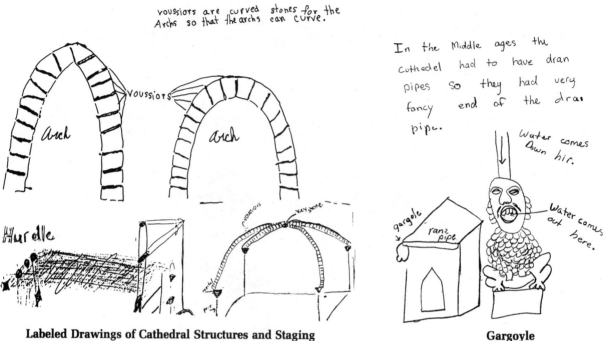

voussiors are curved stones for the
Archs so that the archs can curve.

voussiors

arch

arch

Hurdle

In the Middle ages the
cathedel had to have dran
pipes so they had very
fancy end of the dra
pipe.

Water comes
down hir.

gargole

ranz
pipe.

Water comes
out here.

Labeled Drawings of Cathedral Structures and Staging
Age 9

Gargoyle
Age 9

draw a long, horizontal line and, using dots, divide it in about three equal parts. Now, the first one-third of the line to the left represents the wall on the first section of the floor plan.'' The children watched me do this on the board and then tried to do the same thing in their notebooks.

After following my lead a couple of times, they estimated the proportions for the remaining parts of the drawing. As soon as the group agreed on an estimated proportion, I would draw that part on the board while the children copied it into their notebooks. When dimensions were already given, we added them in the drawings.

When drawing a side wall to visual scale independently, the children proved that they learn best from their mistakes. At first, several children started by drawing a part of the side wall rather than the whole length. When they measured off this section the correct number of times, however, the whole plan did not fit on their papers. Although they had to start all over again, they knew how to draw to visual scale the next time.

The chapter is the group of clergymen who have money to build the Cathedral. The chapter hires the master builders. The master builder hires all the other masters necessary. The masters hire apprentices, journeymen and laborers of thier own trade. The blacksmith made tools mainly for the stone cutter and the carpenter. The master builder draws the plan for the cathedral and others cut timber. The stone cutters start cutting stones. The stones are marked three times. Once to tell where the stone goes in the cathedral once to tell who did the work on it and once to tell which quarry did it. Then they started clearing the space for the cathedral and at the some time they make a trip to skandinavia for wood. Then holes are dug for the foundation 23 feet deep. The mortar is made from sand, limes and water, Then the foundation is made.

When the foundation is finished the piers are made and vaults are put on top. centerings are used to hold the rocks up till the mortar drys.

A scaffold is used for building high up. The scaffold is used so high up that they dont tuch the ground. Spiral staircasers are used to get up and down. The platf-orms is made of woven twigs. It's called a hurdel.

Buttresses are little piers that are

Notes on Stages of Cathedral Construction
Age 10

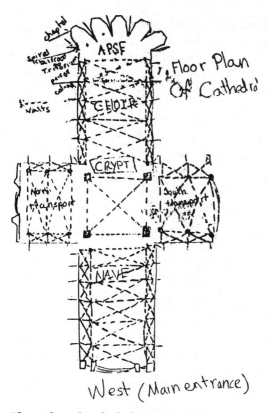

Floor Plan of Cathedral Based on Visual Scale
Age 9

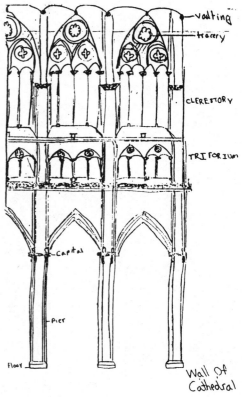

Wall of Cathedral Based on Visual Scale
Age 9

The drawing experience proved fruitful. Later, when the days were warmer, we took a whole morning off to visit some churches and a cathedral and to have a look at some other buildings on our way. We sat outside an old church and prepared to draw the front of it. The children immediately talked about how to begin: draw the whole outline by looking at proportions and then estimate the rest.

St. Pauls Churc 1749

Freehand Drawing Done During "Church Trip"
Age 10

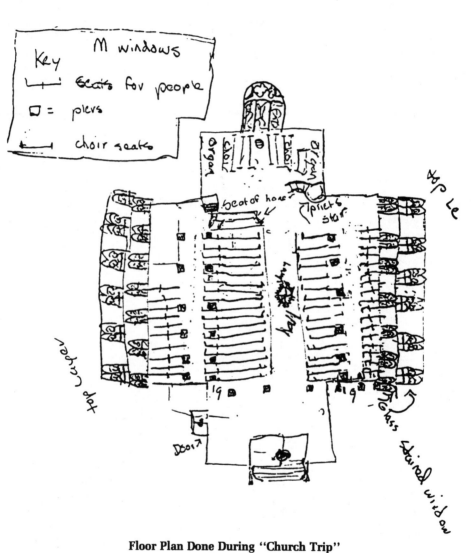

Floor Plan Done During "Church Trip"
Age 9

After the drawings were finished, we entered the church and looked around, and each child drew a floor plan. Some children even included the walls.

When we examined the structure from the inside and outside, the children checked to see if they could find all the parts they had learned about (arcade, capital, triforium, clerestory, vault, tracery, nave, transept, apse, buttress, pier, and so on), constantly using the newly acquired terminology. Finding everything the way "it's supposed to be," they commented on how much muscle power it must have taken to build the cathedral they had read about, especially because it was even larger than this church and had been built with fairly simple tools.

Subsequently, the children and I spent a bit of time learning about stones that were quarried for use in the construction of the cathedral. The children got information by reading:

> *The Rock Quarry Book,* by Michael Kehoe. Carolrhoda Books, Inc. Minneapolis, 1981.

We tried to organize a visit to a quarry but could not do so. Unfortunately, a film on quarrying was not available either.

We also learned that in the Middle Ages producing glass was still very difficult

An Account of Glaziers in the Middle Ages
Age 9

and that it did not look like the glass we are used to. For one session, we looked for information on glass in:

> *The Marvel of Glass,* by Walter Buehr. William Morrow and Company, New York, 1963.
>
> *The First Book of Glass,* by Sam and Beryl Epstein. Franklin Watts Inc., New York, 1955.

Then we organized a visit to a glassblower who did some work in our presence, explained what he was doing, and answered our questions. He told us why the tools and knowledge of glaziers in the Middle Ages were insufficient to produce the clear glass we now have. He helped us realize why glass was very expensive then and why, as a result, houses and other buildings were rather dark places in those days.

Glass Blowing

We visited a glass blower
who made a nice little glass swan
made out of glass tubes.
He told us about soft and hard glass.
Hard glass means if you put it
under a flame it doesn't break as
easily as soft glass. It is made of sand
and soda and the more sand you
make it with the stronger it is under
a high temperature.
After that he took two different
kinds of glass pyrex and quartz
and stuck the under a flame
and then in cold water and then
in the flame again the quartz didn
do anything because it had more
sand. but the pyrex shattered because it
had less sand.

Excerpt from Write-Up of Field Trip to Glassblower
Age 9

Having looked at many pictures of old churches and cathedrals and of stained glass windows, we decided that we could make a "rose window," a particular kind of stained glass window, out of heavy paper and colorful tissue paper. The children had to cut a rectangular or square piece of heavy paper into as large a circle as possible. After they solved this mathematical puzzle without the use of compass, lids, or plates I then presented them with another difficult task—drawing and cutting out intricate shapes in a symmetrical pattern inside the circle. When the children had accomplished this feat, they pasted colored pieces of tissue paper over the holes on one side and colored the connecting, or "lead," parts black on the reverse side. These "rose windows," which we taped onto the windows, certainly cheered up the room.

Every day, just before lunch or near the end of the school day, the children sat together, curled up in a corner, while I read to them from the historical novel:

> *The Door in the Wall*, by Marguerite de Angeli. Doubleday & Co., New York, 1949.

Although this reading was helpful in giving them a better idea of life in the Middle Ages, I certainly was glad when some of the films I had ordered finally arrived:

> *Medieval Manor,* Encyclopedia Britannica Films. 20 minutes, B & W, 1956.
> *Medieval Knights,* Encyclopedia Britannica Films. 20 minutes, B & W, 1956.
> *Medieval Guilds,* Encyclopedia Britannica Films. 20 minutes, B & W, 1956.

Before watching each of the films, the children and I brainstormed together while I recorded all questions and ideas on the board. When I thought the children were sufficiently focused on the topic of the film, we watched it and took notes. Afterward, we discussed what we had seen and raised more questions. When some children remembered or understood a few things differently from other children, we watched the film again. The children understood much more the second time, and their notes improved and were completed. The next step was to write an essay about what they had just learned. Each child wrote a rough copy, a revised and edited one, and a neat copy. The same procedure was followed with all three films.[6]

Meanwhile, whenever the children finished an assignment or were tired from long periods of reading and writing, we looked through and read sections of the many photobooks and other materials about the Middle Ages that we had in the room. The following seemed to be among the children's favorites:

> *The Time Traveller Book of Knights and Castles*, by Judy Hindley. Usborne Hayes, London, U.K., 1976.
> *Medieval Hunting Scenes: Illuminated Manuscripts* (The Hunting Book, by Gaston Phoebus), text by Gabriel Bise. Translated by J. Peter Tallon. Miller Graphics, Productions Liber SA, Geneva, 1978.
> Books of paintings by Pieter Brueghel and others of that period in history.

For several days, the children read about and discussed the organization of the

Notes Written on the Medieval Manor While Watching Film
Age 10

medieval church, the manor, and the guilds. They also learned about lords, serfs, and artisans.[7] They made their own notes and used them to write on these topics. While some chose to write short essays, others preferred to use other formats—a story, a labeled caricature, a comic strip, and others. The amount of time required for these assignments varied from two days to a week.

Village life in the middle ages

In the middle ages people lived in village
Every village was owned by a lord.
the land was divided in to strips.
Every serf (serf are people working for the
lord because the lord gives them protection
has 3 strips in different places
so that every serf got his share
of the good and bad land. Every serf
has to pay ten percent of what he grew to the
lord. If a new lord came he would send
a bailif and two soldiers around to see
how wealthy the serfs were and figure
out how much taxes they should pay.

Excerpt from Write-Up of Village Life in the Middle Ages: Neat Copy
Age 9

In addition, small groups of children read, discussed, and occasionally sum-
marized sections from books on the history of houses.[8] At times I asked the
children to tell the group something about this subject or to read us their summaries.
A lively discussion usually ensued in which the children eagerly suggested reasons
for changes in houses and the development of towns and cities, made comparisons
with modern homes, and so forth. The fact that they talked enthusiastically with

Fate of a Serf

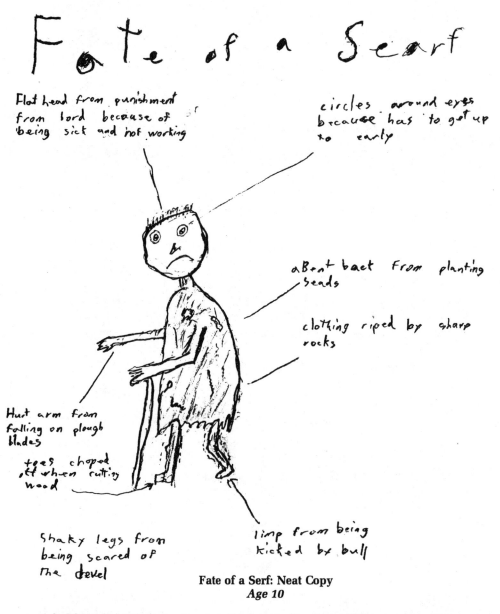

Flat head from punishment from lord because of being sick and not working

circles around eyes because has to get up to early

a Bent baet From planting seads

clothing riped by sharp rocks

Hurt arm from falling on plough blades

toes choped off when cutting wood

Shaky legs from being scared of the devel

limp from being kicked by bull

Fate of a Serf: Neat Copy
Age 10

each other about these topics was the best indication of their interest. They were also developing a good sense of history. Because the children were becoming much better informed, my role in these discussions was now reduced to that of chairperson at a meeting.

Building a Castle

From the end of March on, the children and I were mainly occupied with the study of the following:

Castle, by David MacAulay. Houghton Mifflin & Co., New York, 1980.

Once again there was only one copy available. So I read from the book, and we all discussed it and made notes and sketches.[9] As soon as the children heard me read some dates, they announced that we had to make a chronology for the construction of the castle and take notes of everything else that we did not know yet. Again we discussed the text and illustrations, but now the children took the lead, demonstrating how much more informed they were this time. When they tried to draw some of the illustrations, one of the children uttered a sigh and said, "I wish I could draw like MacAulay" (the author) and someone responded, "He had to practice too!"

Midway through *Castle,* the children asked if we could build a model of a castle. I agreed that it seemed the perfect thing to do and, from then on, notes and drawings became much more detailed and were done faster. Suddenly all information seemed vitally necessary in order to build the model. At the same time, because they knew a lot about the Middle Ages, everyone talked more, raised more questions, and offered more ideas, including suggestions for how to build the model.

After we finished reading *Castle,* we planned our model. I told them that it had to be a scale model. At first, the children did not quite know what scale meant, but after a few examples, they seemed to understand the concept and tried to decide on an easy scale. However, the scale they came up with meant that the model would be as small as the seat of a chair. Once they realized how small the people in such a model would be—mere grains of sand—they concluded that the model, and therefore the scale, had to be much larger to be able to make every part of the castle a sensible size. So the children and I had to decide how small we should make the paper people. We figured that for this purpose, a scale of 1 cm : 100 cm was manageable. Using this scale, we calculated that the castle would fit on a table and therefore agreed that 1 : 100 was a good scale to use.

But there was yet another problem. As one child noted, "Making a model of only a castle is like making a sword without the handle. That's silly! People in a castle can't live by themselves." We had to agree; the model should include more than a castle. After some discussion, the group decided that we would build a walled village for serfs and a few free people and that we should include plenty of land. The book did not give specific information on the amounts of land, so we had to figure them out ourselves. We decided that the whole model should cover no more than a third of the classroom. In addition, some space would be required for building the model because we would have to be able to walk around it, which would leave little more than half the room for doing other work. The

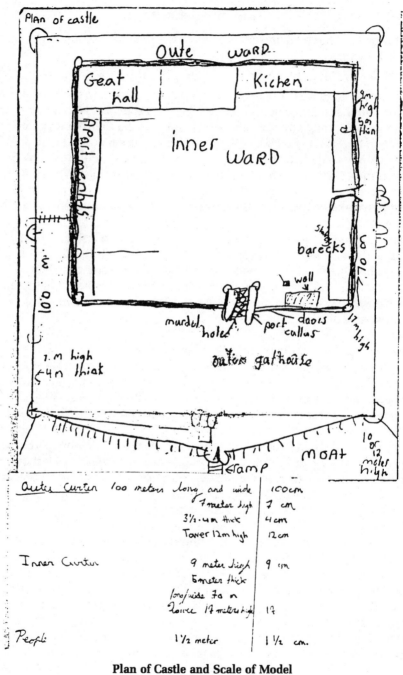

Plan of Castle and Scale of Model
Age 10

children were as overwhelmed as they were excited about this venture. I realized with a shock how near open house was—only seven weeks away!

As soon as we had decided on the scale, all the children looked up the measurements in their notes and calculated the area of the castle and the size of the walls, towers, gates, people, dwellings, and so forth in centimeters. When the children's figures agreed, they went ahead and dragged large sheets of cardboard into the room, arranged the furniture to make one large table that would accommodate the sheets, measured the cardboard base, and then taped and glued the cardboard sheets together. We all cleaned up the room, rearranged the remaining furniture, stood together around the one small table that was left in our cramped quarters, and stared in awe at the large, empty L-shaped cardboard on which somehow our castle and village would grow.

Next we made a list of all the tools and materials we would need to build the model. For many days, the children brought in boxes, cardboard cylinders, and books and pictures of castles and the Middle Ages in general. Then we discussed how we would build the model and what other work still needed to be finished. The tasks and their sequence, insofar as we could predict them, were listed. We decided that working in shifts would be best to make sure that everyone worked on the model and finished other assignments as well. The children looked forward to such great variation in their daily work.

The tasks were to raise the area where the castle itself would be located and to measure the floor plan to scale on the cardboard base; to cut the cardboard boxes and cylinders that we would use for the walls and towers to scale and to mount them onto the base; to decide how and where to make gates in the walls; to build a ramp for a road to the castle; to make a gate to the castle; to make the buildings inside the castle walls; to cover the whole castle with papier mâché and paint it; to draw building stones on the walls; to make the village; and to make paper people, carts, and horses. Many of these tasks had to be researched before the children would know what to do. Furthermore, everything had to be made according to scale! In order not to forget this, one child decided to print the scale in large numbers on the board.

For a long time we did nothing but build the walls and towers of the castle and cover them with papier mâché. A helpful parent provided us with a bagful of small pieces of wood of almost similar size that we used to represent miniature stones. We proceeded to build the walls with these. Gluing the pieces of wood together proved quite interesting because some children had no idea how bricklaying is done. This problem was soon solved by others who knew how to lay bricks and why it is done that way. It did not take us long to realize that we needed many bags of small pieces of wood, something that proved impossible to get. Instead, we used cardboard boxes, which first had to be changed to fit the scale but provided the children with good, purposeful experience in using scale.

Working in shifts, everyone did everything possible to get all tasks completed in time for open house. While some worked on walls and towers, others researched

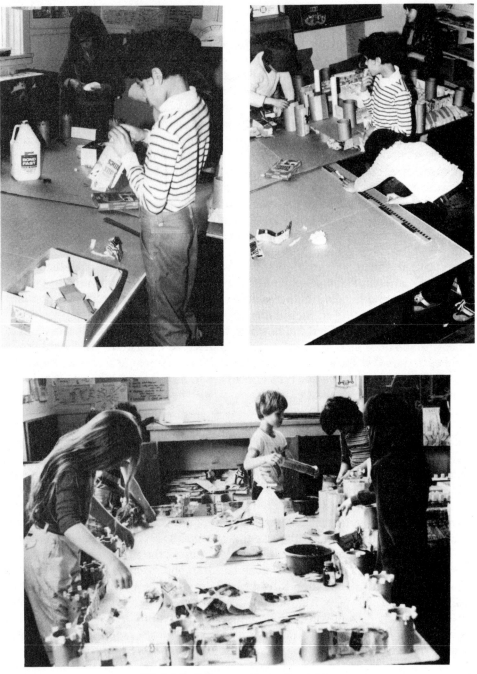

Model Building . . . From Scratch!

and designed other parts of the model, and still others finished their reading and writing assignments. Some children turned out to be excellent model builders, a talent which had not surfaced earlier.* Once the basic structure was finished, some children researched and worked on the buildings inside the castle walls while others researched and worked on the village. All the children wrote up and illustrated the information they had uncovered for display purposes.

When they figured out how many people would have lived in a village such as this, they knew they had to find a way of "mass-producing" houses of specific sizes and different designs. Taking an average of five people per house, they found they would need about 100 paper houses! The children realized that the houses should not all look alike and that some of them had to include the workshops of the craftsmen. They decided that two different designs would suffice—one for the craftsmen and one for all the other villagers.

The next step was to make master models of the two houses. Using a piece of paper, the children and I traced all sides of a cube, which formed a net, and cut the outline out, hoping that we would be able to use this as a folding pattern for a cube shape. The folding pattern worked, but now the children had to adapt it to suit the required measurements and add a peaked roof. To solve these problems, the children had to think about the size of the people, the height of the roof or ceiling, whether there was a second floor, and the size of the overhang of the second floor over the main floor. Once they had calculated the measurements in centimeters, they adapted the paper folding pattern to these measurements. However, when the design was cut out, folded, and glued to form a miniature house, it turned out that improvements needed to be made for easier folding and gluing! The children made many mistakes before the master models were satisfactory and suitable for mass production. Once they had found an efficient way of making a great number of paper houses, mass-producing paper people, horses, and carts was no problem.

Meanwhile, as if there were not enough work to do, the children wanted to try some of the games played in the Middle Ages. They decided to make several different games—checkers, chess, backgammon, and a tilting game. Each game needed a short description of the rules and the background, all of which required more research and writing. The children worked in four groups; each group selected, made, and wrote about one of the games. Once finished, all the children played all the games.

---

*While working on the model, we received an invitation to visit a construction site of an old house being converted into a health food store. Because we thought this might help us learn about changes in tools, building materials, and construction over the past 150 years, we grabbed the opportunity and prepared for the trip as usual. We got more information than anticipated. The carpenter dropped terms such as "apprentice," "journeyman," and "master." This unexpected link with the Middle Ages led the children to ask questions about guilds and, as a result, to discover that guilds were not quite the same as unions. The enthusiastic reports of the trip and the tone of the thank-you letters were evidence of a very successful trip.

As we were nearing completion of our model, one of the boys from a younger group in the school could no longer hide his envy about our activities. He challenged the children by saying that he could make just as good a model as we had in a weekend or less. One of the children responded, "No you can't. We've been learning about building and about the Middle Ages for months, and you haven't. We can build the model because we know a lot about it. And we know that it's a lot of work because you have to build so many different things and do it all to scale so everything is the right size." The challenger did not give up in spite of what the older child had said. After the weekend, he came to school with a model of a castle. There was no comparison, and he knew it. This incident showed that the children had come to appreciate the results of their in-depth study and realized that it had required much varied work over a long period of time.

Finally, two days before open house, the children finished the model, labeled it, and surrounded it with descriptions of the various parts. They only had to put the finishing touches on. However, something seemed to be wrong. The children thought that the model would be boring for visitors because there was nothing to do but look at it. True, but there was not much time left. Undaunted, they suggested adding riddles and quizzes.

So back we went to form small groups and dream up some riddles and questions about the Middle Ages. The results were read aloud and judged by the class. Those that were selected were written on colored paper and added to the display. Everyone agreed that the display was now interesting.

Everything was completed to the children's satisfaction, and we could proceed with the finishing touches. We divided the tasks: the large scrapbooks were updated and put on display; fliers announcing the open house were designed, run off, and distributed among all the children in the school so they could be taken home and hung on bulletin boards in selected buildings; decisions were made about the topics for speeches, which the children then wrote, revised, edited, rewrote, practiced, and rehearsed; displays of written work and the games were labeled; large colorful arrows to show visitors the sequence of displays were put up; the room was cleaned.

A last look around. We were ready to receive guests.

"It sure took a long time before we knew enough to build the model," a child remarked. The others were all beaming!

Looking Back

When we started working on the theme "History of Buildings," I had vaguely in mind that most of our study would concern housing around the world in the twentieth century with some attention to the problems of shelter in the underdeveloped parts of the world. However, the children's tremendous interest in buildings of the Middle Ages and their readiness to do a great amount of work on that period determined our focus.

Finally . . . Finished

Nevertheless, the entire study, even before we hit upon the Middle Ages, bene-fited the children. The first two months were useful in providing an understanding of the relationship between social and technological developments, insight into the reasons behind various building designs, and opportunities to plan a topic of study and gather information about it in a variety of ways. Then, when the main area of interest became clear, through the work involved in planning the study, gathering information, organizing and integrating it by building the scale model of a castle, writing about life in the Middle Ages, and so forth, and presenting what had been learned to others, the benefits to the children were obvious.

While all this was happening, the children were also learning a great deal about the traditional subject areas. However, we never had to drill. All the ''subjects'' were integrated into work that was purposeful and therefore interesting.

Working with a partner and in groups had to be learned as well. Through these grouping arrangements, the children developed an appreciation for cooperation as a pleasant, efficient, and productive way to work and learn.

Building Learning,
Learning from Building:
The Olds and Middles Cooperate—
With Impressive Results

On a chilly day in late November, a crowd assembled in the schoolyard. All eyes fixed on the three children standing before a freshly painted playhouse. The smallest of the three turned to the playhouse, grasped the red ribbon that spanned

This chapter chronicles the experiences of the Middles and the Olds. The text is divided at times into two columns. The column on the left specifically discusses the Middles' activities and therefore is of particular interest to teachers of at least grades one and two. The column on the right tells about the corresponding experiences of the Olds and is of interest to teachers of at least grades three and four. Text that extends the width of the page applies to both groups of children.

the open doorway, and cut the ribbon. The crowd burst into applause. After near-ly three months of planning, researching, and building, the children declared their playhouse officially open.

For this unit on construction, we, the teachers, had gone through the usual preparatory steps—selecting a theme, brainstorming ideas, and then finding resources. We had consulted with architects, construction workers, and building suppliers, including a lumber company and hardware store. Many of these sources offered free printed matter on building projects. Nevertheless, our main source of reading materials was, as usual, the library. We had looked for fictional as well as factual books and those that are not necessarily considered children's books.[1] We had then done some studying on the topic and some initial planning.

When we decided to build the playhouse, we felt a bit apprehensive. None of us had ever done anything remotely related to constructing a building before. This theme study clearly was going to be a learning experience for us as well as the children.

Introducing the Theme to the Children and Planning our Study

Six- to Eight-Year-Olds

The Middles began by brainstorming about the idea of work. To assist them, I raised questions such as "What is work? What is play? How are they different?" "If work is something you don't especially like doing, and play is something you do enjoy, what about people who enjoy their jobs? Are they working or playing?"

The group considered asking these questions in a survey to find out how other people think about work. The original plan was to survey parents at home, but one of the children suggested they also survey peers and school friends. Everyone liked the idea, so that is what they did.

I included the children in the planning to show them that their ideas are valid as well as to give them input in

Eight- to Ten-Year-Olds

The Olds began their year by thinking about and discussing how they would survive in the wilderness. As a result of the first brainstorm, they agreed that the bare essentials for life would be food, water, fire, and shelter. The brainstorm also led to many questions and poten-tial problems. For example, the children wondered how they would know which plants were edible. One child suggested using trial and error as a method, but after the group discussed the possibili-ty of someone being poisoned, perhaps fatally, they dismissed this suggestion. The children also talked about the amount of work required to survive and how survival would be easier with tools. But tools don't just appear out of nowhere, and with no corner hardware store to go to, the children faced the

Six- to Eight-Year-Olds

deciding class activities. The children also set learning goals for themselves whenever possible, but always with my guidance. Learning to establish goals helped the children concentrate their energies and made large tasks easier by breaking them down into manageable pieces.

We then talked about tools and how they make our work easier. I encouraged the children to think of books they have at home about the topic and of tools they have and to bring them in the next day. Several children brought in common household tools from home. I wanted the children to understand that they must take an active part in gathering the information to further the inquiry. In other words, information doesn't exist only because teachers supply it; the children must also contribute their share.

Planning a Field Trip

We concluded our brainstorming by talking about work in relation to the basics of life. What are the basics for life? If you lived in the woods, what kinds of things would you need to survive? The children thought of a number of items, such as a trailer, recreational vehicles, and a speedboat. To help them focus on the more basic requirements I asked some pointed questions such as: Can a speedboat keep you from going hungry? and Will it keep you warm and dry? This time the children decided they would need food, clothes, shelter, and a fire as well as tools to help supply themselves with these things. From

Eight- to Ten-Year-Olds

alternatives to do without or to make the tools themselves.

After discussing these and other questions, the Olds brainstormed once again and added these criteria for survival: selection of good territory with abundant resources, development of tools and skills, and organization of work.

These first brainstorms brought out many suggestions and many more questions. More information was needed. I read the children a book about early settlements and the development of tools. They then read a simpler version about the settlements of early peoples.

The additional information gained through the reading sparked even more lively discussion and debate among the children. After a couple of days, I suggested that we go to the woods and see for ourselves just how difficult it might be to survive in the wilderness.

Planning a Field Trip

Using their recorded brainstorm on surviving in the wilderness, the children planned the details of the trip. They decided to begin by finding a good location. As they had agreed earlier, the site should be close to water and food with plenty of trees and building materials not far off the trail, and safe for building a fire. Then they would try to find food, build a shelter, and make some tools. Because they were also to make a map of the park from the entrance to the place where they would work, they planned to find and record a variety of landmarks.

The children talked about the many

Six- to Eight-Year-Olds

this point, it was an easy step to suggest that we go to the park and see firsthand how difficult it might be to supply some of these basic needs.

Eight- to Ten-Year-Olds

animals that depend upon the forest environment for their survival. This discussion led to the decision to be as quiet as possible in order not to disturb the natural environment.

After all tasks had been listed, the groups discussed the matter of organization. Do you try to do the tasks all by yourself? No. You work with a partner and you divide the workload.

To make our "wilderness" experience more real, we planned to leave our snacks and lunches at the park entrance and return there only after we had completed our tasks and it was time to go home. Furthermore, with the exception of pencil and paper, no one would bring any tools.

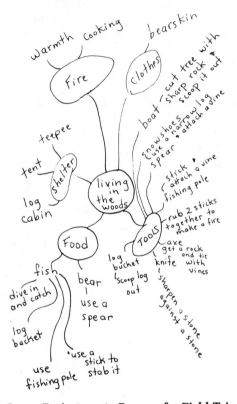

Group Brainstorm to Prepare for Field Trip
Middles (Recorded by Teacher)

Survival in the "Wilderness"

We use the community for our activities as much as possible, and for this theme study, we decided to begin with a trip to the park to establish our study in the context of the "real world." By saying real world, we don't mean to suggest that what happens in the classroom isn't valuable or that it has less importance than outside activities. It's just that too often what happens in schools is totally unrelated to what happens in students' lives outside the classroom. We try to avoid this problem first of all by choosing a theme that has importance to all our lives and second by always emphasizing that what we are doing has a purpose. The reasons for building houses may seem obvious to us as adults, but to six- to ten-year-olds they are not as clear. For children to see for themselves, in the woods in the cold and with the threat of rainfall, is the best way to make some of the reasons clear to them.

Shubie Park is a public recreation area several kilometers from the school. We were able to use public transportation, but it required three buses to get there. We had previously discussed how to behave on public buses as well as in the woods. We planned to try to leave the park the way we found it. When we arrived at the park, the Middles and the Olds were to find two separate areas and set to work on the lists of tasks they had prepared in the classroom. Within each group, children would work with a partner.

Six- to Eight-Year-Olds

The Middles began by trying to make some crude tools. They looked around for sources of food and actually discovered some blueberries and blackberries. Two six-year-olds had the initiative to try their hand at fishing. They made a pole from a long branch and used some string for a line and a leaf for bait. The few minutes that they stood at the water's edge produced no edible results. Nevertheless, it was an encouraging start that two such young

Eight- to Ten-Year-Olds

The Olds began work as soon as we reached the park. Taking note of landmarks along the way, they drew maps of our path to their site. Then they set about finding materials for a shelter.

The results of the building efforts ranged from the surprisingly sophisticated to the quite crude. One team built a very good lean-to from fern-covered branches supported by a tree trunk and a boulder, but another team simply placed a couple of long thin branches on the high interlacing branches of two trees and was quite happy with

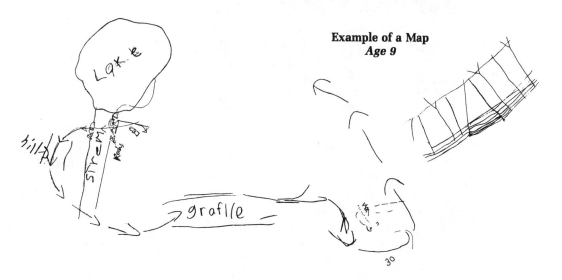

Example of a Map
Age 9

Six- to Eight-Year-Olds

children should not only come up with the idea but also cooperate with each other to act upon it.

Most members of the group also attempted to build simple shelters. At first the shelters were very sparse. One had a spindly little branch supported only by a few rocks as a corner post. In other cases, basic design was neglected in favor of relatively unimportant details.

> I found some Black baries.
> we made a tool with a rock and a Stick.

(I found some black berries. We made a tool with a rock and a stick.)
Age 7

> I FAND BAK BARS
> I WATFSHING
> WE MAD ASHLTR
> WE RAD A KOS

(I found black berries.
I went fishing.
We made a shelter. We found
a house.)
Age 6

Examples of Field Notes

Eight- to Ten-Year-Olds

that. While most children were building one-room shelters, one pair was busily designing a shelter with several rooms but forgot to construct a roof. Another team added a moss-covered floor to their hut. At the end of the day, the Olds made notes and drew pictures of what they had done.

> we made a shelter it was a good spot becuse The Prey cold not see The hunter behind The wall we made it with furns and a log and barmchis and we also made a spear with a sharptek and a roof and po

Example of Field Notes
Age 8

Six- to Eight-Year-Olds

OURARIP

○ tools
a hamUR We t8K
a SiK and a RaKi and a
weD and tat is thaw
we maD a hamR

② fiRe
tac 2
SiS and
RaB and
RaB and
you wall
hav a fiRe

③ Place to Live
Logs and Sis
and wood
we maD a Lag caBin But
the Ligs wiR Soking wa
So we coDit mak a
④ food Lag caBin
we v soND BaK BiReS and BtLS

Example of Field Notes
Age 6

(Our Trip
1. *Tools*
   A hammer. We took a stick and a rock and a weed and that is how we made a hammer.
2. *Fire*
   Take 2 sticks and rub and rub and you will have a fire.
3. *Place to Live*
   Logs and sticks and wood. We tried to make a log cabin. But the logs were soaking wet so we couldn't make a log cabin.
4. *Food*
   We have some blackberries and beetles.)

For example, one shelter was equipped with coat hooks made from roots arranged neatly in a row before the rest of the shelter was even started. After some discussion, some of the pairs started using more appropriate shelter designs such as fern-covered branches in a lean-to shape, but by now it was too late in the afternoon to finish them.

Everyone was responsible for making notes or illustrations about what he or she had observed and tried out.

The field trip was a valuable exercise for the children in how to gather first-hand information. It was also a good opportunity for us to observe the children at work. Because the trip took place very early in the school year, we were still getting to know the children. Therefore, we were not only looking for what they knew about building but were also observing how they organized their learning, how willing they were to take risks, and how they worked together.

Gathering Information on How to Build

Back in the classroom the next day, we again used brainstorms to discuss what we had learned. The children talked about the difficulties they had encountered and about the successes they had experienced. It is at this time that the teacher can influence the direction of the theme inquiry. Because children are eager to learn and are curious about everything, our trip to Shubie Park could have been used for a variety of theme studies. For instance, we could have focused on plant life for a theme on living things, or we might have pursued the survival aspects for a theme on settlements and urbanization. Instead, for our theme of "People and Their Work," we settled on the subtopic of "Building Construction."

Experiments

Six- to Eight-Year-Olds

The first thing the Middles needed to understand was the importance of support and bracing in relation to size and shape in order to make a stable structure. To grasp this concept, they experimented with building structures as tall and as strong as they could out of paper strips and glue. The children tested the stability of their structures by trying to blow them down. Afterward

Testing the Stability of Paper Structures—"The Blow Test"
Age 7

Eight- to Ten-Year-Olds

In the follow-up discussions about the children's experiences with building a shelter in the forest, I focused the children's attention on the quality of the structures by asking such questions as, Would it survive a storm? Would you be warm there? Would it keep out wild animals? and Which of the materials you worked with were most useful—rigid or flexible, heavy or light?

I suggested that the children do an experiment to further investigate the quality of structures. I gave them blocks and Cuisinaire Rods to build stable structures. The children then tested the stability of the structures by fanning and blowing on them. During the testing, they had to determine not only which size, shape, and weight of blocks were best but also how the blocks should be placed to form sturdy shapes. For example, one child had constructed a large walled area and was attempting to stabilize it by adding a roof. She placed

Six- to Eight-Year-Olds

everyone discussed the results of the experiments and listed the factors that made for strong structures, such as good bracing and multiple layers of strips.

I had planned to take the children out to look at actual houses for the next lesson, but wet weather made a change in plans necessary. Instead I showed them a large variety of house designs using pictures of buildings from many different cultures. The children identified a number of basic shapes, such as cube, semisphere, and pyramid.

Working in pairs, they once again made paper strip structures using these basic shapes. Then they tested the strength of each structure by putting blocks one by one on top of it to see how many it could hold before sagging or collapsing. They recorded their observations as they worked by drawing a picture of what the paper structures looked like with the blocks on top.

When everyone had finished, the class discussed the activity. The results of the tests revealed that certain shapes are better for bracing than others. Through their own hands-on, trial-and-error activity, the children were able to recognize and to appreciate the bracing qualities of shapes in building designs. The Middles were now ready to discuss more detailed aspects of building design and materials.

Eight- to Ten-Year-Olds

a piece of paper on top, and it immediately sagged in the middle. She was able to blow the structure over easily and hypothesized that the paper was not rigid and heavy enough to provide stability. She proved her hypothesis by placing a hardcover book on top of her structure and once again blowing. This time she had to exert a much greater effort to knock the structure down.

This activity provided a natural context for me to introduce such building terms as sill, posts, beams, studs, joists, and bracing. The experiment also brought up related concerns about roof structures. Would a peaked, slanted, or spherical shape be best, and which materials might be used?

Learning from Building Construction Workers

After these shape and construction experiments, we told the children that they were going to build a playhouse. Because none of us, including the teachers, had any experience with building, we decided to begin by watching someone else building. A trip to a house being renovated would provide firsthand information that couldn't be duplicated in any other way. We knew of such a house and had talked with the owners and received permission to visit.

As usual the children used brainstorming to prepare for the trip. In addition to observing at the renovation site, they also wanted to ask questions. They began by examining and discussing some real blueprints. Based on this discussion they thought of as many aspects of house building as they could—digging a foundation, putting up the walls, and so forth. Then they composed their questions. Some of the older children prepared really interesting questions on subjects such as unions, safety, what it is like to be a carpenter, and improvements in tools and houses. We grouped the children into pairs and divided the list of questions among

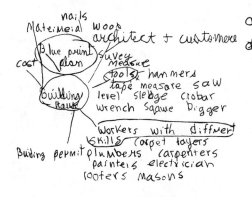

Brainstorm Before Trip to
Building Construction Site
Age 9

do you Like work
do How do you aTach The
wood To The cogcreT
do you PuT The wood
or The concreT on The
ouT Side how do you
Make Sher The Wales wonT
faII over. do you use
na les

Questions to Ask Building
Construction Workers
Age 8

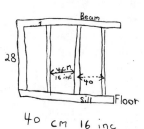

Example of Notes Made During Trip
to Building Construction Site
Age 9

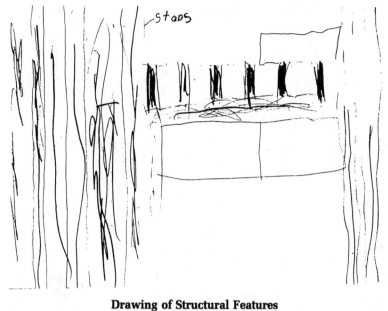

Drawing of Structural Features
Age 8

the pairs. Teamwork is of particular importance for interviews because interviewing is not easy. It requires asking a question, making note of the answer, and deciding whether to ask a new question that occurs to the interviewer or sticking to the list of previously formulated questions. With partners, one person can ask the question while the other records the answer, thus sharing the responsibility.

In addition to interviewing the workers, each group made a few drawings of the house illustrating the interior as best they could. For children to accurately draw what they see is as good a way of clarifying and recording information as taking notes because they must understand what they are looking at in order to draw it accurately. For example, to indicate the joining of a post and a beam, many of the children drew pictures such as the following:

Age 6

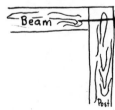

(Not strong: Beam is hanging on nails only.)

(Strong: Beam rests on posts.)

(Thickness of wood and joining of wood are not shown.)

These illustrations indicate different levels of understanding about the basic structure. However, the children who drew pictures like this:

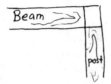

revealed that they simply didn't understand the concept of support because in this drawing, the beam is not supported at all.

Learning from a Road Construction Crew

A second convenient opportunity occurred for gathering firsthand information. It so happened that repairs were being made to the sidewalk in front of a building not far from the school. The timing was perfect because we had been discussing how to build the foundation for the playhouse. The children very quickly brainstormed a list of questions and rushed over to learn what they could. Once again the workers were very helpful and willingly answered all questions. The children asked about the ingredients of concrete, how it is made, how you learn to make it, and what accidents can happen. Some of the children were even able to help the workers a little by shoveling some concrete into the frame.

(*Use:* sidewalks, foundations of buildings and houses, steps, streets, plant pots.

What is concrete? a mixture of gravel, sand, cement powder, lime powder, water.

Pouring concrete: before pouring concrete you have to make a mold out of wood.

wood frame fencing

Before pouring concrete you have to spray the wood.

thin layer of gravel)

Example of Notes Made During Trip to Road Construction Site
Age 9

What ikind of stenght does concrete have?
it can take much compression but concrete can not take presser it is not flexible. That why people put a faceing or steel bars it wont crack as much

(What kind of strength does concrete have?
It can take much compression but concrete cannot take pressure. It is not flexible. That's why people put a facing or steel bars so it won't crack as much.)

Example of Notes Made During Trip to Road Construction Site
Age 9

While both groups were involved with the next stage of the theme study (drawing blueprints and building scale models of the playhouse), we had another opportunity to visit a renovation site. Only the Olds interrupted their work in order to take advantage of this.

Flexibility in Lesson Plans

We maintain flexibility in our lesson plans so that it is possible to take advantage of such opportunities. During our initial planning, we decide upon a number of information-gathering trips. However, when you use the community as a teaching resource, it is not always possible to plan every detail in advance. You can plan only certain excursions and keep your eyes and ears open for others.

Six- to Eight-Year-Olds

The Middles were coping with many difficulties at this challenging stage, so they didn't go on this latest field trip to a renovation site. To send them on another information-gathering trip would have been counterproductive. They were discovering that construction is a very involved activity. The questions they had asked of the workers at the first renovation site had not always received simple, short replies. Each new idea seemed to open a whole book of possibilities.

Eight- to Ten-Year-Olds

The Olds were capable of handling most of the information and, in fact, benefited from the second visit to a building construction site. They were able to revise the questions they had asked the first time to make them more focused and pertinent. When one is first finding out about a new topic, very often one doesn't know enough to ask the right questions. When the questions are poor, the answers are usually not very informative. Therefore, the second visit provided a chance for the children to ask

Six- to Eight-Year-Olds

So that the Middles would not feel overwhelmed and frustrated, I pared down their activities to the fundamentals of the building process. For this age group, that meant hands-on activities to focus on what makes a stable structure, the sequence of frame house construction, and a few basic techniques and terms.

A classroom activitiy that helped to clarify the new ideas about frame construction was an experiment with Tinker Toys. These toys consist of wooden sticks and round attachments into which the ends of the sticks can be placed. Using these, the children tried making the frame of a house. This exercise helped them understand a couple of things. To begin with, they could see

Eight- to Ten-Year-Olds

better questions as well as new ones that had since occurred to them.

The children noticed a number of differences between the first and second renovation sites. At the first site, an architect had designed the blueprints, and, as a result, they were highly detailed. A contractor had made the blueprints for the second renovation work. Being a carpenter himself, he had left out many details that he knew would be assumed by the workers.

Another contrast was provided by the age of the buildings. The walls of the two buildings that had been broken open revealed different materials and construction methods. The workers themselves made a further difference. Those at the first construction site used

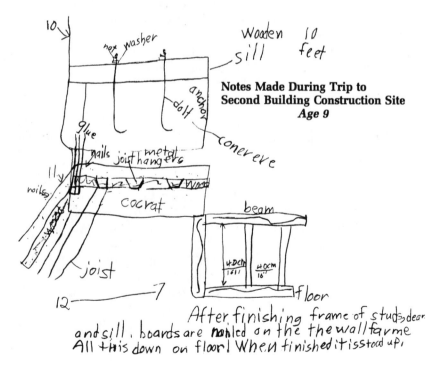

Notes Made During Trip to Second Building Construction Site
Age 9

Six- to Eight-Year-Olds

that some sort of logical building sequence is necessary: first you build the foundation, then the walls, and then the top structure. They could also see the necessity of using braces to make their frames more stable. Although they had seen the workers using studs and braces at the renovation site, using these support structures themselves made the wisdom of this building practice very clear.

Eight- to Ten-Year-Olds

mainly electric tools and, although friendly and willing to answer our questions, continued to work. Those at the second site used many more hand tools and stopped working not only to answer our questions but also to add much information and to show us examples. These workers also included many new ideas and terms in their explanations.

Integrating and Applying Information: Making Models and Blueprints of the Playhouse

Our classroom activities and field trips had provided us with a foundation of information and experiences. However, we were still a long way from being ready to build the playhouse. The next step was to become familiar with all aspects of constructing a playhouse. We also had to integrate what we had learned so far. To accomplish these two goals, we planned to draw blueprints and make scale models of the playhouse. Architects very often do this, although it is not standard building procedure.

Six- to Eight-Year-Olds

The Middles began by building a paper playhouse. To ask them to begin by drawing blueprints, even without scale, would have been too abstract a task for them. Consequently, a different approach was necessary. The children would collectively build a model of the playhouse.

They started by using blueprints that I had prepared. I had made one blueprint for each section of the house—the floor, the four walls, and the roof. I had drawn the blueprints to a scale of one centimeter to twenty because the larger pieces were easier for these young children to manipulate. The building materials for the model were cardboard

Eight- to Ten-Year-Olds

The Olds began their playhouse construction activities by discussing the shape and purpose of the playhouse. They also began considering the difficulties they might encounter when building.

They decided that a square house with a large door opening and a window on each of the three remaining sides would be best. The door and windows would provide ample light for the interior and at the same time would allow people to see immediately if someone inside the house was hurt. We decided on a slanted roof structure, because a peaked roof would be too difficult to construct, and a flat roof, though easy to

Six- to Eight-Year-Olds

strips representing two-by-fours (that I had precut) and sheets of heavy paper representing plywood sheets.

Each team of two children took one blueprint and cut the two-by-fours by laying the cardboard strips down on the blueprint to measure the correct length. Next the children glued the strips together to form the frame. They followed the same procedure for measuring and cutting the paper sheets representing plywood. Then as a group, we assembled the floor, the four walls, and the roof to finish the model. This sequence was the same as assembling a real frame house and functioned as a rehearsal for the playhouse construction.

Actually, the process didn't go as smoothly as the above description may suggest. The children found that great accuracy in measuring and cutting was necessary; otherwise the parts wouldn't fit together when we tried assembling the whole. Consequently, many sections had to be redone. However, this process provided a valuable example of the consequences of inaccurate measurement. As the pile of paper errors grew, the children began to appreciate the potential waste of materials, time, and energy that could occur and recur when building the real playhouse.

When the paper playhouse was finished, the children made paper models of themselves to scale. We did this particular activity so that the children would have a clearer understanding of the actual size of the proposed playhouse. Comparing their paper figures to the model helped make the playhouse real in their minds.

First the children measured each

Eight- to Ten-Year-Olds

build, would eventually rot from accumulated water.

Next the children sketched each side of the playhouse. They didn't worry about scale at this point. They also tried to make one drawing of the total house in perspective just to get an idea of what the sides of the playhouse were going to look like.

Once the pictures were drawn, the measurements had to be added. These had been decided upon previously by the teachers, but it was a valuable exercise for the children to determine the measurements for themselves. Through discussion, they agreed that the floor space should be suitable for about four or five "medium-sized" children to play in. They also decided that four big children were roughly equivalent to five medium-sized children. The four largest children then sat together on small chairs in a corner of the classroom while others placed two metersticks on the floor and marked off the space. The four then moved around a bit to be sure there was enough space for playing. After adjusting the metersticks a couple of times, the children measured the area. They finally decided on an area of approximately two meters by two meters for the floor space.

The next consideration was the height of the door, the three windows, and the roof. The children suggested that the door opening should be high enough for the tallest child to pass through and that the sills of the windows should be lower than the shoulders of the smallest child in the school. As for the roof, they suggested that it be high enough so that an adult

Six- to Eight-Year-Olds

other using metersticks. Then they made scale models of themselves using the proportion of one centimeter to twenty centimeters. This activity turned out to have an unexpected benefit. When one of the girls stood her paper figure by the door of the playhouse, she realized that her head was going to hit the door frame. We had underestimated the height of the children when we had worked out the measurements. Fortunately, this discovery allowed us to correct our mistake and save costly adjustments to the real playhouse later.

It wasn't until this point that the children made their own blueprints. Before beginning, we examined samples of actual blueprints and brainstormed about the kinds of information they contained. We talked about why particular information is included and how it helps the builder. Then, using my blueprints as models, each team of two drew a blueprint of the part of the paper model that they had worked on.

This activity wasn't simply a case of copying the teacher's work. There were many new skills the children had to learn to turn this three-dimensional model back into two-dimensional blueprints. They had to learn to measure and count accurately using the graph paper. Because the squares on the graph paper represented ten centimeters, the children had to count by tens to find the correct length of each beam and post on the blueprint. This was no easy task. When a pair had difficulties counting, I helped by counting out loud with them and encouraging others to join in. This procedure reinforced the process of counting and measuring for the par-

Eight- to Ten-Year-Olds

could comfortably stand inside the playhouse. The children determined all these measurements and added them to a sketch of the playhouse on the blackboard.

When I compared the measurements that the children had worked out to those of the teachers, I discovered that the figures were very similar. One important difference was the height of the door. The measurements the children had worked out were more sensible and, therefore, would be used.

Once again the children drew sketches of the playhouse. This time they added the measurements as well as the placements of joists, studs, and rafters. Booklets from the Canadian Mortgage and Housing Company, which contained many diagrams, proved very helpful. We noticed that not only were the spaces between the joists, studs, and rafters uniform, but they were prescribed by the building code. Remembering our experiments making stable structures, we briefly discussed the necessity of a building code to ensure safety.

Although the children did not draw these last sketches to scale, they made great efforts to keep them proportional. Much math was involved, including rounding off numbers and estimating lengths and fractions when drawing door and window openings. The children also had to consider perspective when drawing the two-by-fours: which side of the beam would be facing up—the two-inch side or the four-inch side?

Because these sketches were meant just as diagrams prior to making the real

Six- to Eight-Year-Olds

ticular pair as well as for all those who had listened or chimed in. At the same time, the children pointed to each line with a pencil tip so that it was easy to keep accurate count. Thin pencil tips were a big improvement over fat fingers that covered up more than one line on the graph paper.

Drawing the lines was also challenging because using a ruler to draw straight lines was a new experience for many of the children. Demonstrations of bracing the ruler before drawing became part of our daily routine. As soon as any of the children had gained competence in counting or drawing, they were encouraged to help others.

Most of the children, however, continued to have the greatest difficulty drawing the posts, beams, and sills so that they were structurally correct. Even though the children had my blueprint as an example, they were not able to accurately duplicate it until they completely understood why the beam had to rest on top of the post, or why the posts and beams had to have thickness and could not be represented simply by line drawings.

I circulated from group to group and helped with each difficulty as it arose. I referred to the blocks, Tinker Toys, and model many times in order to clarify the necessity for adequate bracing and support as well as drawing what the children saw. Whenever everyone experienced similar troubles, I stopped the pair activities and got the whole group to investigate and discuss the difficulty together. Slowly but surely, the first

Eight- to Ten-Year-Olds

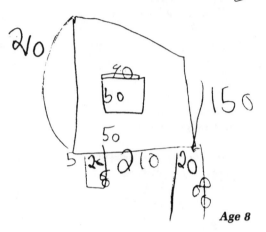

Age 8

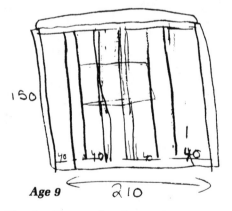

Age 9

Sketches Prepared Before Making Blueprints

Six- to Eight-Year-Olds

hesitant and scratchy trials were replaced by drawings that actually looked like blueprints.

Eight- to Ten-Year-Olds

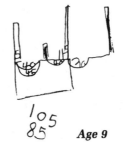

$\frac{105}{85}$ *Age 9*

Sketch Prepared Before Making Blueprints
Age 9

blueprints, we completed drawings for only two or three of the six parts of the playhouse. We also used these drawings to begin discussing the building sequence: first the foundation, then the floor, the walls, and finally the roof.

The children were now ready to draw the blueprints, and this meant drawing to scale. To help with this task, they could refer to their first sketches, and they would also construct scale models. The children would work on the blueprints and the scale models at the same time. Having three-dimensional models to refer to would be of great help to the children during this difficult work.

Using cardboard strips to represent two-by-fours and paper for plywood

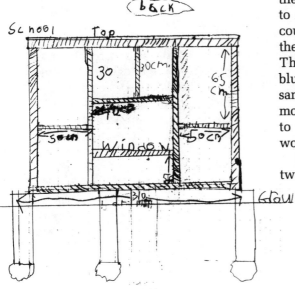

Example of Blueprint: Back Wall Frame
Ages 6 and 7

Eight- to Ten-Year-Olds

sheets, they would build the model a section at a time. They would use their first drawings with the measurements to make the model. Once one section was completed, they would draw a corresponding blueprint to scale. Each team of two children would draw a set of blueprints.

They began the models by building the floor. The children used the actual measurements of the floor and reduced them to a scale of one centimeter to ten. This scale had been chosen because it would be easy for the children to use, thus making the task as simple as possible. There was no need to further complicate an already difficult task by using an unfamiliar scale of one to six, for example, that would have served no useful teaching purpose. In fact, such a complication would probably have defeated the children from the outset.

Using the reduced measurements, the children cut the cardboard sills and joists and glued them together to form the frame of the floor and the front side with its door opening. Then, as a class, we drew the scale representation on graph paper. First I drew a part on the board, and then the children counted the appropriate number of squares on the graph paper to draw the same part to scale. One square of graph paper represented ten centimeters. At times it was helpful for the children to use Cuisinaire Rods as models to accurately draw the joining of two pieces of wood.

These first blueprints took about four hours of observing, building, calculating, measuring, drawing, and erasing. The children had to consider many

Eight- to Ten-Year-Olds

things: how to place and space the studs; how to make a door opening that would still ensure adequate support for the roof; how to accurately calculate and transfer the measurements; and so on. At first there was much moaning and groaning and erasing and redrawing, but eventually all the children produced blueprints that they were satisfied could not be improved.

After this first effort, the children worked on their own, helping each other and learning from their mistakes. Using this procedure of alternating building with drawing, the children completed both the model and the blueprints of the five remaining parts (four walls and roof). As the group gained experience, this work went much faster and became enjoyable. Building the model while drawing was especially useful for clarifying such details as joining the walls at the corners and constructing the roof and the overhang.

The roof posed more building problems than we had anticipated. The rafters had to be cut at an angle so that they could easily rest on the front and back beams. However, because there had to be room for cutting notches in them, the rafters had to be made out of two-by-sixes, instead of two-by-fours. This meant that the weight per rafter would increase and that the roof might possibly be too heavy for the walls to support. We again consulted the Canadian Mortgage and Housing Company booklets and found, to our great relief, that they included information on guidelines for support of lumber of specific sizes and weights per foot. A

Eight- to Ten-Year-Olds

quick calculation showed that it would be safe to use as many two-by-six rafters as we needed for the size of our roof. One child, remembering our experiment with the paper and notebook roof, remarked, "And now the walls will be stronger too, and the roof will not blow off in a storm!"

Next we faced the problem of the purpose, placement, and size of roof overhang. Looking at the roofs of buildings near the school, we noticed that there was overhang on one set of opposite sides but not on the other. We reasoned that the placement of the overhang was probably related to the direction of prevailing wind and rain and that the purpose of the overhang was to help protect the structure from rain and snow and eventual rot. Thus, we decided to build our overhang on the same two opposite sides of our playhouse as the buildings near the school.

Yet, how much overhang was enough? After a lengthy discussion, the children built the roofs as best they could. The result was three different kinds of roofs. Another discussion followed. Finally we decided to ask advice from an expert, either a carpenter or an architect.

Once the children had finished all their models, they discussed putting paper "plywood" on the floor, walls, and roof. Because sheets of plywood come in specific sizes, the children had to reduce these sizes to scale and, using squared paper of that size, they put up the "plywood." This was difficult because the "plywood sheet" had to extend from the middle of one stud, joist,

Eight- to Ten-Year-Olds

Step 5 put ply wood on Joist and nail it This will be the floor

Not good

plywood   crat

good

Example of Notes on How to Build the Playhouse, Made Before Actual Construction

Age 8

or rafter to the middle of the next one. The children finished off by leaving some sides uncovered so that they could see the inside of the model and therefore make better use of the model when building the real playhouse.

When the blueprints and models were finally completed, the children were visibly proud of their work. They commented on how difficult it had been and how good it had been to try building with cardboard, paper, and glue before using wood, tools, and nails. Two difficulties the Olds particularly mentioned were building and drawing the corners of the walls and the roof. One child commented, ''It sounded so easy when the carpenters told us how to do it, but it wasn't at all! They didn't explain it well because for them it is so clear!''

To make the models more realistic, the children drew themselves to scale.

Eight- to Ten-Year-Olds

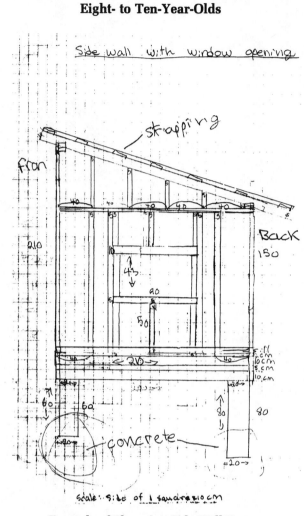

Example of Blueprint: Side Wall Frame
Age 9

They measured each other's length and width and reduced them to the same scale of one centimeter to ten. Next they marked the dimensions off on a piece of stiff paper and drew themselves to fit the dimensions. Then they colored the paper children, cut them out, and glued them onto the model playhouse in a standing position.

This whole process of drawing blueprints and building the scale models took both groups about three weeks.

Building Permit

Back in the summer when we, the teachers, had planned the theme activities, we had spoken to the architect who works in the University Planning Department, not only to make sure the university would have no objections to our plans to build on their land, but also to consult him for any advice he could give us. We now approached him again to ask if he would participate in the next phase of our construction process. Because we wanted the experience of planning and building the playhouse to be as realistic as possible for the children, we had decided that they should apply for a building permit. The university architect was our person. He readily agreed to serve as the "city building inspector" and receive our request for a building permit. The Olds would give a presentation explaining what they had learned about building and what their plans were for building the playhouse, and hopefully, our inspector would decide that we could proceed. He took his participation very seriously and even came to the school the day before the presentation to take a look at the work that the children had done so that he could make his comments appropriate to their knowledge and understanding. He left that day assuring us, the teachers, that he would treat the children and their presentation with the same seriousness he would give to an adult presentation.

Six- to Eight-Year-Olds

The Middles' part in the presentation would be less demanding than that of the Olds. When they brainstormed about the proposed visit, they expressed curiosity about the job of an architect. They didn't really understand what an architect was—how the job differed from that of a carpenter, for instance. So they decided to interview the architect and brainstormed a list of questions to ask him. It was agreed that each child would ask one question and that the group as a whole would record the answers.

Eight- to Ten-Year-Olds

The concept of a building permit was not new to the Olds. They had heard of it at one of the building sites we had visited and had seen references to it in the Canadian Mortgage and Housing Company booklets. The children's own experience building the scale models had shown them that there were many ways to go wrong and had led to discussions about building a safe structure and about government regulations and inspectors. They understood that a building permit was necessary and required by law. So they knew that their

Six- to Eight-Year-Olds

Middles Questions for Architect

① Will our house be secure enough if we build it like the model? it will be sacuere a note. some people might come in it

② Is the model too big or too small compared to other models? there all the same

③ What do you need to know to be an architect? you try to bild a toy house first then when you grow up you lern to be a arkatect

④ Do we have enough studs for keeping the house up? there are a note studs you have to do bracing betan you bild it

⑤ Is our house going to work out? we are going to be carePull

⑥ Do you build a model when you build a house? he sometimes dose it he bild one of the climer

⑦ How do you learn to be an architect? you need to have a lot of intarest

(Text:
1. It will be secure enough. Some people might come in it.
2. They are all the same.
3. You try to build a toy house first. Then when you grow up you learn to be an architect.
4. There are enough studs. You have to do bracing before you build it.
5. We are going to be careful.
6. He sometimes doesn't. He built one of the climbers.
7. You need to have a lot of interest.)

Notes on Interview with Architect
Age 7

Eight- to Ten-Year-Olds

major task was to convince the "building inspector" that they knew enough about building to go ahead and construct a safe playhouse.

They assembled all the materials they had collected so far—their notes from the field trips, the models, and the blueprints. Then they brainstormed the content of the presentation and decided that the request for the permit should cover the following points:

- why the children wanted to build the playhouse;
- what they could learn from building it; and
- what they had learned so far about how to build.

Using these three points, each child wrote a rough copy of a "Request for a Building Permit." The children helped each other revise and edit and then wrote final neat copies. Next each one assembled a booklet made up of the written request for a building permit, a list of materials to be used, and the blueprints.

The group then brainstormed how the presentation should be made. We listed the responsibilities and divided them among the group. Two children were to read their requests for the permit. Then one child was to speak about constructing the floor using short pieces of two-by-fours to represent the joists and the sills. Another was to discuss how to build the frames for the four walls; this child would be followed by another who would speak about raising the walls. All of the children would refer to their models, which they would bring along to the presentation. Because the

Building materials

2"x4" wood for studs, sills, posts, joists, rafters.

2"x6" wood for door and window header
        Plywood for the floor, roof, and
        walls. 2½" nails (6 cm)
tarpaper roof, walls
shingles for roof }
shingles for wall } depends on price
wolmanized posts concrete for posts outdoor
later paint

Building tools

hammer
saw
level
measuring tape
square
pencil

Age 9

Request for Building permit for constructing a playhouse in the playground of the Dalhousie University Elementary School, of the Department of Education

We would like to have a playhouse because: It helps us learn about building & tools, It will improve the playground and give some more playspace. It will give them some experience about building things

We interviewed people & visited construction sites, We made a model on scale for more practice, and we had to get help & permission from teachers and parents. for all these reasons we feel we are now able to build the house.

please examine our model & blueprints. We hope that you except them and give us a building permit
        yours, sincerely

Pages from Proposal Presented to Architect
Age 9

Eight- to Ten-Year-Olds

children had been unsure of how to build the roof and had, therefore, made three different kinds on the models, three children would explain their solutions to the roof problem and would ask the architect for advice. One child would then speak about the sequence of the building tasks and the finishing touches such as shingling and painting. In conclusion, a child would give a list of materials needed and another would talk about safety during construction. After helping each other polish and rehearse their presentations, they were ready to see the architect.

The following morning, equipped with their models, blueprints, demonstration items, written speeches, and questions, the Middles and the Olds found themselves seated in plush swivel armchairs around the huge conference table of the University Planning Department. The Olds made their presentation and the

(Courtesy of The Chronicle-Herald)

STUDENT PROJECT—Students from Dalhousie Elementary School, a school sponsored by Dalhousie University's department of education, drew up blueprints for a playhouse to be built on the Studley campus. Senior staff architect Martin Giddy discusses the project with grade five* student David Mitchell, left.

Note: Should be grade 4.

Wamboldt-Waterfield

Coverage of Our Trip to Architect in Local Newspaper

Middles asked their questions. The architect commented on each presentation, answered some questions, and asked others. Then he gave a brief talk about the building codes and models, showing books that architects use as well as a scale model he had made. When the roof problem was raised, he explained that there wasn't one right answer and that it was often better to discuss such problems with carpenters.

Other than the furious scribbling of pencils in notebooks, there was not a single fidget among the twenty-five children for two full hours! They were deeply impressed by the seriousness of the occasion as well as by the architect's manner. At the end of the session, he thanked the children for coming and said that he had examined the models, which they could now take back to the school, but that he would hold on to the requests and blueprints to consider the matter further.

The children's disappointment when they saw they weren't to receive the permit right away, and perhaps not at all, was immediately visible in their long faces. Their expressions did not escape the notice of the architect who ran after us down the hall, catching us before we reached the elevator to say that the models were good and that he really didn't think there would be any problems. The children greeted his pronouncement with many grins of relief! That same day at four o'clock after the children had gone home, the official looking permit arrived along with the children's blueprints.

BUILDING PERMIT

Dalhousie   University

YOU HAVE BEEN GRANTED
PERMISSION TO CONSTRUCT A
PLAYHOUSE IN THE EDUCATION
PLAYGROUND.
DURING THE CONSTRUCTION OF THIS
BUILDING ALL SAFETY STANDARDS
MUST BE MET. THE BUILDING
MUST MEET THE NATIONAL
BUILDING CODE, CITY
REGULATIONS AND BY-LAWS
IN CONSTRUCTION.

Martin Giddy

MARTIN GIDDY M.A.A.I.C

SENIOR STAFF ARCHITECT.
DALHOUSIE UNIVERSITY.

Official Building Permit for Playhouse

Integrating and Applying Information:
Building the Playhouse

It was now early October, and at last construction could begin. We teachers had been collecting the wood for the playhouse since the beginning of September and now had enough. Most of it, by the way, had been generously donated by lumber companies and parents. We, rather than the children, cut the lumber to the appropriate sizes to save time and to ensure accurate cutting under safe conditions.

The Foundation

A company that donated labor and materials had dug and constructed the foundation at the end of September. The workers had even come on a Friday afternoon during school time so that the children could watch, ask questions, take notes, and draw pictures as the work progressed. The children participated by taking turns using some of the tools, and all the Middles and Olds got a chance to stand in the holes dug for the posts. That way each child could appreciate how deep the holes were.

tools
post hole digger
hammers
digger rod
shovel

step 1 measure wood
step 2 saw wood
step 3 measure wood
step 4 dig holes
step 5 nail wood together
step 6 make a circle
step 7 I helped
step 8 move wood
step 9

Notes Taken During Building of Foundation
Age 9

During all this time the Young Ones had also been studying buildings but at their own level of understanding, interest, and pace, of course (see Chapter 6). Although interested in all the commotion about the playhouse-to-be, they were simply too small and immature to participate in building it. However, they contributed in an important way by making signs for our construction site.

Building Teams

The afternoon of the day they visited the architect, the children divided into building teams of five each. Each of the teams, which consisted of both Middles and Olds, would have an adult (a teacher or a parent) as a group leader and would be responsible for one of five parts of the playhouse—the floor or one of the four walls. Using their notes of the measurements and their models in front of them, the teams prepared a "shopping list" of the number of pieces and lengths of wood needed for their assigned part of the playhouse. The children and teachers decided to begin building the next morning at nine o'clock sharp if the building permit had arrived. Each child, who was to bring a hammer and helmet, went home that day with a letter to parents reminding them of this special activity.

	Sizes of wood								
	CM	CM	CM	CM	CM	CM	CM	CM	CM
floor	10×210								
front	8×210	3×90	2×140						
Back	Studs 6×150	Cripple Jacks 3×40	Cripple Jacks 3×50	Header Sill 3×90					
Side	Sill Beam 3×210	Studs 6×150	Header Sill 3×90	Cripple Jacks 3×40	Cripple Jacks 3×50	1×20	1×20½	1×30	
Side	Sill+post 1×210	Studs 6×150	Header Sill 3×90	Cripple Jacks 3×40	Cripple Jacks 3×50	Beam 1×20	Beam 1×2½	Beam 1×30	beam 210-5/200
Roof	Rafters 7×20	?rafters 6×310							

Master Chart of Wood Needed for the Playhouse
Age 9

Volunteer Helpers

Parents are an integral part of our school activities. Not only do we keep them informed as much as possible about their children's progress, we also enlist their participation in many of the activities. It should be said that very often parents volunteer without being asked. When they see their children coming home excited about school work, they often are eager to participate, and we encourage them. Not only does their participation give us extra help with the activities, but it also gives them a chance to gain a greater understanding of how the school operates. This understanding, in turn, encourages them to carry over our teaching practices to the home.

Safety

It was at this point that all of us turned our full attention to the question of working safely. The children had been thinking about the issue of safety all along. Many of their questions to the workers had been concerned with this issue. However, we, the teachers, now wanted to stress safety more than ever. The groups spent a good deal of time brainstorming and discussing how to work safely—including being aware of others in the work area, using a hammer properly, watching for electrical cords, and handling frustration when a nail proves contrary. We told the children that absolutely no carelessness would be tolerated and that anyone fooling around would be asked to go inside immediately and work on other tasks. As it turned out, they took the safety concern very seriously, and no one was hurt during the construction. No one even had to be told not to go near the unfinished playhouse during playtime.

Building the Frames

The cut lumber was stacked outside, our work teams were gathered and everyone knew what to do. We were all ready to begin. Our goal for the first day was to build the frames for the floor and the four walls. At nine o'clock each team received the blueprint for its section plus the "shopping list" to go with it. The children then went to the woodpile and chose and counted their pieces. After carrying the wood to their assigned work sites, they placed the pieces on the ground and got ready to hammer them together. As you can imagine with nails ten centimeters long, this wasn't an easy job. By taking turns, however, the frames began to take shape. Amazingly by one o'clock that day, we had fulfilled our goal. The frames for the floor and all four walls were ready to be put together, which we left for the next day because by now everyone was exhausted. We deviated slightly from standard building practice at this point. Normally the plywood is put on the wall frames before they are raised. However, we were concerned that our measurements might not have been precise enough and that the frames would require a bit of persuasion to fit properly. We concluded that fitting the frames would be much easier to accomplish without the plywood.

Putting Up the Walls

The next day each team went back to the same section they had worked on the day before and carried it over to the floor that now covered the foundation. Only the teachers and the parents held their breaths worrying that the wall frames would not fit properly when raised. In anticipation of such a disaster, we teachers had asked a carpenter to come and had told the parent volunteers to be prepared to knock the frames together if necessary. When the teams raised the wall frames we all discovered, to our utter delight, that they fit perfectly! They fit so snugly that the clamps a parent had thought to bring weren't really necessary.

Then began the symphony of hammers. Twenty-five children, each with a hammer, went to it. The adults put an "X" wherever nails were needed and the children happily hammered them in. More than one shining face gave evidence of how much they enjoyed their work. "This is the best day of my life!" commented one seven-year-old. In fifteen minutes the children had nailed the four wall frames securely to each other and to the floor.

Next we had to nail on the plywood. Putting it on required some care. Each piece had to extend from the middle of one stud to the middle of the next. This was not so difficult with the beginning pieces because they were large, though being large they were hard to maneuver. However, when we ran out of the large plywood sheets, we had to piece the smaller ones together and that was trickier. We used an electric jigsaw to cut the pieces to the right size. The adults did most of the cutting, although a couple of the children did get to help with the saw under strict one-to-one adult supervision. The adults then cut out the windows and covered the highest areas of the frames with plywood. We thus concluded the second day's work.

Building the Roof

The next step was to build the roof. Because we weren't sure about how to do this, we asked a carpenter, who was the father of one of the children, for some help. He came in one rainy day and looked at the models we had made. One of the things we still weren't sure of was how much overhang was necessary. He advised us that the roof needed to overhang only on the front and the back. Taking a two-by-six, he told us about the crown of the wood, which simply means that the wood, because of its grain formation, curves slightly more one way than the other. The crown is important to check because plywood nailed on top will buckle if the crowns of the wood underneath aren't on the same side of the frame. After everyone had a chance to check and mark the crown, he let the children help measure and cut the lumber to size. Then he cut the notches on the two-by-sixes that were to be the rafters, explaining as he worked. Finally, we all trudged out into the rain and he helped us put up the scaffolding we needed to do the work. He put up half, and then we did the rest.

Eight- to Ten-Year-Olds

Learning from the Roofers

About the time that we were building the roof a lucky coincidence occurred. On an errand during lunch hour one day, I noticed some men working on the roof of a nearby house. This was too good a chance to pass up. I rushed back

Eight- to Ten-Year-Olds

to the school and, assuring the Olds of playtime later, asked them to very quickly brainstorm some questions. Then they raced over to see if the workers were willing to be interviewed. They were, and the children learned quite a bit from them. The workers gave the Olds information about the materials to use for roofing, what types of nails to use, and how much area a roll of tar paper and a bundle of tar shingles covered. They talked about the nature of their work. For example, they mentioned that roofing is seasonal and that they travel all over Nova Scotia to do jobs. Most of the children were surprised to learn that the workers had come from 150 kilometers away, where the company is based, to do this particular job.

1 Q wich is betTer Tarpaper or shingles
a shingles

2 What size nails do you need To
b wild a roof   (What size nails do you need to build a roof?)
3 1/2 a 3 inch

3 What size raffers do you   (What size rafters do you use mostly?)
uroe NoTsicy
2X6

4 whaT do you use For safTey   staging

5 what is The lagesT nail   (What is the largest nail you ever used?)
you ever yousTed
pinch

5 how Meny carpenTers working
on This house
5

6 1G you hale a accidint   (If you have an accident you get compensation.)
you geT upen raTion
do latters fall dewn

7 olot

Example of Questions for Roofers
Age 8

Eight- to Ten-Year-Olds

The roofers also stressed working safely and explained the dangers of the job. One man told of how he had suffered many accidents slipping off a ladder and sliding down a roof. One of the children asked him how he would support himself if he fell and had to go to the hospital. He replied that he would receive workers' compensation. Although the children probably didn't fully understand what workers' compensation meant, they seemed to be duly impressed because nearly everyone made some attempt to write this in their notes. Some creative spelling was

Trip to Roofers

One day at lunchtime winnie went out on a errand and she saw people working on a roof. because we had to lern how to shingle the roof we now had a opportunity to find how to do what. Winnie rushed back to school called the olds together and read that we could have 20 minutes playtime but we had to come see the roofers so we got our pencels papers and wrote down questions. we went there and asked them questions

the end

noah

Description of Trip to Roofers
Age 8

Eight- to Ten-Year-Olds

necessary, however, and the results ranged from "comensation" to "comsaching" to "campsinshin."

After this visit everyone felt more confident about working on the roof, and so we proceeded.

Illustration of Trip to Roofers
Age 9

Once again the teams had to take extra time with the plywood because we were using pieces of different sizes, but eventually we managed to cover the frames. We then put tar paper on the plywood and covered it with shingles. We had to learn as we went along when we put on the shingles. Trial and error is sometimes the only way to go. Not all the children worked on the roof. Some were just too afraid to do so, and we left it at that. Others, however, were eager to do it. This activity, which required good coordination and motor skills and no fear of heights, gave some children a chance to excel. Every theme, because of its variety of activities, allows the different strengths of children to emerge and therefore, provides a natural opportunity for praise, not only from the teachers, but from peers as well. Although the young roofers were closely supervised, the adults did the few parts that were highest and most dangerous.

Shingling the Sides

All that was left to do now was the wood shingling and the painting. We hadn't intended to shingle the sides of the house, but since a parent donated some used and new wood shingles we decided to use them. Though we had gained some experience in shingling from working on the roof, we couldn't follow exactly the same procedure. For one thing, the shingles for the sides were made of wood and, as a result, weren't as pliable as the tar paper shingles we had used on the roof. The wood shingles were also uneven in size and thickness whereas the roof shingles had all been of uniform size, and we now had to apply them to a vertical surface as opposed to laying them down on the sloping surface of the roof. We knew enough to start at the bottom and knew that a slight gap should be left between shingles to allow for expansion. After putting on the tar paper, some children used a two-by-four to draw a straight line as a guide. Then they nailed on the first row. Using the two-by-four as a guide again, they put on the next row, and so on. The highest parts of the walls were shingled by adults for safety reasons.

Painting

The Youngs did most of the painting. Up to this point, their participation had consisted of making and putting up signs around the construction site. Now they could contribute once again. Covered in garbage bags from neck to toe, they gleefully went to it. Later some Olds and Middles helped because the smallest ones couldn't reach the high parts. Inside and out, the playhouse was covered with paint, which, like so many other things, had been generously donated by the parents. A bit of trim around the windows and doorway, and the playhouse was completed.

One last detail arose that we teachers hadn't originally foreseen. After a rainstorm one day, we noticed water on the floor of the playhouse. The water had come through the uncovered windows. To prevent eventual rot to the floor, we decided to cover the windows with plexiglass that we were lucky to get at a reduced price. The doorway was left open because of the potential danger to children playing in the playhouse after school and getting trapped when no one was around to help. Earlier we had talked about this danger with the children. We had also discussed the possibility that someone could use the playhouse to hurt a child if it were totally enclosed, which was one of the reasons we had designed the playhouse with three windows and why it was built so close to the schoolyard fence. We wanted to be sure that the security guards who patrol the campus could easily see inside the structure.

After the first two days of construction when all twenty-five children had worked together, work outside had proceeded in small rotating teams of five to ten children with one teacher. When the children were not building, they were in the classroom working on activities related to building the playhouse. All in all, the actual construction took about a month and a half. This included a few delays due to poor weather.

Explaining and Presenting What Has Been Learned

Writing about Building

Beginning in September, we had stressed that writing has a purpose and that the first thing the children had to know was what they wanted to say. Therefore, we had told them to think about the topic and to talk about it with their partner, their teacher, and the whole group.

We had encouraged the children to brainstorm, individually or in a group, as an especially good way of organizing writing. The children would organize the information by identifying categories wherever they could. The teacher would help them make charts using all the relevant categories they could think of. She would elicit new ones and sometimes add a few. As the weeks went by, the children would add to or revise their charts as they learned more through activities and reading. The teachers always emphasized that the children should think about what they were doing, why they were doing it, and how their work fit into the larger context.

As one of the major activities of the construction theme, we had assigned the children to write a book about how to build a house (see excerpts on pages 132–133). Both the Olds and the Middles did this assignment but in slightly different ways.

Six- to Eight-Year-Olds	Eight- to Ten-Year-Olds
The teacher has to make the writing process explicit for the Middles, and they need much time to gain experience in this work. They started writing their	I began the writing assignment by asking the children to write everything they knew about building the playhouse. They wrote for an hour and a half for

Six- to Eight-Year-Olds

books when construction began. Their usual writing procedure is to gather the information and record it right away. Thus, they recorded each step of the building process as it happened. However, because the building extended over a relatively long period of time, the children had to integrate a number of construction steps. I wanted to use the writing exercise to help them keep the whole picture of building a frame house in mind. Children of this age need help with the larger concepts; they can get too caught up in details and lose sight of the framework within which the details fit. Having to work on a written record, of not only what is happening now, but also of what has gone on before, would help the Middles maintain that sense of the whole topic. Therefore, they frequently rewrote sections of their books. Many children even decided to start all over again because, as construction proceeded, they were gaining knowledge and experience that made them realize that what they had already written wasn't complete or, in some cases, accurate. Knowing that these books were to be used for display purposes, the children were anxious to make them as good as possible.

The fact that the Middles, at their own initiative, undertook to rewrite their books was indicative of how far they had come in learning about the writing process.

Eight- to Ten-Year-Olds

two days in a row. Then I suggested that they read aloud to each other what they had written. By the fourth reading, everyone could see that while the information was there, it was so jumbled that no sense could be made of it. The children agreed that the information needed to be organized. Therefore, they brainstormed a list of the major ideas and decided which one should come first, which one second, and so on. They also discussed starting the book with an introduction and ending with some concluding statements. Then, using the list as an outline, they all rewrote their pieces. As usual, when the children finished writing, they read their work to each other to check that it made sense. Where necessary, they made revisions. After one final editing for spelling and punctuation, they prepared the good copies and illustrated them.

Another important writing activity that both groups of children did in connection with the playhouse was to write thank-you letters to all those who had contributed to their work. Once again the children first made a rough copy and then a neat copy. The letter writing was a good opportunity for them to practice another kind of important writing format and to get practice using different styles of writing. Not only does the content of a letter change according to the person being written to, but the style of the letter must change too. A letter to a company requires a more formal style than a letter to a friend.

All the Middles and Olds chose thirteen names from a list of twenty-three and wrote a letter to each. The letters were good reminders to the children that building the playhouse wouldn't have been possible without the help of many people.

Dear Fuller Thomas construction thank you for all the pieces of plywood you supplied us. We couldn't have done i with out the plywood at all. Now the walls of the playhouse are up and all the plywood is on except for the samll pieces. We will use the other pieces for the roof and we put signs up about your company giving us wood. We hope that this will help aboutizing your business.
thant you very much again from all of us.

yours sincerely **Age 10**

dear Louann morehouse.

thank you for the help.

we are almaost finished the

play howse. thankyou for helping

us saw the wood.   *Age 6*

Thank-you Letters: Neat Copies

Preparing for Open House

Time for the open house was now very near, and we had to begin our planning. Preparing for open house gives the children a chance to synthesize what they have learned. Looked at in retrospect, each step is more easily seen as a piece of the whole pattern. This leads to such revelations as, ''Oh, now I see! We made the model so that we would know how to build the real playhouse,'' or ''We made the blueprints so that we would know which pieces of wood to use.''

Six- to Eight-Year-Olds

The Middles started planning for the open house by considering the major question: "How will we present what we have learned so that others will understand it?" They began by making a list of the things they thought they should tell people. Then they brainstormed how they were to do it. One little boy suggested that we erect partitions and do a slide and tape presentation such as he had recently seen at the museum. Everyone liked the idea, but we decided, due to a lack of time (not to mention funds), we would do a modified version. We agreed that there were six major areas to be presented—the foundation, the floor, the walls, the roof, the shingling, and the painting. We decided to have six stations with two people each who would talk about their particular area.

The next step was to decide what kind of information should be presented at each station and in what form. One child suggested that the best way to decide would be for the group to put their heads together and brainstorm again, which they did. The result of this brainstorm was that each station would display a step-by-step poster explaining how the work involved in their area had been accomplished. The four stations responsible for the foundation, the floor, the walls, and the roof would also exhibit Tinker Toy models, and all six stations would display a neat copy of the brainstorm they had recorded when planning their presentation. By now brainstorms had become such a useful technique for the children that they considered them important enough to be included in their presentations. When the

Eight- to Ten-Year-Olds

The Olds began brainstorming for the open house when they had completed their books about houses and the thank-you letters. Each year one Old who won't be returning in the fall opens the event with a short speech. This time there would be a grand opening of the playhouse as well. The group decided that three children would lead this event: an Old to give the speech, a Middle to add some brief remarks, and a Young to cut the ribbon.

In addition to the opening, the Olds would make presentations about building the playhouse. They agreed on what the content of the presentations should be and divided the topics among the group. Then each child wrote a speech about her or his topic, beginning with a rough copy, followed by revising

Speech Prepared for Guided Tour of Playhouse: Rough Draft with Revisions Added

Age 9

Six- to Eight-Year-Olds

stations were ready, partners worked out what they were going to say and then practiced their presentations.

Eight- to Ten-Year-Olds

and editing, and ending with a neat copy. It was up to each child or team of children to decide what they were going to say and how they were going to say it. One team of three who were to speak about the blueprints came up with a question-and-answer format. For instance, one team member would ask, "Why were the blueprints necessary?" and another would answer.

Another group made a chart and prepared a short talk about the cost of the playhouse, which had been worked out earlier by all the Olds together. This was an estimated cost, of course, because most of the materials had been donated, and we had done the bulk of the work ourselves. However, it was important for the children to realize just how much the goods and services would have cost if we had paid for all of them. The children had done some phoning to ask about the price of tool rentals and building supplies. This posed some difficulties because different businesses charge different rates, and nobody rents hammers. In such cases, the costs had to be estimated. To arrive at the price of the various building supplies, the children had done numerous calculations. For example, many different sizes of wood had been used, and so the children had to estimate the amount of each kind. They used the same process for the sheets of plywood. They also estimated that it would have taken one adult five days working eight hours a day to build the playhouse. They made inquiries about the minimum wage. They then estimated that the cost of a worker's labor, and the

Eight- to Ten-Year-Olds

materials and tools needed to build the playhouse would have come to over seventeen hundred dollars! This was a revelation to us all.

total tool rental   278. —
total costs of materials   1313. 75
labour costs   150. —
_____
Price of the playhouse:
$ 1,741..75

"Bottom Line" of Detailed Account
Showing Cost of Building the Playhouse
Olds

In addition to finishing off the playhouse and preparing for their specific presentations, both the Middles and the Youngs worked on all the other details of the open house. They made fliers and wrote invitations to the families of the children in the school as well as the families of prospective students, all those who had contributed to the playhouse, and anyone else we thought might be interested. The children hand delivered the invitations when possible and mailed them when not. The teachers prepared a schedule of events, and the children made poster-sized copies of it.

They made labels and captions for photo displays and decided how they would staff a number of display tables on a rotating basis. They put up a wall exhibit with pictures of our trip to Shubie Park and many brainstorms and set up a table displaying the experiment of making a stable structure from paper strips. The children

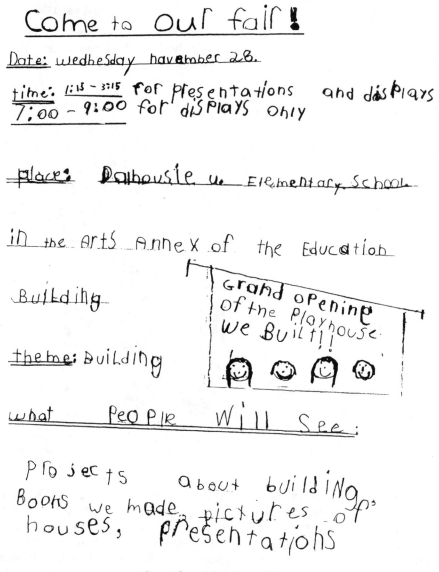

Flier Advertising Open House
Age 7

also arranged several displays of the models and the blueprints, a wall containing exhibits of the rough and neat copies of the books, another display of the thank-you letters, and photo displays of the construction itself.

Finally, the children rehearsed their musical presentation and planned the guided tours they would conduct of the playhouse and, of course, the grand opening

Age 7

puTing up The Walls

The way you puT The walls up you get some people To lifT each side up. put iT on The Floor. and nail a side To a side (be for doing This clomp The side Together) Till you have each side nailD To each side Then puT ply wood over Them. Then Then Tar pape Then wood shingles

Age 6

How to make the FLooR.

when the foundanon is done. We put the 2x4's around the foundation. it makes the sill. Then we put the joists across the foundation. Than we put the plywood on the joists than we are finished.

(Putting up the walls:
The way you put the walls up—you get some people to lift each side up. Put it on the floor and nail a side to a side (before doing this clamp the sides together) till you have each side nailed to each side. Then put plywood over them. Then tarpaper. Then wood shingles.)

Part of Brainstorm, "Putting Up the Walls": Neat Copy for Fair

(How to make the floor:
When the foundation is done we put the 2 x 4's around the foundation. It makes the sill. Then we put the joists across the foundation. Then we put the plywood on the joists. Then we are finished.)

Part of Brainstorm, "How to Make the Floor": Neat Copy for Fair

of the playhouse. They revised, edited, and rehearsed their speeches, and we discussed appropriate behavior for the open house. We talked about being attentive not just to parents and brothers and sisters, but to other guests as well. We also went through the events to be sure everyone knew what was to happen.

Age 6

a trip to Martin Giddy

① he looked at all the models

and showed all the changes we can do

② We asked Questions about or house.

③ he showed us Books about differents house

④ then he told us that he made play house when he was little and it was to small for him.

⑤ then he told us more changes we can do

⑥ then we asked him if he ever made a model of or school

⑧ then he told us he made the art gauery with some friens

Account of Trip to Architect: Neat Copy

Age 9

'Help! We got many donations from parents and companies. We put signs up that said: (for example) "Foundation By FR.s Fencing" and "Framing Wood By Peircy Construction L.D" to advertise that they helped us.

We got some tools from the parents and We were even lucky enough to get some parents to help building.

We had to write many thank you letters but it was worth it.

Excerpt from Book on Playhouse Construction: Neat Copy

Age 6

Then We put up The Wals. and Then We The roof ad made The rafters we cored the rafter With plywood

(Then we put up the walls and then we (made) the roof and made the rafters. We covered the rafters with plywood.)

Excerpt from Booklet, ''How to Build a House'': Neat Copy

Age 9

The shingles were a bit harder because we had to make sure that they were the right distance apart.

Age 10

nailed on. Then plywood was nailed onto the rafters. The shingles for the roof were nailed on the plywood before the side shingles were nailed on the wall because the roof would leak. Working on the roof was difficult, dangerous and fun because you had to climb high up between the rafters and later sit and slide down the roof. We nailed the shingling on the sides we painted the playhouse and it was done.

Excerpts from Books on Playhouse Construction: Neat Copy

And Later

The crowd has gone home, the paint has long since dried, and only a few posted signs remain to give evidence of the planning, activity, and work that went into building that simple structure. But the effects of the learning process that took place are still felt.

To accomplish their goal, the children had learned to organize their study; to collect, record, compare, and organize new information and ideas; and to synthesize these new concepts into a meaningful whole. Beyond this, they had discovered that learning is a valuable social activity and that many people working together complement each other's abilities.

We as teachers learned much from the process also. The study confirmed for us again that risk-taking happens on both sides and that teaching this way is a rewarding joint enterprise. Above all, we all enjoyed it.

Ribbon-Cutting Ceremony Marking the Grand Opening of the Playhouse

From Stones to Bricks:
A Study of Housing with the Youngs
(Ages Five and Six)

It was open house at last. This special day found the five- and six-year-olds, the youngest group in the school, at their stations giving explanations to visitors about the work they had done during the past three months, which was now on display. Some children were explaining the process of building model rock houses; others, how they had made model brick houses; and still others, the use of Lego to build model houses. In another part of the room, several children were showing and discussing books they had made on house building. A couple of others were displaying other work they had done outside of their theme study. At the end of a specified time period, the children changed positions, thus rotating their tasks. The keen interest and sense of responsibility for learning that accompanies participation of this kind represent great achievements for these small children.

Teacher Preparation

Several months before this long-anticipated day, I had laid the plans for the children to study housing. They would begin by thinking about their own houses in detail. Then the children and I would make field trips to look at a number of finished structures in the neighborhood, paying attention to differences in materials and styles of building. Finally the children would build a number of model houses from different materials, such as rock, brick, Lego, sod, and wood. At each stage, I would read books to them and we would discuss the ideas. The information we obtained would be recorded, mostly by me but also by the children to the extent they could manage. Throughout our housing study, we would keep tabs on the progress of the playhouse construction being done by the older children. (See Chapter 5.)

To allow the children to explore the material on housing and to incorporate it into their own body of knowledge would take the entire fall term. Taking this much time would have several advantages. It would provide an opportunity for the children to expand their knowledge of the world around them and to develop their thinking skills by dealing with problems such as figuring out which building materials were appropriate for certain structures and how best to use these materials. The children would also be able to observe others making similar decisions in real life as they watched the older children in the school struggling with their task of building a playhouse.

Necessary Supplementary Work

Throughout the term, the children would see that reading and writing are an integral part of the learning process and thereby feel motivated to learn these skills. Although I incorporated reading and writing into the theme study, their function, at this point, was more to demonstrate their usefulness and to provide practice and reinforcement than to serve fundamentally as vehicles for teaching and learning the skills. Certain additional work was needed to get the children started in reading and writing. I separated learning to read and write from theme study activities for part of the time in order to make it easier to provide the support required by beginning readers and writers. I did this because there are simply not enough suitable (for example, predictable) materials available at a beginner's level that are also suitable for our theme study. I also separated these areas because, at the early stages, reading and writing demand so much effort of concentration that the further requirement of also recalling newly acquired content makes the combined task too difficult. Thus, from September to December, a portion of the time allotted to theme study was spent on beginning reading and writing within the contexts most familiar to children of this age.*

With the exception of some separate reading and writing experiences, then, the remainder of the time scheduled for theme study was spent on learning about the theme. In theme study, the children used skills in which they already had some proficiency—listening, discussing, and thinking. The children's abilities varied greatly in these three areas, but some children were proficient enough to carry the rest of the children while they developed their skills.

Getting Started

During the first week of school, the children began thinking about their own houses. I chose this starting point because new information is more easily understood when it is an extension of something the learners already know. In addition, the children needed to deal with the familiar at the start of the school year to make the newness of the school surroundings and organization easier to manage.

With the use of a brainstorm, the children started thinking about their houses. I asked them to mention all the things they could remember about the outside of their houses and recorded their responses on chart paper. As with any new learn-

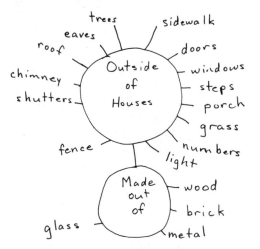

First Group Brainstorm on Houses

* It should be emphasized that this separation of reading and writing from theme study is both partial and temporary. Nor is this kind of separation unique in our curriculum. There are many occasions when something must be taught and learned separately. (See the weekly timetable on page 11.) Even in our non-theme study periods, we incorporate as much theme-related work as possible, while at the same time recognizing that there are limitations. We accept the fact that, although theme studies are broad, they cannot be all-encompassing. This qualification, however, in no way diminishes what can be and is accomplished through theme studies.

ing activity that encourages thinking, the children needed lots of practice, but in the meantime, they also needed to experience success. In time they would learn to stay on a topic and to elaborate on other people's ideas, but for the time being I accepted all the children's ideas in a noncritical fashion.

Our simple brainstorm served a number of purposes. It showed the children that they have valuable information, that the other children are also valuable sources of information, and that learning is a cooperative process. The brainstorm stimulated the children's various thought processes such as recall, deductive thinking, and associative thinking. Because each child had information on the topic, it was possible to get participation from all the children without putting anyone on the spot. I involved all the children right from the start so that none of them would develop the habit of letting other people do the thinking for them.

"My House" Books

Next I gave each child several blank sheets of paper stapled together. These would become the children's own individually made books. On the covers, I asked them to draw their houses from memory, copy the title "My House," and write their names.

Drawing

It is important to focus on drawing as one of the skills to be learned. Drawing improves fine-motor coordination and develops observation skills. When dealing with factual material, learning to draw representatively and accurately is useful for recording information. In addition, it is crucial that children develop confidence in their ability to draw when they are young. Gaining confidence requires lots of opportunity to develop the skill and lots of encouragement.

When I noticed that a few children were reluctant to draw, I handled it in one or both of two different ways: I explained to the children that everything they had learned to do—walk, talk, eat, and so forth—had started off with some problems and had improved with experience. "Do you think you would be walking now if you just sat around and waited to be good at walking?" In like manner, I explained to them that their drawings would not be as good now as the ones they would be able to produce by the end of the year and that what was important was the effort that went into the work, not the quality of the picture. My second strategy for helping a reluctant budding artist was to ask for a volunteer to draw a house on a piece of scrap paper and then have the first child do his or her own drawing using the volunteer's drawing as a guide. This approach usually benefited both children and helped diminish the idea of the teacher as the absolute and only expert.

I did not, however, accept the resulting pictures without reservation because that does not help children grow in their ability to visualize objects and reproduce them. So, for example, I commented positively on details such as the individual bricks drawn for the chimney but also asked questions about the lack of a front door or lack of paint on the house. The children's confidence in their drawing and an improved ability to draw developed slowly but steadily from then on.

At this stage, I made sure that each child had finished one activity before starting the next. Although the children gradually learn that they will have time to complete their work even if it takes them longer than it takes others, at the beginning of the year, some children may be confused or worried if they see others continuing without them. Thus, I instructed those who worked more quickly and finished their assignments early to look at books—a choice of children's literature or books on the theme topic ranging from simple picture books to illustrated adult materials. I then permitted the children to build with various kinds of blocks until everyone was ready for the next activity. Looking at books and working with building materials gave the children additional practice in getting information from books and in developing construction skills that fit well with our theme study.

The next step was to draw a picture of each room in their houses. The children began with the living room, again brainstorming together about what they had in their living rooms. As I recorded the brainstorm on chart paper, I said each word slowly and asked the children what letters I needed in order to write the word. After a few minutes, I shifted to writing their responses more quickly to get them thinking faster. With my assistance, they then reread the brainstorm to see what was missing.

This completed, the children drew a diagram of their living rooms in their house books. The next day, I paired the children, putting more experienced or adventuresome writers with less experienced or less confident writers, gave them each a piece of lined paper, and asked them to write the names of the things they had drawn in their pictures. The children relied on sounding out the words, sometimes discussing the sounds with their partners. Then they wrote down the letters they knew and glued their writing into their books on the page opposite their drawing of the living room.

For the children new to the school, this assignment was perhaps their first experience using writing for recording information. These early attempts were virtually illegible, but the children could remember what they had written well enough to read back at least some of their writing. This kind of activity not only gave the children practice in writing but also helped them develop familiarity with the format. Over the long haul, such work eventually produces confident writers.

The children worked on the books regularly over the next two months using the same format, one result being that the less experienced writers gradually wrote more independently. In retrospect, I would incorporate a discussion on the purposes of houses in general as well as discussions about the uses of the particular rooms.

"A Book about Houses"

Having used the information they had in their heads about their own houses and having been introduced to recording through writing and drawing, the children were ready to move on to new information. So we went on small field trips. I divided the children into groups of four and recruited an adult helper for each group. The children carried pencils and cardboard with scrap paper to serve as a notepad. On our first field trip, we roamed the neighborhood and discussed interesting features of the houses we saw—this one was two stories high; that one had windows with round tops; another had a skylight in the roof, and so forth. We also looked at some rock walls to become familiar with rock as a building material because one of the model houses the children were going to build later would be made of rock. This is a widely used material in many parts of the world but presents some inherent problems to builders. Thus, I drew the children's attention to some of the difficulties experienced by early house builders.

During the trip, I asked the children to make drawings of two houses that I had selected because of differences in their styles. One was a two-story box style house with narrow rectangular windows; the other was a house with several roofs at various levels and a skylight in one roof. The children put their notepads on the sidewalk, knelt down, and drew what they could see. Their drawings and our discussions while they were drawing revealed that they had gleaned the following information: squares, rectangles, and triangles are shapes used in buildings;

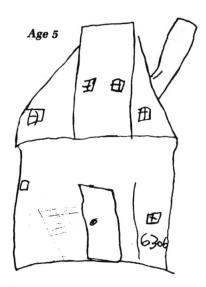

Age 5

Age 5

Drawings of Houses Seen on Field Trip: Rough Copies

stone, brick, wood, and aluminum are materials used in buildings; and the outsides of houses have windows, doors, balconies, and verandas.

When we returned to school, the children and I discussed our observations. They then began work on another book that they called "A Book about Houses." I had told them that the notes and drawings done on a field trip constitute a rough copy. I now asked the children to draw a neat copy of one of the houses they had drawn on the field trip. The neat copy in almost all cases bore no resemblance to the rough sketch. Nevertheless, it was worth doing even when there was no visible improvement because improvement comes with practice.

Because the children learn the functions of rough and finished copies early, the appropriate use of such copies eventually becomes second nature. Although the procedure of writing more than one draft is constantly stressed at all levels in the school, it is, of course, unrealistic to expect all work by five- and six-year-olds to be done in both rough copy and final drafts. However, the children did both drafts whenever practical and through this means learned to concentrate on content first and then deal with form separately. They gradually became adept at spotting parts that could be improved and took pride in producing good quality finished products.

The following week we went on another field trip to see a garage under construction. This time we looked more closely at the structure of the building and checked such features as the placement of studs, the attachment of the roof, and what the foundation was made of. I asked the children to choose one side of the garage to draw. Although the drawings they produced all showed a skeletal structure, they reflected little or no accuracy in recording details of the support structures.

Age 5   *Age 5*

Drawings of Garage Under Construction Seen on Field Trips, with Emphasis on Structural Features: Rough Copies

The children also drew pictures of the materials and tools needed to build a garage and tried to write down the names beside them. There was great variation in how they did this. Some children simply made a list, knowing that this would be enough to help them remember the materials and tools when they got back to school. Others needed pictures to help them interpret their writing, and so they did both. Still others only drew pictures. For most of the children, this task was quite arduous.

This open-ended way of approaching work helped the children understand that

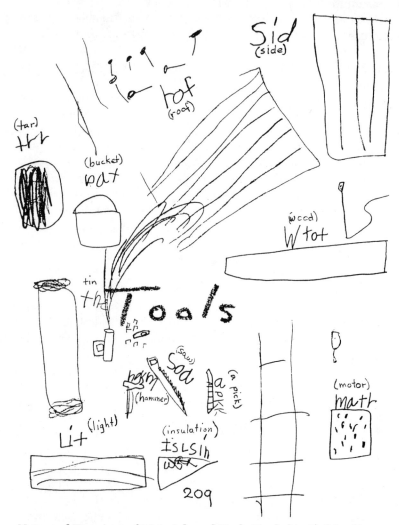

Notes and Drawings of Materials and Tools Needed to Build a Garage
Age 6

while they were all expected to do their best, they had different strengths and were at different stages of learning so that what was expected of one might be unrealistic for another. In general, the children made efforts to forge ahead and become more competent. However, there were some exceptions. One child in particular, who was quite insecure about his ability to learn and produce acceptable work, would use any kind of strategy to avoid committing his pencil to paper. It took me the better part of the year to convince him that there is not just one right way to do things before he could finally begin to feel good about his work.

When we returned from this field trip, the children, as usual, made their neat copy of the garage in their "Book about Houses." Then we did two group brainstorms: one was a list of materials needed to make a house or garage and the other a list of the tools. The children came up with very impressive lists and even suggested that one would need to draw a "picture" (blueprint) of a house or garage before building it.

In the early brainstorm sessions, I had accepted ideas from any child who volunteered them, but I soon realized that the quieter children were letting others do their thinking while those impatient for a turn were doing all the talking. Therefore, I changed to a system of going around the circle and taking turns, with everyone being required to contribute the first few times around. (One painfully shy child was an exception, but I asked him to think of one idea and tell me about it when the group activity was over; gradually he was able to participate with the others.) This system allowed the impulsive children to calculate how long they had to wait for a turn, thereby making the delay more bearable. Going around in a circle also taught the children to listen to and respect other people's contributions and helped create a cooperative working atmosphere.

During one of these brainstorms, the longest we had attempted so far, some children were restless and inattentive due to their lack of background information. They were unable to ask questions or understand some of the points being made. Knowing that the discussion was relevant and potentially interesting to the children, I persisted in spite of this problem. As they gradually realized that they were expected to try to concentrate and to follow the discussion, the children indeed did refocus their attention more constructively. Over time, they learned to attend to a subject for longer periods, demonstrating that practicing the skill of concentration helps to build concentration.

However, there was another problem. Two of the girls had so little ability to focus their attention and were so totally disruptive that they needed special treatment. I arranged a work space for them close to the circle and gave them paper, pencils, and pencil crayons for drawing pictures. They were required to ask permission to leave the circle when they were unable to manage their behavior and to go to the work space where they were still able to listen to the discussion. If one of them had something to say, she could return to the group and raise her hand. They gradually became more able to manage discussions and did not need the special arrangement.

More Sources of Information

Throughout this period of about two months, I read books about houses and house building to the children.[1] The reading proceeded very slowly at times because I stopped frequently to answer questions, discuss new concepts, and hear about related experiences. By hearing information from books and discussing it in depth, the children get an excellent demonstration of how to be fluent readers at a later stage. This approach centers on the importance of understanding what one is reading, of thinking about how it relates to what one knows, and of applying it to the world around us.

With readings, field trips, and discussions under our belts, the children and I did two synthesizing brainstorms, both reviews of what the children had learned. One was about what the outside of houses can be made of, and the other was about the inside parts of houses. The children came up with a wide range of ideas. For example, in the first brainstorm, they decided that houses could be made of rock, bricks, animal skins, grass, and other materials.

Building Model Houses

During this time, the children had started to build model houses. They were replicas of primitive early houses made of rocks. The children used gravel from a driveway for the rocks and were, therefore, building with irregular shapes. They cemented these ''rocks'' together with a mixture of white glue, sand, flour, and water. I had experimented with several mixtures in the presence of the children and had asked them to check the results. Because there were no noticeable differences in the mixtures, the children went ahead with the simplest one, and then used popsicle sticks for the roofs.

Each child worked with a partner, and each pair built one house. When I paired the children, I tried to get combinations that would cooperate and help each other's thinking. The pairs worked well together, but the results were quite varied. Some of the children's structures were very houselike in appearance; others were just jumbled collections of rocks. Since the effort put into the jumbles of rocks was appropriate for the children involved, their work was accepted with some minor improvements. Working three or four hours a week, the children completed the models in three weeks.

Once the houses were built, I asked the children to draw a picture of the one they had worked on in their ''Book about Houses.'' I also gave them lined paper and asked them to write about their house. Through these two activities the children continued the record-keeping process of illustrating and writing about what they were doing and learning. As usual, I emphasized the content of the children's work rather than the accuracy of spelling or letter formation or the superficial appearance of the finished product.

For their second building effort, the children made Lego houses, which were to serve as plans for the model brick houses that they would build later. I assigned the children to work with different partners to gain experience cooperating with a variety of people. Each pair completed a Lego house, and each member of the pair drew a picture of it in her or his ''Book about Houses.''

The children were then ready to work on their model brick houses using cardboard ''bricks.'' They used cardboard cut into brick shapes with the white glue mixture for mortar and sheets of cardboard for the roof. In actual fact, the brick houses looked much more like houses than the rock houses had. However, even though I had encouraged the children to use the Lego model and drawing as guides in building the brick houses, they did not look like the Lego houses or the pictures of them. Young children need time to train their eyes and their hands to achieve the desired carry-over, but, as with all skills, proficiency comes with practice. All the children again drew a picture of their finished house and wrote about building it.

Playhouse Construction

During this time, the children in my group also worked periodically on the playhouse that was being built in the schoolyard by the older children. Using stencils, they traced the letters for signs such as: DANGER; PLAYHOUSE UNDER CONSTRUCTION; FOUNDATION BY FRIIS FENCING; WOOD FROM DALHOUSIE U. onto pieces of plywood, colored the letters with permanent markers, and nailed the signs to the fence at the construction site. They also helped put wooden shingles on the outside walls and did most of the painting on the outside of the playhouse. These young children had observed the work being done by the older ones at all stages of construction. Consequently, they had acquired a good knowledge of the basic steps involved in building a simple structure.

Nailing Up Some Construction Signs

Painting the Playhouse

Preparing for Open House

By now, the end of November was approaching. It was almost time for the school fair. In preparation, the children put the finishing touches on their models, completed their books, and made name labels for their work. The more fluent writers also made captions for theirs. During the three-hour open house, the children would explain their various displays to the visitors. To prepare for these explanations, we spent some time talking about building the houses. As part of the discussion, I asked the children which were easier to build, the rock houses or the brick houses. Without exception, they said that the brick houses were easier, but they had trouble explaining why. After several minutes, someone finally said, ''Well, the bricks were flat, and the rocks were round and wouldn't stay where you wanted them to.'' The other children thought about the comment and agreed, ''Yes, that's what it is,'' showing once again that children need lots of concrete experience to be able to develop insights and many thoughtful discussions to learn to articulate them.

During this theme study, the children gained a great deal of knowledge about houses and their construction. More importantly, they learned to work together, to formulate and ask questions, and to discuss ideas. In addition, they learned the reasons for recording information and ideas through drawing and writing, and they developed some initial skills at doing these things. They learned how to listen for important information contained in factual books and increased their familiarity with print. Their attention span and ability to work for long periods of time grew, and most important of all, their formal education had gotten off to a good start: every child, without exception, had become actively and enthusiastically engaged in the learning process.

SPECIALIZED
THEME STUDIES

Chili Enterprise Ltd.:
A Minitheme Involving Lots of Math
and All the Children

Although all theme studies include math, it is generally difficult to include as much as the children need. Therefore, we have separate daily math periods during which all the math that cannot be covered during theme time is studied. As with the theme work, we try in these math periods to engage the children in activities in which they can apply math, that is, those in which the children can learn and practice math in a meaningful context. Meanwhile, we have also tried to develop special minithemes (small-scale investigations of topics) that provide a context for math. Such a minitheme is one in which:

- math is a major component and opens up new avenues for learning and applying mathematical concepts and skills;
- the other components are valuable learning experiences as well and are not too far beyond the children's existing abilities;
- the amount of time and effort required can be accommodated in the schedule without unreasonable sacrifices.

One minitheme we thought of, which would provide a rather exciting context for math, was setting up a "restaurant business" with the children. This minitheme would include the whole range of activities from planning the business, buying food and cooking it, to advertising, selling lunch, and calculating the price and the profit or loss. We developed this minitheme because it would provide the children with an opportunity to learn and apply math while gaining firsthand experiences in almost all aspects of the business and to integrate math, nutrition, and art in an interesting and purposeful context. It would also be conducive to cross-age grouping, with all the children in the school involved in the enterprise at their own levels.

We developed the following plan. Each week for six weeks, a team of six children representing the three age groups would be responsible for most aspects of the lunch sale. The children who were not part of the team of the week would take care of the remaining responsibilities. During math time, in a period coinciding with the six weeks of lunch sales, all the children would learn and practice, at their own levels, the various aspects of the minitheme: handling money; making charts; learning about volume; discussing nutrition; doing layout in artwork; and so forth. As a result, all children would experience all aspects of the business during the full six-week period.

Almost all the time spent on this minitheme would be scheduled during math time, which totaled a bit over five hours a week, while the remainder would take place during a lunch period that would be extended for the team of the week. In addition, the team of six children would have to be excused from classes for one-and-a-half hours on one day, and half an hour on another day in the same week for shopping and other tasks. We thought the additional time would be well spent, considering the benefits of the minitheme—the joys of shopping, cooking, eating, and selling as well as the meaningful study of math, nutrition, and art.

Because the school has a small but fully equipped kitchen, there was no worry about cooking facilities. The teachers, however, had to prepare for the business in a number of other ways before presenting it to the children: selecting possible recipes that would be suitable; finding sources of information on the nutritional composition of the ingredients and their caloric value; borrowing pots, pans, utensils, and measuring cups for preparing the food as well as a hot plate for serving it; arranging the timetable to accommodate the various aspects of the minitheme; and finding parents willing to help the children cook.

It was decided that Wednesdays were most suitable for selling lunches. We could make bread dough and shop on Mondays, and on Tuesdays a parent could help with the cooking. The other aspects could be handled throughout the week during math periods.

Planning a Lunch Business

Having estimated the work involved and having located the resources, we proposed the lunch sale to the children during one of our regular school meetings.

Needless to say, they were wildly enthusiastic about the idea and immediately responded by listing their favorite dishes and offering their parents' help in cooking and supplying kitchenware. However, because the many aspects of the project had to be thought through and discussed, we told the children to think about how to organize a lunch sale and voice their ideas at the next day's meeting. The school was buzzing with comments and plans for the new business we were about to launch.

The following day, we all brainstormed about the jobs that needed to be done for a lunch sale. Everyone made suggestions about shopping, cooking, and selling, and some children mentioned advertising. In no time we had a great variety of jobs listed on the board—deciding what food would be sold and getting the recipes for them; estimating the quantity of food to be cooked and of each ingredient needed; purchasing supplies and calculating the prices; advertising; organizing and then doing the cooking, serving, and selling; calculating profit or loss; cleaning up; and handling complaints.

The children enthusiastically raised many specific questions about the organization of this enterprise. Their most urgent questions were whether they could cook spaghetti and pizza, when their turn would come, and when they would start. We again pointed out that they would have to think about these questions first. We would all discuss them at our next meeting, and to make sure we would not forget, we wrote them on the next day's agenda.

When discussing what food we would cook, the children asked countless questions beginning with the type of customers we were likely to have and what kind of lunch people would want to spend money on. This led to other questions such as where the customers would eat the lunch, how much time they would have to buy and eat it, how much time it would take us to serve the lunch and get the money aspect figured out, how much time it would take six children and a parent to cook all that food, whether we should cook it on the day of the sale or earlier, what kind of food could be stored properly without losing its quality, and so on. A whole new world had opened up for them and the more we talked about it, the more they thought through and realized the complexity of the many aspects of setting up a business.

The issues mentioned were written on the board and, beside each one, the name of the child who raised it. As the group went through the list, we wrote down the solutions. There are several reasons for writing the list on the board:

- to show the children how to keep track of important issues and to make sure that all matters are addressed;
- to demonstrate how to select and write down only those suggestions and questions that deserve attention because they concern the topic at hand and because they matter to the whole group (after demonstrating the process a couple of times ourselves, we began asking the children whether we should write an item down, and before long they could tell us what to write down or explain to each other why an item should be omitted);

- to be able to include the name of the child who raised the particular issue, thereby ensuring that this child would be the first one to speak about it and would receive credit for bringing it up;
- to show how writing is an efficient way of handling a complicated topic at a meeting.

The children were impressed with the results, and, at the end of the discussion, one child observed that a lot can be accomplished when you work as a group, thus making it unnecessary for a teacher to point out the value of group work. One result of using this method is that, with experience, the children have learned to independently hold their own meetings about work and playground problems and to make lists of the issues.

In dealing with the children's specific questions, everyone agreed that decisions about who would do the various jobs would be left to the teachers. The names of six children for each of the six lunch teams were posted next to six dates so that all the children could find their names, be assured of a turn, and know when that turn would be.

Because the children were exploring all eventualities, one child asked, "What if my mother takes me to the dentist when it's my turn?" to which another child replied, "That doesn't matter. Someone else will take your place, and you'll get to do it the next week." "What if you forget and I don't get a turn?" "We'll write it on the schedule." The children solved such problems themselves; we, the teachers, only chaired the meeting.

When we asked the children how they would pay for the groceries, they responded, "That's easy. We'll make money from the sale." However, they realized from the discussion that ensued that to start a business and "make money," they would have to have money in the first place or be able to borrow it. They were quite relieved to hear that the teachers would initially lend them the money. However, after each lunch sale, the fact that expenses had to be deducted from the large pile of money taken in was always slightly disappointing.

Having discussed and cooperatively solved most of the initial problems and concerns, the children then addressed the scheduling and finer details. We worked out the following timetable and division of labor with the children.

Running a Lunch Business

Thursday and Friday: Recipe, Shopping List, Nutrition

On these days, a few of the Olds calculated the amount of each ingredient for a selected recipe and the number of plastic utensils, paper plates, and paper napkins that had to be purchased for fifty people. They found that the most difficult part of this task was calculating the ingredients. Because most of the recipes were intended for eight to ten servings, they had to figure out how to increase the quantities to serve fifty people. In most cases, this was done by repeat addition rather than multiplication because that was the level of most of the children.

Meanwhile, one of the Olds copied the recipe on a large sheet of paper that would be used during cooking and would later be put up near our food counter. A few other Olds listed all the ingredients used in the recipe and found the nutritional value of each one per serving. For this purpose they looked up and calculated the number of calories of the most important food groups (proteins, carbohydrates, and fats) and some of the most important elements (iron, calcium, potassium, iodine, and phosphorus). During the lunch sale, this information would be posted near the food counter. The children completed all these tasks during two math periods totaling about one hour and forty minutes.

Monday: Shopping, Bread Dough, Price, Advertisements

On Monday mornings during recess, two Olds made a shopping list, checking off or changing the quantities depending upon whether we had leftover supplies that could be used for that week's lunch. On occasion, when the shopping list showed an unlikely quantity of an ingredient, the children had to look up the original recipe again, redo the calculations, and check the adjustments they had made for provisions already on hand. In this way, they usually found their error. Occasionally, however, they did not and had to make an extra trip to the store after school if they were short an ingredient or save it for the following week if they had bought too much.

Once in the store, the children sometimes found that the shopping list was illegible and that they had to try and remember or to guess what might have been meant. As a result, they sometimes lost valuable shopping time and became annoyed with the guilty party's carelessness. Such experiences made it very clear how important it is to write legibly. Back in school, the shoppers would relate their experiences to the others; their implication was: write clearly when you make a shopping list. If we had intervened to prevent or correct these mistakes, the children would not have learned to take responsibility for their work or to deal with the consequences of carelessness. In spite of the inconvenience to both children and teachers of sometimes having to return to the store, we waited for the children to solve these problems themselves. To do otherwise would have contradicted the very reason for doing lunch sales with the children in the first place.

In the store, the six children had to locate all the items on the shopping list and put the indicated quantities in the grocery cart. This meant that they had to solve a variety of problems such as: where to find flour; what brand of margarine to buy; whether to buy three separate 1-kg packages of hamburger for $2.88 each or one 3-kg. family pack for $7.29; how many 398-ml and 156-ml cans of tomato paste to buy to get 1800 ml; whether to choose one 10-kg bag of flour or one 5-kg and three 1-kg bags to make a total of 8 kgs of flour; and how to buy 50 plates when there are only packages of 12, 15, 24, and 100. After solving these problems with each other, the children had to pay the grocery bill at the cash register and, therefore, solve another math problem. Then we returned to school with the groceries.

On Monday afternoons, while most of the children were swimming, one teacher made bread dough with the team and a few children who had not gone swimming. The teacher presented the recipe, in large print but purposely with its original small quantities. She posted the recipe in a convenient place to be read together. Each child worked with a partner making double batch after double batch of the recipe and thereby gained lots of practice measuring and calculating quantities. After making the dough, the children put it in plastic bags and placed the bags in the refrigerator. Making bread dough and cleaning up usually took about fifty minutes.

The Olds were responsible for calculating the price of the lunch per serving. After swimming, they unpacked the groceries and then made a list of the quantities and prices of all the ingredients based on the fifty-serving recipe. If there was a discrepancy between the required quantities and the amounts actually purchased (e.g., the 10-kg bag-of-flour problem above), the Olds had to include the surplus in the following week's expenses.

Children's Calculations for Meal Sales

To calculate the price per serving requires adding and subtracting numbers with decimals and multiplying, dividing, and rounding off figures. Because most of the children were not yet familiar with complex dividing, they had to find another way to figure out the price per serving. They had the bill for the groceries; so they knew how much money they had to earn. They set an arbitrary price, and then, by repeat addition, they found out if fifty servings would cover the total cost. After a few tries, someone in the class came up with a suitable price. These calculations took a lot of time. If the Olds were unable to finish all this work on Monday, they would continue it on Tuesday morning, still in time for the Youngs and Middles to write the prices on the posters and fliers.

Meanwhile, the Youngs and Middles worked on the advertisements. Because this task required some discussion and planning, the children talked about the various ways of informing people about the lunch sale and where we should distribute advertisements. One of the teachers listed all the ideas on the board. Often there was a child who suggested that we get our ad on TV, on the radio, or in the local newspapers. This would lead to intriguing questions: How many portions could we cook and how many people might come if we advertised that widely? How many fish would we have to buy to serve fish chowder to 800 people? How many big cooking pots and how many stoves would we need to cook the chowder? How much money would we need to take in to pay for a TV ad? A perfect time and reason to demonstrate large numbers!

Cost of groceries to make chili and buns   43.95

Number of servings   50

Estimate by children of what we should charge to make a small profit.

1. Chili 50¢   bun 10¢
   $.60 × 50 = $30.00

2. Chili 80¢   bun 10¢
   $.90 × 50 = $45.00

3. Chili 90¢   bun 10¢
   $1.00 × 50 = $50.00

We decided to use number 3 - Chili 90¢ bun 10¢

Summary of Calculation of Price and Profit

For the more practical suggestions, she asked the children to list the information we would need to include on posters that would be hung up and in fliers and letters that would be taken home. She continued to write all their ideas on the board—the type of lunch we would sell, the price, date, time and location of the lunches, as well as who was running the business. The next question that the children raised was about how to present this information in a way that would cause people to want to come and buy our lunches.

To demonstrate the need for attractive posters, the teacher wrote all the information about the lunch in normal-sized writing on a regular piece of paper and put it up on the wall at some distance from the children. She then asked, "Does this poster inform people of our lunch sale?" The children's comments invariably included, "I can't even see it," "I didn't notice it," and "It looks boring."

To solve these problems, she brainstormed with the children about what a good poster should look like. She wrote down all the solutions the children offered—for example, use a large sheet of paper with large printing and a simple, small, colored picture of someone eating in the corner. The teacher then made another poster, following the children's suggestions to the letter, and hung it up at some distance. The children again evaluated the poster, and in this manner added new criteria for a good poster.

During the brainstorm, the children also started to think about layout; various kinds of illustrations that relate to the printed message on the poster; and the need for clear, large, neat letters, accurate information, and attractive and neat coloring. The children and teacher concluded the brainstorm with a discussion of what would happen to the lunch business if the children didn't make good posters. They suggested that they would lose money, be disappointed, have spoiled food, and so on. The brainstorm helped all the children realize the importance of their jobs in the lunch business. Without this discussion, they would not necessarily have become aware of their responsibilities and, therefore, of the consequences of careless work.

Next the teacher wrote all the information needed for the poster on the board. The younger children asked the Olds what food would be sold and at what price. The teacher added this information on the board. Then all the children got to work, either in small groups or alone, whichever they preferred. One child who could write small, usually a Middle, would be made responsible for a letter-sized flier.

The children frequently examined their own and each other's work. For example, a child might hold up a poster at the opposite end of the room and ask: "Can you see it?" or "Does it look good?" or "Does it make you want to buy the lunch?"

As the children examined each other's work, they also commented on how accurately and clearly the information was copied. If one child remarked that it was not clear or neat enough, the other child would improve the text with or without help from others. The teacher demanded improvements only when a child had very clearly been careless. She accepted and praised all other work.

Dalhousie Elementary School Chicken
Soup and Buns Wed April 13 Hallway
of the Education Building cost chicken
Soup and Buns :25cts

Age 6

Age 5
Posters Advertising Lunch Sales

Usually the children finished the posters and fliers in an hour. Those who did not finish would generally complete them the next morning before school or certainly before recess. Given the importance of the posters, volunteers were always available to help get all the posters done on time. When the flier was finished and approved, the child who made it usually helped to duplicate it for distribution.

After the group discussed what kinds of places would be good for distributing the ads, a few children left with a teacher to put up posters and fliers in strategic places near the school. Since the teachers had already informed the parents and invited them to come to school to buy lunch, the children needed to take home only a small strip of paper as a reminder of the time, place, type, and price of the lunch.

Tuesday: Cooking

Early in the morning, a teacher took the bread dough, which had risen in spite of the low temperature, out of the refrigerator and placed it on the counter to reach room temperature. Two children from the lunch team of the week helped her get ready for cooking by organizing the utensils, bowls, measuring cups, cutting boards, and ingredients that the team would need.

The children finished most of the food preparation before recess and all of it usually by the end of lunch time. A parent came in and helped the team (who had just washed their hands) shape the bread dough into buns and put them on greased pans. Shaping the buns is not an easy job as it requires a particular way of folding the dough to make the buns, and care has to be taken that they are of similar size, not too large and not too small. We discussed what would happen if the team made buns of very different sizes. The children suggested that the customers would complain if they had to pay ten cents for a very small bun, but of course at least one child solved this problem by proposing to give the disgruntled customer two small buns for the price of one big one. The rest of the group, however, decided that this was not a good solution because we would risk running out of buns.

The other reason for making sure that the buns were not too large was more difficult for the children to figure out. However, a child with baking experience eventually suggested that big buns may be raw on the inside because it took more time for heat to reach the inside and to bake a big bun than it would to bake one half its size. Convinced, the children diligently cut dough and shaped buns while commenting on the sizes each teammate was producing. "That's too big because it's a thick piece of dough," "Oh no, when I was cutting, I forgot that the dough is thin, and now the bun is too small, and I have to start all over again!" and "Someone is going to complain about that bun!" were some of the comments heard around the floured tables.

Cutting a batch of dough into pieces of almost equal size meant solving a math problem. At first, the children tried to solve this problem by cutting the irregularly shaped dough each time into two parts until the desired size was attained.

However, these pieces were often not of the same shape nor of the same thickness, and as a result the sizes of the buns varied a great deal. Later the children discovered that by flattening and shaping or cutting the dough into a square or rectangular shape of almost uniform thickness, they could achieve better results than by cutting the dough into pieces of almost equal size. When the team had finished all the buns and had placed them on greased pans, they left them to rise on the kitchen counters and other available surfaces.

Then they had to prepare the main dish. First the children read and discussed the recipe for fifty servings, which was posted on the wall, and distributed the ingredients. Then they got to work singly or with a partner if they wished. When they all had finished the peeling and chopping, one or two children, under the supervision of the parent helper, used the stove and cooked the lunch. The others cleaned the tables, swept the floor, washed their hands (sometimes more than that!), and returned to the classroom. When the cooks were finished, they cleaned up as well.

After recess, when the buns had risen, they had to be baked in many batches in the oven. If we were lucky, a parent looked after the baking for us. Otherwise, we, the teachers, did so during lunch and in the afternoon, asking the children to alert us whenever the timer went off. For safety reasons, the children were not allowed to take the hot pans with buns out of the oven or to put unbaked dough in the hot oven. Because the bread cooled off after the children had gone home,

Youngs Preparing Homemade Buns from Scratch

we took on the job of storing it for the next day. By the end of the school day, the wonderful smell of freshly baked buns reminded everyone to bring money for lunch the following day.

Wednesday: Lunch Sale, Bookkeeping

The children sell lunches! At the start of the school day, one of the teachers put the two large pots of food on the stove to heat up. During recess, the lunch team organized everything needed for the sale and set it out in two places: the area where the children would buy and eat their lunch (or eat their home-prepared lunch) and the area where other customers would buy and eat their lunch. The children had many items to remember: paper plates, plastic utensils, paper napkins, pepper, salt, margarine and knife, signs with prices of buns and hot lunch, tables to put everything on, hot plate, extension cord, chairs, and the poster with information about the nutritional value of the food.

Finally the children put the "cash registers" (boxes with dividers) with change, a pencil and a sheet of squared paper to mark off the number of buns and hot lunches sold, baskets containing the buns, and the pots of hot food with ladles on the two food counters. Sometimes, when selling chicken soup, we set up a tape recorder and played the song "Chicken Soup with Rice" while serving the meal.

The lunch team sold the lunches between twelve and one o'clock. Three children—a Young, a Middle, and an Old—staffed each of the two food counters. Before the children started their work at the counters, we had a brief discussion about how to treat customers and when the children were allowed to leave the counters. The jobs were divided as follows:

- To keep track of the sales, the Young one recorded each purchase on squared paper (folded in half to distinguish between the two different items) by marking a square on the appropriate side when one bun or one serving of hot lunch was bought. We did not sell drinks because the business was already difficult enough for the children.
- Either the Middle or the Old one, depending on maturity and size, served the hot dish.
- The third child took care of the money, making sure that the cash register was never left during the lunch sale. The Middle and the Old usually discussed the total cost of each sale and how to make change while the Young child offered opinions.
- One teacher stayed near each food counter to help with money, to make sure that the children were careful with the hot food, and to refill the pots when necessary. Sometimes a parent or older child helped as well.

The children discovered that selling lunches is serious and taxing work. They knew that they could not eat until business was slow or finished. Meanwhile, they had to attend to customers who were standing in line and waiting patiently for their turn to buy lunch. The waiting time was usually quite long because selling and serving were time-consuming. To reduce the waiting somewhat, the lunch team used a card showing the prices of the most common combinations of purchases. The children had prepared this card beforehand. However, calculating change still took time. One child was overheard saying, "I'm dizzy from doing all that math for the sale."

The customers usually complimented the children on their business and praised the food. On occasion, though, a customer had a problem: "This bun is horrible; it's too salty!" or "I don't like fish chowder. What are you selling next week?" or "You gave me too small a serving," or "You didn't give me enough change; I'm missing a dime." In handling complaints, the children always tried to make up for shortcomings, for example, by giving more food or returning the money paid for something that was substandard. However, back in school, the children elaborated on the complaint during our regular school meeting. This discussion invariably led to numerous comments about how poor quality food and cooking would result in losing customers and, therefore, money, which eventually could lead to closing down the business. After the children had painted the worst scenario possible, we led the discussion back to the question of how we could solve these problems. In no time, one of us was busy listing the children's ideas on the many ways the restaurant business could be saved from doom and, in fact, be improved: "We should double check when measuring and calculating the amount of salt for the buns," "Maybe we should read the recipe two or even three times before we do any mixing," "We should make a list of the price of one bun and one hot lunch together and write that down so we don't have to think about adding and can think only about how much change to give," and so on with many more suggestions.

At one o'clock it was time to clean up. The lunch team, with the help of the teachers, put everything back, washed the used plastic utensils, pots, and ladles, wiped the tables, swept the floor, and returned all furniture. Usually there was no time left to go out and play, just enough to get a few minutes of fresh air, demonstrating to the children that running a business involves making some sacrifices.

On Wednesday afternoons during math period, the Olds on the lunch team counted the money in the two cash registers and calculated how much profit they had made. The profit included the money from the leftovers that were usually sold to the teachers and some parents. Frequently, at the sight of so much money, the children's initial reaction was that they had made a lot of profit, until they remembered that the costs still had to be deducted. In the end, we usually broke even or showed a small profit. All records were kept in a separate notebook.

While the Olds calculated profit or loss, the Youngs and Middles cut and pasted together the records of the sales to compare what they had sold most of, buns or hot lunches, as well as to find out which counter had sold more. These children recorded the results of this work on a chart and dated it. We then discussed the findings on the chart, counting how many buns and servings of hot lunch had been sold, calculating the differences in sales between the two lunch counters, and guessing how many people had eaten, how many servings and buns might be left over, and whether there was a profit or a loss.

That afternoon at the end of the math period, a Young and a Middle accompanied the teacher to retrieve the posters and remove the fliers. As soon as we had completed the last task for that week, the children began planning the following week with such questions as "Is it my turn next week?" and "What should we cook next?"

After the children had sold lunches on six Wednesdays and everyone had had a turn, the children wrote thank-you letters to the parents who helped with the cooking. Before writing the letters we had a brief discussion. We brainstormed about what we should put in the letters and wrote this list on the board along with the names of the parents. Then everyone wrote a rough copy, edited it, and finally prepared a neat copy. Although the children did most of the work involved in the lunch sales, it was important for them to realize that very little could have been accomplished without help from others.

Chili Enterprise Is Born

After we had been in the "restaurant business" for a while, a parent proposed to the teachers that the children cater a lunch that was going to be held at a nearby place of work. The workplace was the Chemistry Department at the university, and the lunch was for a large group of visiting high school students. To make sure that this idea was acceptable to the Chemistry Department, the teachers invited a delegation of two tasters to one of the lunch sales to taste the children's chili and buns before informing the children of this catering possibility. They passed the test. We welcomed this opportunity for the children to experience another aspect of the restaurant business and suggested to them that they try to cater a lunch for the Chemistry Department.

The teachers decided that the Olds, with some help from the Middles and Youngs, would organize and carry out the catering service. The Olds then brainstormed how to provide the service. They divided their problem into two parts: (a) what price to ask, and (b) how to write a letter to the Chemistry Department that would convince them that we could do the job well and therefore should be hired.

We decided that, unlike the small or nonexistent profit we made when selling school lunches, we wanted to be sure of a profit when catering. The children suggested calculating the price based on prices charged at fast-food restaurants. We did this and then compared the figure we arrived at with the grocery bill for chili and buns for forty people. The difference, of course, was huge. In further discussion, the children attributed the difference to the fame of the fast-food restaurants and the cost involved in buying equipment and maintaining the building. They did not think of labor costs at the time, and we left it at that. Because our customers most likely would expect a lower price from a business run by children than from a fast-food restaurant, we finally decided on an amount higher than our costs but much lower than that of a restaurant.

Next we had to write a letter offering our catering service and trying to persuade the Chemistry Department to give us the job. The children told the teacher what to write on the board: what food we cook and how it tastes, how many people we can cook for, the price of the food, what is included in the price, and the quality of our service and cleanup. Using this list, each child then wrote a letter that was aimed at convincing the reader that we should be hired. We all listened to what each child had written. The children chose one of the letters for the teacher to write on the board and then edited it using the ideas of all the other children. The effects of advertisements on the children were obvious; they wanted to put an abundance of adjectives and superlatives into the text. After rereading the letter together, we discussed the virtues of modesty and, as a result, eliminated some words and replaced others with milder synonyms. One child pointed out that our business lacked a name. After several suggestions, we decided to call it "Chili Enterprise Ltd." because everyone agreed that our best lunch was chili and buns. The whole letter writing session for the purpose of getting this job was quite exciting and useful for the children.

The edited and approved version of the letter had to be copied very neatly. But who was to do that? Some children suggested that one person should be the manager of the business. But how is a manager chosen? The children offered various criteria, and the teacher wrote them on the board. In the end we agreed that a manager should be someone who could organize activities, would be conscientious about the job, would discuss with others what needed to be done and how to do it, would make sure that everyone was working, and, in general, could be counted on to be a responsible person. After listing all the leadership qualities the children could think of, they chose a manager. The manager's first job was to write the letter to the Chemistry Department.

Very soon we received a reply. We got the job! The children were thrilled.

Now we could go over to see where the meal was to be served and make arrangements. A delegation from Chili Enterprise Ltd., including the manager and a teacher, visited the Chemistry Department. Using a previously formulated list, which included everything from hot plates to vases for flowers, the delegation made notes on the availability of all the needed items. We also noted where the guests would enter and exit and where we would be at those times, how much time we would need to set up our "restaurant," when we could get access to the rooms, and so on.

As usual, we asked a parent to help with the cooking. We maintained most of our lunch preparation routine and made only a few necessary changes. Although some of the Youngs and Middles continued to participate in the cooking, only the Olds went to the Chemistry Department to serve the meal. The children kept the same cooking schedule, but in order to serve the meal on time, they had to miss

Dr. W. Jones
Chemistry Department
Dalhousie University

Dear Sir

We are more than pleased to cater a home made meal for 40 adults, if you are fully satisfied with our offer.

We are known for our excellent recipe for piping hot, scrumptious chili with bread and butter.

We will supply paper plates, napkins and utensils.

We will serve it at a time suitable for you, but hopefully between 9 and 3 on weekdays.

This entire set is yours for only $80,00.

We hope to hear from you soon

Yours Sincerely

Daria Manos

Manager of Chili Enterprise Ltd.

DEPARTMENT OF EDUCATION
DALHOUSIE UNIVERSITY
HALIFAX, N. S.
B3H 3J5

Chili Enterprise Ltd.
Daria Manos
Manager
c/o Elementary
School

Dr. W. Jones
Chemistry Department
Dalhousie University

Cooperatively Written Letter Offering the Services of "Chili Enterprise Ltd."

recess and lesson time until lunch. The ''manager'' compiled a list of things we needed to carry to the Chemistry Department and gave everyone a job to do, including the one of gathering flowers near the school.

At last the moment arrived. We walked there, heated the chili, moved furniture, set the tables, decided on a division of labor for serving the food, and ate our own lunch. Meanwhile, we discussed how to behave and what was expected of waiters and waitresses. When the lunch guests arrived, our ''manager'' was introduced to the person who had written to us confirming the catering job, and then we started. Everything went without a hitch between the eager and efficient waiters and waitresses, and the delighted guests.

Chili Enterprise Ltd. in Action

Serving the Customers Our Scrumptious Homemade Chili and Buns

After lunch, the manager received payment for the meal from the department representative, gave a self-made receipt in return, and expressed our wish for an opportunity to cater for them again. Meanwhile everyone else cleaned up, and then we walked back to school carrying our gear and brimming with stories about this experience. We shared the leftovers and the stories with the Youngs and Middles who had just returned from their lunch break.

Now we took care of the last items remaining from the catering job: calculating profit or loss and writing thank-you letters to the parent who had helped us cook.

Received $_____ in cash/cheque

From: _____

Date: _____

    Signed _____

Dalhousie University, Manager
Elementary School Chili Enterprises Ltd.
Halifax, N.S.

Receipt for Payment

The children were excited because, for the first time, they had made a reasonable profit! And for the first time, an important aspect of business surfaced: namely, what to do with the profit. "We did the work, and, therefore, we should divide the profit among ourselves," said one child, who was immediately supported in this claim by the others.

This was an excellent opportunity to discuss wages, prices, and profits and losses, which we did at length. The children finally concluded that, in fact, the whole school and the parents had worked at the business and that dividing the profit would give each person only a negligible amount. The children also thought that, in order to maintain a business, they had to set aside money for repairing, replacing, and adding equipment. Therefore, everyone agreed that, for the moment, the money should be saved to pay for past losses, to buy things that the business needed such as aprons and kitchenware, and, if possible, to trade in our existing stove for a larger one. In this way, everyone would benefit from the profit.

Proof of the success of Chili Enterprise Ltd. was the fact that we have been invited back by the Chemistry Department to provide our catering services for their annual hosting of high school students every year since. Our success is also in evidence by our growing popularity. We have recently picked up another customer; the Education Department at the university now wants us to provide our famous chili and buns meal at a reception they hold in the fall for their new students.

Conclusion

We have carried out this program now for four years and have developed a routine for the organizational aspects, such as using only one or two recipes that have reliable results, organizing the transportation and shopping with children, collecting and bringing our own kitchenware to school on time, having enough change for the sales, and fitting lunch sale activities into the general program.

From the outset, we decided that the six weeks of lunch sales should not be done during the fall term because, after two months of summer vacation, the children have to get back into a school routine first and have to get fully involved in the major theme study. Although the lunch sales hardly disturb the daily routine, some commotion is felt throughout the school. Consequently, we set up and carry out the lunch business during February and March. The catering service usually operates in May, and now, with our new customer, in September as well. Since it mainly concerns the Olds, it can take place almost any time during the school year. Although the lunch sales and the catering service are now a routine for us, each year the children look forward to them.

One year we decided to give the children more business experience by adding a weekly bake sale of buns only. The children were able to get almost everything else, with the exception of shopping, done in one day. At the end of the day, the children bought bags of half a dozen warm buns to take home. However, it proved too hectic, and the project was dropped.

SCHOOL ENTERPRISE — Children at the elementary school of Dalhousie University's education department have set up their own company, Chile Enterprises, to cater to visiting high school groups on the campus. From left, Naomi Buckland-Nicks, 7; Luanna Robinson, 7; Carol Baker-Toombs and Helen Jones, parents; Dustin York, 7, and David Althein, 9.

(Wamboldt-Waterfield)

"Chili Enterprise" in Local Newspaper

The lunch sales have been useful for obvious reasons and have fulfilled all our initial objectives. But in addition, they have been positive learning experiences in a number of other ways as well: cross-age cooperation has required that some children assume leadership roles, new friendships have developed, and everyone has had to work with others who have different views, temperaments, and talents. As one child commented, "You know, I always thought X was weird, but since we've been cooking together, I decided he's not so bad."

The children have applied their new knowledge to other situations. Thus, when the Youngs and Middles went on a field trip to a restaurant, when the Olds went to bakeries, and when they all visited other places of work related to the theme they were studying, they raised questions that were clearly based on their experience with the lunches: "How many double batches of the recipe do you make per day?" "How much bread do you make every day?" "How often do you clean up the bakery?" "How much profit do you make?" When we had to raise the price of the lunches at school, the children, remembering the previous year's prices, asked for the reason. Then the older children explained that there had been an increase in the cost of groceries and that we had to charge more if we didn't want to lose money.

In sum, the benefits of setting up a business with five- to ten-year-old children have been many and have been noticeable in the children's other activities. The business has indeed provided a context for learning math. It also has given the children some understanding of an important aspect of everyone's life, the economy.

Encouraging Children to Act Up: The Whole School Becomes a Theater

Imagine one activity that encourages children to appreciate literature, provides plenty of opportunity for reading, writing, music, and art, and gets children to work cooperatively toward a goal, a goal that they share with their families. Each year in December, the children give their families a Christmas surprise in the form of an evening's entertainment. For about an hour, all thirty-six children in the school bring to life a favorite children's novel by putting it on as a play. This event is the result of more than three months' preparation that involves selecting a book, adapting it to play form by writing the script, making sets and props, designing programs, posters, and invitations, and rehearsing.

The actual process of play production is not as difficult as it may seem at first glance. The way we do it, the process is relatively uncomplicated and smooth.

Overall Schedule and Division of Labor

We divide all the children in the school into two groups for this work. From early September until late November, we make adjustments in the timetable so that the older children (generally those who read and write at about a second grade or higher level or are at least eight years old) have a two- to three-hour drama session each week. During these sessions, the children choose a book and rewrite it into a script. Occasionally they need extra sessions to complete the script before the end of November.

Once a book is chosen, the younger children meet once a week to hear the story. One of the teachers reads the book to them chapter by chapter and allows plenty of time for discussion. Because everyone will have a part in the final production, it is important that all the children understand the plot and become familiar with the main characters.

December brings ''play mania'' as we set aside the regular school schedule for two-and-a-half weeks before the Christmas break. Each day is devoted almost exclusively to rehearsing, making sets and props, and preparing invitations and

Some of the Action from *Fantastic Mr. Fox*

advertisements. Then, two days before vacation, we hold an afternoon dress rehearsal for a small audience consisting of those unable to attend later, and finally that evening the children put on their gala performance usually to a standing-room-only audience.

The teachers also divide the chores among themselves. One teacher takes responsibility for the weekly drama sessions during which the older children select the book and write the script. In addition, she serves as director during rehearsals in December. Another teacher reads and discusses the book with the younger children. She is also in charge of designing and helping the children make the sets and collect the props. During the performances, she is the backstage manager. The third teacher assists with the props and sets and is responsible for providing other activities—math, silent reading, journal writing, and so on—as a change of pace from rehearsing and set making. During the performances, this teacher has the job of keeping the children occupied between their appearances on stage.

While there is a necessary division of labor among the teachers, there is no division of ingenuity. Throughout the fall, all three teachers discuss problems about the play and try to solve such wild problems as how to make a spider web on stage and how to make a boat move through a swamp.

Choosing the Book

Perhaps the most difficult part of producing a play with young children is finding the right book. Although there are lots of excellent children's books, we have found that many of them are not suitable for adapting into a play. Through trial and error, we have narrowed down our selection criteria to the following:

- the book should have an exciting, nonmoralizing plot and be of interest to children from ages five to ten;
- it should have, or be capable of being adapted to have, at least as many main characters as there are older children and enough minor characters to give everyone in the school a part;
- it should be at a level that permits at least a few of the older children to read it independently and the other older children to read it with some help.

Using these criteria, we have adapted some of the best-known and best-loved children's books into wonderful plays—*Charlotte's Web, Charlie and the Chocolate Factory, Jacob Two-Two Meets the Hooded Fang* (put on twice, once as *Jenny Two-Two Meets the Hooded Fang*), *Fantastic Mr. Fox,* and *The Phantom Tollbooth.*

Generally the selection process for a book for the next play begins as soon as the last play is finished. It is then that teachers, children, and parents look at every book they come across with an eye toward a potential future production. Thus, by the beginning of a school year, the teachers generally have a few possible candidates for the next play.

With these titles in mind, one teacher initiates early September discussions about the play with the older chilren who will be doing the writing. Returning students give animated descriptions of previous productions to the new children. Meanwhile the teacher guides the discussions to help the children develop their own list of criteria for a suitable book. Then she introduces possible books for this year's production and encourages everyone to recommend other books as well. She and the children weigh all suggestions carefully against the criteria. In the end, the three teachers balance all the factors and name, with the excitement of an Academy Award announcement, the final choice.

As soon as the immediate squeals of excitement have subsided, the children confront one of the hardest aspects of the play production they will have to face. The title of the play must be kept a secret! The teachers explain that the play is like an enormous present to all of their families, who will enjoy it most if they are completely surprised. As difficult as keeping this secret may sound, the children delight in the thought of a special surprise, and even the youngest members of the school take the responsibility seriously. The children often remind each other to keep the secret and can be seen quickly hiding their books if a parent unexpectedly enters the room during a drama session.

Planning the Production Schedule

The next job for the older group is to establish a production schedule for themselves. As with all aspects of producing the play, this is accomplished by having the children generate ideas while a teacher guides the group discussion. In this case, the teacher also records the ideas so that a calendar of events results. Although this process takes longer than one in which the teacher simply presents a timetable to the children, it is more beneficial because the children feel responsible for a schedule of their making and, therefore, more serious about adhering to it.

Reading the Book

Now the actual play production can get under way. First the older group must read the book. Depending on the length, the reading takes from one to two weeks. If necessary, the children can take the book home as long as everyone remembers to keep the play a secret. Many of the children can read the book independently. However, there are always some who need assistance. Fluent readers are asked to help them with the difficult passages. Learning to be supportive of other people's strengths without being critical of their weaknesses often requires direction from the teacher.

In spite of the help, some children need even more assistance. These are hesitant and unsuccessful readers (usually newcomers to the school) who can understand the ideas in the book but simply cannot read at the required levels. They are nevertheless included because it is crucial that they come to see reading and writing as useful and purposeful and because the need for these skills is obvious in this situation. Moreover, the constant review involved in adapting a book into a play provides these children with many opportunities to reread and rewrite the

<u>Play Preparation Schedule</u>

① choose a book
② read the book
③ discuss the book   } September
④ choose partner & assign part of the book to each set of partners
⑤ reread the part with partner & discuss
⑥ write the script

⑦ finish rough draft of script   } October
⑧ make changes to rough draft
⑨ write songs

⑩ revise the script as a group
⑪ type the script
⑫ read over the script with the whole school   } November
⑬ get parts - memorize

⑭ rehearse
⑮ make props and sets
⑯ practise with props and sets   } December
⑰ dress rehearsal — make posters and program
⑱ final performance

Group Generated Schedule for Play Production
Older Group

same material without any stigma attached because everyone in the group must reread and rewrite the material many times.

For these children, the book is read aloud by a teacher, another child, or a family member (amazingly, even in this situation, the children find ways of keeping the purpose of reading the book a secret). Frequent discussions about what is going on in the story keep the children focused on the meaning. With this support, they can often eventually read parts of the book chorally or even independently.

Meanwhile the younger children spend all of their drama sessions from September through November listening to a teacher read the story bit by bit and discussing each new event thoroughly. They make drawings of what has been read and discussed. The drawings help the children visualize scenes for the prop making and scenery production that will come later. The drawings will also be used to decorate the walls at the gala party after the performance.

Analyzing the Book with the Play in Mind

After the allotted week or two to read the book, the older group discusses the plot and characters. First the children are asked to recall the main events of the book. The teacher again acts as a catalyst, guide, and recorder for these sessions. What results is a chapter by chapter outline of the plot.

During the sessions that produce this outline, the children are often very animated as they urge each other to recall the events of the book accurately. In

Jacob Two-Two Meets the Hooded Fang
PLOT

Ch. 1 J22 is at home and asks his older brothers and sisters if he can play and they say "No!" Asks his mother if he can help and she says "No!" Asks his father if he can run an errand, and he says "yes".

Ch. 2 J22 is afraid of the grocer Mr. Cooper. J22 asks 2x for tomatoes and Mr. Cooper doesn't like it and calls a policeman and J22 runs away to the park. J22 is afraid of the park because of stories he has heard from his sister. J22 falls asleep and has a dream. (Song)

Ch. 3 J22 is taken to a courthouse cell and Mr. Loser says he will defend J22 in court. But Mr. Loser tells J22 how he always loses in court.

Ch. 4 J22 goes to court. The big people in the jury yell that big people are never wrong. Mr. Loser loses the case. J22 is sentenced to jail. Child Power comes and scares the big people and say they will appear again. (Song)

Ch. 5 J22 is taken to the court-house cell and Child Power sneaks him a bleeper. Master Fish and Mistress Fowl take J22 to the children's prison.

Ch. 6 J22 meets the Hooded Fang and he tries to scare J22 by telling him why he hates children.

Part of Group Generated Plot Outline of *Jacob Two-Two Meets the Hooded Fang*
Older Group

order to locate sections in the book to support their ideas, the children must do a good deal of rereading. The less secure readers need not be intimidated by this, however, since everyone is expected to flip through the book at the same time in an effort to find and reread the appropriate sections.

Using the plot outline, the group easily makes a list of characters in the book, both major and minor. Then the children discuss each character's personality and how it could be personified on stage ("What kinds of things would this character have to say or do in order for his/her personality to be clear to the audience?''). The children often need to reread parts of the book to find evidence for their positions. If guided carefully, they can make some interesting observations about particular personality traits. These discussions bring the characters to life for the children, and so it is helpful, as well as fun, to act out some of the characters in order to clarify their personalities. The teacher again records the ideas that emerge from these lively acting-discussing sessions.

Armed with the plot outline and the character charts, the children can now make some important decisions about the organization of the play. For example, some of the events of the book may have to be left out of the play because they are too long, uninteresting, too difficult to put on stage, unnecessary for the plot, too complicated or too repetitive. This kind of exercise gives the children practice in editing within a much larger context than usual. They must make decisions carefully to be sure that the final story line of the script will make sense to the audience.

In a similar manner they also plan how the personalities of the characters might be written into the script. For example, the children thought that the young foxes in *Fantastic Mr. Fox* should always be asking about the meaning of the long words used by the father fox. The humor that this would add to the play became evident as the children tried improvising possible scenes. Also, the scenes including the young foxes became easier to write. Decisions like these are made democratically and after thoughtful debate. However, when agreement does not prevail, the teacher has the final say.

In tallying up the number of characters, the older children discover whether there are enough main characters to give each child in their group at least one speaking part and each of the younger children a minor part. If there are not enough parts, they discuss possible solutions and usually deal with the problem by adding children to a family, clerks or customers in a store, and so forth. Eliminating extra characters is a more difficult, but luckily less common, problem because this can necessitate rewriting sections of the plot. Experience has shown that it is easier to simply have some children act out more than one character.

The plot outline is also helpful for deciding where songs might be added. Generally, songs have been peppered throughout the plays, especially when the younger children are on stage. These songs have familiar tunes but new words that match the action of a particular scene. By singing the songs, which are often accompanied by little dances or actions to go with the words, even the youngest children can remember more easily when to get on and off the stage.

With the plot so clearly laid out and the places where there should be songs

Fantastic Mr. Fox Characters

	Characteristics	Ways to Write These Into Script
Mr. Fox	- fantastic - kind, especially for family - thoughtful - brave - clever, smart, IQ over normal - sneaky (thief? robber?) - respectful of digging creatures community	- he thinks of the ideas - makes little speeches
Mrs. Fox	- afraid, worried in times of difficulty - calm - respectful of her family - she gets hungrier + more starving	- reminds children to be careful all the time - fussing - she speaks softer and slower when she's hungry
Little Foxes	- talkative - excited - questioning - jumpy - obedient - eager	- little voices - ask a lot of questions - copy Mr. Fox's speech - cheer enthusiastically at ideas - pitch right in to help
Bean (tall farmer)	- jumps to conclusions too quickly - mean - cleverest of farmers but still stupid - cruel - selfish - drinks tons of cider - sneaky	- low, mean voice - says an idea and he doesn't change it no matter what - thinks of it quickly but he doesn't analyze the consequences

Part of a Group Generated Character Chart for *Fantastic Mr. Fox*
Older Group

already determined, the children have at least a rough idea of what kinds of songs will be needed. And so, one of the most enjoyable activities associated with the playwriting begins. From this time on, all the older children are busy humming popular tunes that lend themselves to new lyrics. The lyrics must not only fit the basic mood of particular scenes, but they must also be easy for the young ones to sing. Selecting tunes and composing lyrics is an ongoing activity that extends throughout the period of playwriting. It adds a dose of comic relief for everyone to take a break during scriptwriting and to try to think of a "washing-the-pig" song or a "baby-spiders-being-born" song.

To The Tune of *animal fair*

. Boggis and Bunce and Bean
One fat one short one lean
these horible crooks so diffrent in looks
are nontheless equaly mean mean mean.

Song from *Fantastic Mr. Fox*—Adapted from the Song "Animal Fair"
Older Group

The decisions involved at this stage allow the children to recognize some of the factors that must be taken into consideration when producing a play. However, the children cannot make all the decisions about the play because there is not enough time for such a process, and they are too young and inexperienced to juggle all the factors that need to be considered. Consequently, they learn early on that some decisions will be made by the teachers. For example, the roles they will play will be determined by the teachers and disclosed on the first day of rehearsal. The teachers might also make certain decisions about the flow of the plot, some technical aspects of staging, or the appropriateness of certain parts of the script.

Writing the Script

Having worked out the story line as well as the character traits of the main characters, the children can begin to actually write the play. This is a time-consuming process but not as complicated as one might expect. Depending upon the maturity of the group, either the teacher or the children set up the writing partners. Ideally pairs are formed with a fluent writer working supportively with a less fluent or hesitant writer. However, the personalities of the children are also important. Obviously the partners' relationship must be able to withstand some hard work over a long period of time.

The teacher gives each pair one or more chapters or sections of the book to rewrite into a script for the play. The plot outline helps to identify where the major events begin and end in the book, and so, the teacher can give a pair the responsibility for rewriting an event in its entirety. The more fluent or experienced sets of partners might also be given the longer or more difficult parts of the book to rewrite.

Now each pair may begin work on their section. The children will have to reread the part of the book that they are working on and take notes on the main events to be included in the script. Each pair can also use these notes to help them develop a schedule for the completion of their work, thus getting them off to a realistic start.

Otherwise, they might get bogged down on one part and lose track of their end-of-November deadline.

Just before the writing begins, the teacher shows the group what a script looks like, and they discuss ways of turning narrative passages into dialogue. With only this short introduction, experience takes over as the main teacher. The pairs struggle together to write their sections—reading, discussing ideas, and writing. They are allowed to copy directly from the book when appropriate. With lots of support from the teacher and from others in the group, they attempt to make use of each other's strengths. The working atmosphere is full of discussions as partners talk together and sometimes to other pairs of children. Outstanding ideas or problematic sections of the script are talked over with the whole group, which helps to solve difficulties as they arise. The teacher moves from group to group, assisting those who are stuck as well as keeping tabs on how all of the scripts are progressing and making sure the work is on schedule.

The teacher expects each pair to write their section as best they can without concerning themselves with accurate spelling or beautiful handwriting, which would inhibit the flow of ideas and demand too much time. The children are, however, responsible for writing their section as completely as possible so that it will make sense to an audience and so that they and the teacher can read and understand it easily. Each pair is also responsible for writing whatever songs, if any, are required for their section. Sometimes there are a few children who are particularly interested or talented in suggesting appropriate tunes and adapting suitable words. They may be called upon to assist others.

Hesitant writers benefit from all the discussions about each section. They also benefit from the built-in repetition necessary to write and rewrite their sections. Still, turning narrative passages into dialogue is difficult, and children often find it helpful to act out certain sections before trying to write them. Once they have succeeded in getting some dialogue on paper, children with reading and writing difficulties need to frequently reread what they have written so that they will remember their often difficult-to-read work. The teacher may have to keep very close tabs on these children to make sure their labors are not lost. As hard as writing is for some children, writing a script is often much easier for them than other kinds of writing because a script can so easily be turned into action and because it resembles the forms with which they are familiar from their exposure to television. In addition, of course, this type of writing clearly serves a real purpose, one which most of the children find very exciting.

When a pair thinks their section is complete, they are responsible for rereading it and making any changes that might improve it. Often another pair will listen to the section as well and suggest further changes. Changes usually involve adding or deleting parts and sometimes transferring sections to other, more appropriate, places in the script. Writing on the back of scrap paper makes it easier for children to make these changes because they can see that their work is still in the rough draft stage. Furthermore, if they write on only one side of the paper, they can cut

out or paste in chunks of text easily. Since the writing process is a long and difficult one, the teacher must use discretion in deciding how far to urge the children
to improve their script. Obviously, it is counterproductive for the teacher to push
them to the point where they lose interest in the project. Many changes, even rather
major ones, can be made in a lighthearted manner later on with the whole group.

mr fox: ~~comes in~~ breaks in   fiddles with toys

Shapero ~~ ~~ some wons   here

otool   maby mr fox Jacob 22 said   he   was   doing   toy sabatosh
shapero ~~o tote~~ ~~probably 1?~~   ~~custan~~
otool   ~~are is   its a 2   persant chanse~~   ~~ripping~~
    ~~1%~~ I think   o tool: Look   ~~show~~
shapero ~~make that~~   what
~~this is   boring~~   ~~otool   you shur   he's doing
shapero hes   & mixing up puzzles so   its   impossble to do them
otool ~~I feel sorry for the kids that buy toys~~ here
    changing pepes of different
shapero ~~hes~~ Now he's ~~mixing~~ chemastry sets
otool   What will he think of Next
Shapero shouled / show myself!   [Song - To the tune of PINK PANther
otool   are   you crazy   dont go dont go
Shapero   hes putting Pin Pricks in Kites   he'll see you if you show
otool   and takin king baterys out of toys   mr fox —]   that say   baterys included
Shapero hes ruinig a lot of stuf
otool you better show yourself Now

Excerpt from Rough Draft Script of *Jenny Two-Two Meets the Hooded Fang*
Ages 7 and 9

Finally, after their section of the script is as complete as possible, each set of
partners corrects for spelling mistakes, punctuation errors, and difficult-to-read
handwriting. Because they have time restrictions for completing the script, they
need not edit very thoroughly. As long as the children and the teacher can read
their work, the section is considered ready for the important group revision sessions. Those pairs that finish early can do one of several activities: help other pairs
who are having difficulties, work on songs for the various sections, begin to type
their part into the computer, or help to design sets and props.

Although the quality of the work may vary dramatically depending on the skill
of the different pairs of children, it does not usually take long before there are some
completed sections. At this point the teacher finishes typing them into the computer and puts them together into the first, very rough and incomplete version of
the script. We find that the word processing capabilities of computers are an ex-

cellent timesaving devise when used for scriptwriting. Because there are so many changes made in the script, not only when it is being developed, but even during rehearsals of the production, the computer allows updated versions to be ready quickly, efficiently, and economically. The children also benefit from using the word processor for a real purpose, as it was designed to be used.

Revising the Script

Using individual copies of the preliminary script, the children who have finished their sections sit down with the teacher for the first reading. They read the script through together to get an idea of how the whole thing sounds. Then the script is reread from the beginning; once again, the repetition supports the less fluent readers. This time, it is read slowly with the children and the teacher commenting freely about each section and the teacher recording changes. The fact that the teacher is doing the writing is beneficial at this point because it allows the children to concentrate on composing. The teacher needs to try to keep the comments balanced so that the children who wrote the section under discussion are not discouraged by changes. On the other hand, since everyone is in the same position, they tend not to take changes in their writing personally. Furthermore, because the teacher is the one recording the changes, the children are not always aware of how much of their writing has been altered by the group. By the time they go over the section again, it sounds quite good. Even when the teacher is instrumental in making the changes, most children attribute the improvements to their own excellent writing skills!

These group revision sessions can be both productive and very enjoyable once the children begin to visualize what the characters might be doing on the stage and what kinds of voices they might have. Generally a rather animated reading of the script will suffice to generate some good ideas and dialogue. Depending on the quality of each section, the group may need to add quite a bit to the script before the play makes sense and before some action is evident in each scene. Consequently, these group sessions always take longer than expected, and so we begin group revisions as soon as possible even though that means starting with less polished sections.

More sections are added to the group work as they are ready. For pairs of children to continue working on their sections at the same time as the others are revising in a group creates problems because the teacher's time is now almost exclusively devoted to the group. There is no easy solution, but an experienced child may be able to assist one of these pairs. Alternatively, if the children who are not finished have put enough effort into their writing, they may benefit most by joining the others and adding their unfinished section to be revised by the group. Despite the fact that revising extends over a long period of time, the freedom to try out a variety of ideas as well as the excitement generated by the group can turn composing from an arduous task into a pleasurable experience. Always cheering are the songs

Chapter One

J22: Hello! My name is J22 and I am 2+2+2 years old and I

have two ears and two eyes and two arms and two feet and two

shoes. I have two older sisters and two older brothers.

Daniel: (skips onto stage and does homework)

J22: May I come in your room? May I come in your room?

Daniel : ~~skips onto stage~~ No J22 you can't come in my room

Now you are disturbing me doing my

because you are too small. ~~homework~~ so I'm going to find another

place to do my

Noah & Emma: (come out onto stage homework. (exits)

and play)

J22: May I play with you? (2x)

Noah: ~~runs onto stage~~ I'm the fearless O'toole! J22 you

can't play with us any more because you are too little.

J22:   I'm not too small! I'm not too small!

Emma: ~~she runs out onto the stage~~ I'm the Intrepid

Shapiro! You wrecked our game so get out of here!

Noah & Emma: Let's go out to the back and play our game (exit)

Marfa: (cartwheels and watches TV

~~puddle jumps~~ onto stage) ~~she says~~ You can't watch

any scary movies because you're too small.

Marfa: Hey, that's the ~~Hooded~~ Fang!

J22: What's the ~~Hooded~~ Fang? (2x)

Marfa: ~~X~~ He's ~~the~~ a boxer and he's going

to jump out of the TV and eat you

up.

J22: Are you sure? Are you sure?

Marfa: Yes, I'm sure. You're too small to

watch the Hooded Fang because you'll

get nightmares.

J22: I'm not too small! I'm not too small!

Marfa: Yes you're too small. (goes back to watching TV)

J22: (walks off to kitchen)

J22: (J22's mother walks in and starts to cook) I won't ask

my mother if I can help her cook because I know that she

will say ~~that~~ NO! Mom, can I do a chore?

Excerpt from Script of *Jenny Two-Two Meets the Hooded Fang*
After Group Revision *(Recorded by Teacher)*

that come up in the script from time to time. There is nothing like a rousing chorus of "Dig for your lives, dig for your lives . . . " sung to the tune of "Jingle Bells" to stir up a little energy and enthusiasm.

This process does not work without snags. Some children who have not had much writing experience may not realize what a play is all about until these final stages. But that is enough of an accomplishment for them. Others may make it difficult for the group to generate creative ideas or to accept them. In addition, if there are many skimpy sections, the group may still have a lot of work to do, and yet this work has to be done by children who did not have many ideas in the first place. None of these difficulties is easy to solve, but it must be kept in mind that, if possible, group generated solutions should be tried because they are the most easily accepted. In our case, because we have a play every year, many of the children have accumulated successful play experiences. Therefore, they are willing to take on increasingly larger responsibilities as they get older and to help motivate the uninitiated, who hear about this exciting event through these more seasoned playwrights and actors.

Each week during drama period, as the script continues to grow, the children can see the changes they made added to the latest computer printout. The ease with which additional changes can be made to the text through the use of the computer allows the group the luxury of rereading the already revised sections of the play and of still feeling free to make alterations. However, since there is a definite time limit for the completion of the script, there comes a point when the script must be considered finished.

Preparing for Rehearsals

The teachers decide which parts will be suitable for which children, taking into account their interests, memorization skills, ease with acting in front of groups, and sense of responsibility. We also think about which children will be on stage at the same time and make use of positive combinations of children, while avoiding problematic ones. We consider it of utmost importance that every child participate on stage as a member of the cast. Because of some children's shyness or low self-esteem, we have had to think up creative ways to convince them that they could play successful and necessary parts in the play. These parts have ranged from being the person behind the grandfather clock responsible for turning the hands at the stroke of midnight—unseen but indispensable—to carrying a sign saying "The Next Day" across the stage, to being inside of a tractor (a cardboard box with a wheel that had to be turned to simulate digging)—a role with lots of time on stage and frequent action but no lines and no visibility. Getting children on stage for what they consider relevant parts means that they will be willing to take on more substantial roles the next time. The children's increased self-esteem after such successes also carries over into other endeavors.

By now, the "director" has decided what sets and set changes will be required and has indicated these in the script. The teacher in charge of sets then designs

Jenny Two-Two Meets
The Hooded Fang

Scene One

J22:   Hello! My name is J22 and I am 2+2+2 years old and I
have two ears and two eyes and two arms and two feet and two
shoes. I have two older sisters and two older brothers.

Daniel: (skips onto stage and does homework)

J22:   May I come in your room ? May I come in your room ?

Daniel :   No, J22 you can't come in my room because you are
too small. Now you are disturbing me doing my homework and
so I'm going to find another place to do my homework. (
exits)

Noah and Emma: (run onto stage and play)

J22:   Can I play with you? Can I play with you?

Noah: I'm the fearless O'toole! J22 you can't play with us
any more because you are too little.

J22:   I'm not too small! I'm not too small!

Song :   (To the tune of You'd Better Watch Out)
You'd better watch out,
You'd better not cry,
You'd better not shout ,
I'm telling you why,
Child Power is coming to town. (2X)

Noah: I'm the Fearless O'Toole.
Emma: ...and I'm the Intrepid Shapiro ! Oh, J22. You
wrecked our game so get out of here!

Emma and Noah: Let's get out of here and go back and play
our game Shapiro. (exit)

Marfa: (cartwheels onto stage an watches TV) You can't
watch any scary movies because you're too small. Hey,
that's the Hooded Fang!

J22:   What's the Hooded Fang? What's the Hooded Fang?

Marfa: He's a boxer and he's going to jump out of the TV
and eat you up.

J22:   Are you sure? Are you sure?

Excerpt from Finished Script of *Jenny Two-Two Meets the Hooded Fang*

them and works out the sorts of art techniques that will be possible and most effective given the ages and capabilities of the children. She also prepares a list of props from the finished script while keeping in mind that the number of props should be kept to a minimum and that miming certain actions can be just as effective as having props. Finally the director plans the staging of the production. Once rehearsals begin, the children will have a tremendous amount to remember, and the fewer the changes made during rehearsals, the better. Therefore, prior to rehearsing, the director figures out when and from which side of the stage the characters should enter and generally what they will be doing on the stage.

With copies of the script for every speaking character available and a list of things to be made for sets and props ready, everyone now gears up for the last, all important two-week blitz.

Rehearsing the Play

Generally, we ease into rehearsing by first reading through the play with all thirty-six players. While the whole group reads, the characters find and circle the places in the script where they have to speak. The next two days are devoted to memorizing the script. Where helpful, the children work together in groups to go over lines. Only if a child has great difficulties memorizing is the script allowed to go home, but since the children are eager to keep the play a secret, they usually find ways of memorizing their lines in school. Sometimes, in a discussion with a child a teacher realizes that some parts of the script are too difficult. In such cases, the teacher and the child concerned might remove, reduce, or change certain lines to make them easier for the child to remember. Surprisingly it is often the confident child, the one who has been eagerly reading and writing all fall and has consequently been given a large role, who feels overwhelmed by the task. Usually all that is required to boost sagging confidence is a few reductions in the part and moral support from others in the group.

Now rehearsing can begin in earnest. To get the children used to being prompted if they forget lines we don't allow scripts to be used during rehearsals. We found out one year, when the children attended a mime show at about the same time as we were rehearsing the play, that the show had made a significant impression on the children because it gave them ideas about ad-libbing on stage. However, in the usual course of events, we know of no magic ways of bringing the play to life in this short span of two weeks other than repeating the scenes often with as few changes as possible. Some characters are easier to portray than others, while some children need help to become livelier in their roles. As well as participating in rehearsals for their scenes, the younger children learn their songs separately and sometimes practice them when they are making sets and props. They can also be heard singing during lunch and recess and, of course, during regular rehearsals when they sing with all the older children who will be on stage with them.

Unfortunately, we have generally had to rehearse the play in one of the small classrooms; we have had access to the large room that is actually used for the performance only on occasion and only for the last few days of rehearsal. Obviously, it would be preferable for the children to consistently practice in the same place where the performance will be held.

Preparing Sets, Props, and Costumes

When the children are not practicing the play, they are responsible for helping to make the sets and props. They choose or are assigned a job by a teacher from

```
                         (leaps back into den in one bound)
                         The farmers were waiting for me.  I'm afraid that you can't have
                         any dinner tonight, darlings.
Little Foxes:            What about your tail, won't it grow back?
Mr. Fox:                 No. I'll be tail-less for the rest of my life.
Mrs. Fox:                It was the best tail for miles around.
                         *    *    *    *    *    *    *    *    *    *    *

                         SONG:  (to the tune of "Mary Had a Little Lamb")
                         Oh no, look what's happening now,
                         Happening now, happening now.
                         Oh no, look what's happening now,
                         They've got Mr. Fox's tail.
                         *    *    *    *    *    *    *    *    *    *
3 Farmers:               We got the tail - but we missed the fox.
Bean:                    This tail will go fine in my collection.
                         (whispers)
                         This fox will be too scared to come out any more.
Boggis:                  All right - now we can starve them out.
Bunce:                   Oh come on - can't we dig them out?
3 Farmers:               Yeah!  That's a good idea!
Bunce:                   That's a good idea of mine.
Boggis:                  Your idea?  That was my idea.
Bunce & Boggis:          O.K. - it's our idea.
Boggis:                  (to Bean & Bunce)
                         Go get the shovels.  Quick!
Bean:                    You go get them.  Wasn't it your idea?
Boggis:                  Yeah . . . but.
Bunce:                   No 'buts'.  Move along.
                         (Boggis goes to get shovels)
Bean & Bunce:            (point rifles at hole)
                         We've got you surrounded now!  There's no hope for you.
                         *    *    *    *    *    *    *    *    *    *
                         SONG:  (to the tune of "Maneater")
                         Oh, Oh, Here they come,
                         Watch out fox they'll chew you up,
                         Oh, Oh, Here they come,
                         They're fox-eaters!
                         *    *    *    *    *    *    *    *    *    *
```

Excerpt from *Fantastic Mr. Fox* Script—Lines to Be Memorized Are Circled

a large master list of what is required, and when they finish the job, the teacher checks it off the list. In this way, the children take some responsibility for what needs to be completed.

The sets consist of large pieces of cardboard, 1.2 meters by 2.4 meters (about 4 feet by 8 feet), stapled onto light wooden frames. There are two sides to the frames

Rehearsing the Feast Scene of *Fantastic Mr. Fox*
Both Groups

so that they can simply be turned around on stage to reveal a new scene. Clearly, the designer must plan the sets carefully. The cardboard pieces are reused each year. Usually the stage consists of six frames, two on each side of the stage and two in the middle, although the number might vary for different productions.

Because the older children are often rehearsing, the five- to seven-year-olds make most of the sets and props. Therefore, we keep the steps simple. We make up large batches of finger paint in the colors required, and some of the children simply spread the paint over the cardboard where desired. Then the children color and cut out the shapes of certain articles. Thus, for example, if the set were a toy store, the group would make different kinds of toys. Sometimes these are stuffed to create a three-dimensional effect. One year we made sausages by stuffing newspaper into old nylon stockings. These articles are then carefully glued onto the set. The result is a large, bright, colorful backdrop.

In the process of making sets, the children use numerous art and craft skills: painting, cutting, coloring, stenciling, origami, collage techniques, and many others. Making props can also introduce a range of skills such as building small wooden structures, using papier-mâché, doing macramé, and so on. The children have many ideas for the creation of the props and sets, and, when appropriate, we use them, much to the contributors' delight. It is by taking advantage of this situation that we can draw upon the hidden skills and talents of the children, even those who are more retiring.

Gluing the Chicken House Set for *Fantastic Mr. Fox*
Younger Group

There are always some props that are difficult to find around the school and difficult to make but are essential to the production. For example, some kind of a wagon that can hold a few children seems to be a useful item for a number of plays. Parents are helpful in supplying these props. We also ask parents to provide the costumes. As soon as rehearsals begin, we inform them of the kind of costume their child will need for the play. We don't tell them the name of the play or what role their child has in it. However, we give them a description of the type of costume their child needs—a young fox, a plump pig, and so on. In addition, we assure the parents that the costume need not be elaborate and that, if necessary, other parents or the teachers can help them.

To be sure that our work is on track, that problems are being solved as they arise, and that everyone is aware of what still needs to be done, we hold meetings of all children and teachers first thing in the morning and in the afternoon every day. At these meetings, we discuss the rehearsal schedule and the set- and prop-making timetable, and make adjustments as needed; we also address any problems that the children or teachers wish to discuss. In all their work to produce the play, we urge the children to take great care and to set high standards for themselves, which sometimes results in work being redone until it is acceptable. Of course, with the thought of their families coming to see the play, most children need not be reminded to try hard and to help each other. By the time the sets and props are finished, there is such a collage of different people's labor that the children are well aware that the whole project is a collective creation.

Although the atmosphere of the school is quite positive during this period of rehearsals and set-making, children who feel more secure with a predictable routine may sometimes find this period stressful. Therefore, when necessary, we interrupt the play production work of some or all of the children and engage them in more normal, everyday math, journal, or reading activities for a while.

Making Invitations, Advertisements, and Programs

As the day of the performance nears, we ask the children to turn their attention toward the audience. How will they inform people about the big event? The children come up with suggestions such as posters, invitations, programs, and the usual flashy television promo. With the exception of the latter, these suggestions are added to the list of things to do. Children who are making posters or invitations are asked to consider what information to include, what sort of design will draw people's attention, and how to make important information such as the title of the play, and the date, time, and place of the performance stand out clearly. The finished products are sent home to parents and placed prominently around the school community. The children then prepare the programs to be handed out at the door. Like all programs, they contain the names of the actors and the writers and acknowledge the efforts of all the children who made the sets and props. As with most other jobs, the design and layout of the program are done by the children.

Organizing Lighting and Sound Effects

As the day of the performance draws near, we turn our attention to the finishing touches. The school has a small display of footlights—a simple, three-sided wooden box with a string of light bulbs attached on the bottom and tinfoil behind the bulbs. We add these lights plus a few spotlights to the finished sets in the performance room and figure out a system for turning the required lights on and off. We also prepare necessary sound or other effects. For example, in *Fantastic Mr. Fox,* the tractors dug to the sound of real tractors coming from a tape recorder amplified over a small sound system. To show baby spiders in *Charlotte's Web*, we drew little spiders on transparencies and projected them onto the stage using an overhead projector.

If there are too many things for the teachers to control during the performance, a parent may be asked to assist. Needless to say, however, if there is any way to avoid asking a parent to help, we do; we want all parents to enjoy watching the performance.

Dress Rehearsal

On the afternoon of the big day, we hold a full-blown dress rehearsal complete with costumes, sets, props, sound effects, lights, and audience. All are welcome

Poster Advertising *Fantastic Mr. Fox*

Dalhousie Elementary

School

Presents

Fantastic Mr. Fox

Main characters
BRENDAN M.R fox
Matthew - Bean
JULIA - Ms. fox
ANDREW - Badger
WREN - Bunce
DAVID - Boggis

FOXES
BRENDAN
JULIA
Karen
Bridget
Jason

Farmers
Matthew
WREN
DAVID

RAT
Noah

MOLES
Trevor S.
Trevor M.
Paul.
Troy

BADGERS
ANDREW
Sarah
Stephen John

VISITING farmers
J.B.
Elliott

Chickens
chris
Alexs
Jenna
Ben

Tractors Shawn
Zachary

Program for *Fantastic Mr. Fox*

to this performance, which usually draws a small audience of parents who cannot come at night, young brothers and sisters, and a few members of the general public. Because the children have had a chance to see the play during earlier rehearsals, they are completely backstage this time. Most important is the fact that they get a taste of what it is like to act in front of an audience and to experience pride in successfully accomplishing this big undertaking.

The Big Moment

That evening, the long-awaited and hard-worked-for event takes place. On one such occasion, as the stage lights came on and a child walked to the center of the stage, a hush fell over the crowded room of parents, grandparents, brothers, and sisters. "Welcome to the Dalhousie University Elementary School. Tonight we are pleased to perform *Charlotte's Web* for you, a play written by the older children in the school and adapted from the book by E. B. White. As you can read in your programs, the children have also made all the sets and props. We hope that you enjoy the play." Thus began an hour-long performance in which thirty-six five- to ten-year-olds brought to life the touching and well-known tale of Charlotte, the clever, kind spider, and her endangered friend, Wilbur the pig.

The Grand Performance of *Charlotte's Web*

The Grand Performance of *Charlotte's Web*

What a wonderful Christmas present!

But more importantly, long after the crumbs from the after-the-play potluck dessert party organized by the parents had been swept up, positive effects of the play were visible everywhere. The children worked together more easily and smoothly; many of them were much more willing to share and were more considerate of others. There was general enthusiasm about books and writing, and even hesitant readers and writers made considerable progress, not only in their actual reading and writing, but also in their more positive and self-confident attitudes toward these skills. Self-confidence grew in other areas as well because the production had required so many kinds of skills, ranging from acting, singing, songwriting, dancing, and painting to teaching, exercising leadership, cooperating, having a sense of humor, and even to moving furniture and cleaning up. Because every child's contributions were sincerely appreciated, both individual self-esteem and group pride were enhanced.

YES, BUT WHAT ABOUT . . .

What about "The Basics"?
And Other Sundry Matters

Visitors to the school, commonly practicing teachers and future teachers (education students) who spend time observing the program, as well as others interested in theme studies have a lot of questions about our program. In this and the next two chapters we discuss the most frequently raised issues.

People who are new to the theme study approach as it is implemented in our school always want to know about "the basics." Listed below are their questions and our answers organized into three categories: skills, teacher's role, and "other sundry matters."

Skills

How do you teach reading?

We apply the whole language, or psycholinguistic, approach to reading. Much has been written about this approach.[1] Briefly, it views reading as a process in which the student is an active learner who reads for meaning. While figuring out text, the reader must constantly predict and then confirm a prediction and proceed, making new predictions in the upcoming text, or reject the prediction and reformulate an alternative one. This process of predicting and confirming is ongoing. Fluent readers not only do it all the time, but they do it very well.

In practice, this means that children start to learn to read by having predictable stories read to them and joining in whenever they can. "Big Books" are especially helpful because the text is large enough to be seen and to be followed by young readers. Predictable books (of any size) are those with portions of the text repeated frequently, stories that are already familiar, songs and poems that rhyme and have a definite rhythm, books with illustrations that closely match the text, and so on—books, in other words, in which the children can easily begin to predict what comes next and that they can read independently before long.

After having such books read to them many times, children begin to read the books themselves, gradually matching the words they say, based on prediction and memory, with the printed words on the page. In this way, they develop effective reading strategies, build up a sight vocabulary, and can move on to more complex books. Because the children are successful in reading enjoyable and natural sounding "whole language" stories (as opposed to the fragmented bits presented when drilling sounds or the stilted language that goes with controlled vocabulary), they develop a love for reading.

The main purpose of our reading instruction is to help the children develop good reading strategies, which we interpret to be those strategies that focus attention on what the text means. Thus, when children encounter difficulties in reading a particular text, we encourage the following strategies: read ahead to get context clues about what happens next and then reread the difficult part; sometimes skip over a section completely if reading ahead and rereading do not help and then keep reading until the text is meaningful once again; and substitute one or more words for unknown words to make the passage sound sensible. By such means, the children learn to actively try to understand the text without overly relying on the less effective strategies that divert attention from meaning and fragment language and without feeling an absolute necessity to read every word accurately.

Those children who are experiencing difficulties with reading are given many opportunities to develop effective strategies by having predictable books read to them frequently and by reading these books repeatedly with a teacher, someone else, or independently. The teacher observes how the children handle difficulties and keeps them informed about their progress in developing productive reading strategies.

Once the children show that they have learned some effective reading strategies and can successfully read an unfamiliar story, they are ready to more independently tackle factual material to gain information about a topic. Generally this happens at about age six. From then on, reading is more completely integrated with the theme studies, but of course, we give help as needed. In addition, immersion in theme studies means that the children must do a great deal of reading with concentration on meaning. Consequently, their reading strategies improve rapidly.

How do you make sure the children learn reading skills?

Practicing reading skills for their own sake can be boring and pointless. One always needs a context to put them in and a purpose for using them—to get information and ideas or for just plain enjoyment. There must be ample opportunity to read for these purposes and a high success rate in these efforts without the constant expectation of perfection. We see this process as similar to initial oral language acquisition. If learning to speak required practicing sounds and words without meaning or context and if a high degree of accuracy were expected right from the start, who would learn to speak? Instead, children are constantly exposed to spoken language that has meaning, appears in context, and is whole. Through this means, virtually all children develop highly sophisticated oral language skills. We think that by adhering to the same principles, we can help children become equally competent in their reading and writing language skills. Theme study provides precisely this kind of exposure to print—written language that has meaning, appears in context, and is whole.

How do you teach writing?

Much has been written about the writing process as well.[2] As with reading, there must be a purpose for writing and plenty of opportunities to practice it without having to fear devastating criticisms for being less than perfect at the skill. Just as children learn to read by reading, they learn to write by writing. Consequently, the children write a great deal and for various purposes every day. In their theme study work, they record brainstorms and take notes; they write up observations, label their drawings, and write questions for field trips and guest speakers; they prepare thank-you letters and summarize what they have learned about a topic; they write proposals for projects; they produce games, plays, riddles, and jokes; and they write books, make signs, fliers, posters, advertisements, and shopping lists. The children also do a lot of writing in their non-theme study school activities: they write in their journals; they write stories and messages to each other; they list books they like to read and activities they like to do; they write about a story they have read and suggestions for parties and other activities; they write reminders, apologies, explanations about a problem with a classmate, and agendas for meetings. The lists are endless. As the children get older and more adept at writing, the quantity and variety of their writing increase tremendously and its quality improves greatly. Writing eventually becomes almost as natural as speaking.

To back up for a moment, many children start off with some knowledge of sound-letter correspondence. We build on this knowledge by helping them listen more attentively to sounds in words. For example, the Youngs practice printing the beginning letter of certain words, and then they draw pictures of things they can think of that start with that letter. Encouraging children to write what they hear rather than getting the correct spelling helps them learn to hear an increasing number of letters in words. This strategy also goes far in developing self-reliance and the courage to take risks, both important aspects of learning to write. The children quickly move on to more substantive writing in the form of newsbooks in which they write things of importance to them. They read their entries to the teacher or to peers and get feedback on their ideas or some technical matter—a sound they may be ready to identify, spacing, and so on. These activities are done individually and are geared to each child's development.

Writing is integrated into theme studies from the beginning so that it is clearly purposeful from the start. At first the teacher does the actual printing, but it is not long before the children take over. We introduce the notion of "rough" and "neat" copies at the primary level. At this early stage, the child simply reads the whole sentence or text to the teacher to see if it makes sense and then circles or underlines one or two words that present spelling problems. The teacher then writes in the proper spellings and the child gets another piece of paper and produces a "neat" copy. The effect is dramatic. This process helps the children become aware of three important aspects of writing that have to be considered in a definite order: first, does the writing make sense, and is the meaning clear?; only then, which words are spelled incorrectly?; and finally is it neat and legible?

Only certain kinds of writing require "neat copies," depending on the purpose of the writing. Yet the children experience the need for quality in content, accuracy in spelling, and legibility every day because their partners and others comment on their writing and because they are approached for help and advice. Later during open house, many other people will also look at their displays. Therefore, the children want their writing to be of high quality in all respects.

Although most of the writing is factual, all the children write stories. When a theme study lends itself to this kind of writing, it is readily included. Most story and poetry writing, however, is done outside of theme study.

Why is the children's written work often messy? They need to be taught standards of neatness, don't they?

What is "messy" depends on the level of the child's development, the nature of the task, and the purpose of the writing. Many kinds of writing do not require others (except perhaps the teacher) to read the work. But in almost all cases, children have to use their own work for some purpose or other. Therefore, not being able to read their own writing is a problem with consequences that are immediately felt and must be rectified. As for other people's standards of neatness, as soon as the children are aware of them, they try hard to meet them. In any case, legibility should not be confused with perfection or beauty.

Putting ideas and information on paper is difficult. Deciding what to write and how to express it is the primary task. Anyone of any age who has tried to compose anything understands how all-consuming this task can be. The effort required is at times so great that little attention can be paid to spelling, letter formation, punctuation, and general neatness. When the children revise their work, they again focus mainly on content. It is when they edit that they can devote their attention primarily to spelling, punctuation, and legibility. Good writing is developed by allowing children to begin with rougher, messier first-draft attempts and not by expecting attractive, mistake-free end-products right from the start.

Do you teach spelling, punctuation, and grammar? How do children learn these skills if their work is not corrected? Why do final drafts still contain mistakes?

As with other skills, spelling, punctuation, and grammar are taught and learned when the need arises, which, in fact, is every day because the children need to write every day. The need becomes evident as soon as anyone, the writer or someone else, experiences difficulties reading a piece of written work, which happens often.

We fully agree that correcting children's work is necessary, but the value of correction depends on how it is done. Correcting their writing can easily deteriorate into a hunt for spelling, grammar, and punctuation mistakes that makes the children's work look like a battlefield full of casualties. When this happens, children can see only what they have done wrong rather than becoming aware of and feeling good about the successful aspects of their writing.

Moreover, if the teacher corrects all the mistakes, it is the teacher, not the child, who has done the thinking. Children must learn to become critical of their work and to be able to express and accept constructive criticism; otherwise they will become dependent on the teacher's opinion and will work mainly to please the teacher rather than to become good writers.

Constructive criticism can be given in many ways, but it always has to be limited both in quantity and quality to only those inaccuracies that the child is developmentally able to incorporate. Thus, if we take spelling as an example, the youngest children sound out words they want to write and use invented spelling. Their work is corrected only when the teacher can see that they are ready to make a few small improvements. There is always the danger that children may become overly concerned with accuracy and, therefore, inhibited if correction is started too soon or if there is too much of it. Corrections introduced at this stage are oral and occur incidentally as the opportunity presents itself. For instance, a child may be asked to listen carefully and then add more letters to a word or to add dashes to indicate spaces between words.

Corrections for children in the middle group are also given orally and individually although they tend to be more extensive. From their growing experience with reading and writing, these children become aware that there is a consistent way to spell words, and they can increasingly identify some of their own misspellings. In their written work, they might circle one or two questionable words and then ask the teacher to supply the correct spelling. After a time, they build up a vocabulary of words they know how to spell and try others without becoming dependent on the teacher for every new word they wish to use in their writing. Depending upon the child, the teacher may point out additional misspellings for the child to circle.

To continue with the spelling example, by the time the children reach the Olds group, they are noticing spelling patterns (e.g., make, cake, bake). At this stage, spelling rules, long and short vowels, common word families, and so forth are introduced. Because of their earlier writing experience, the children never limit their written work to only those words they can spell. The Olds also get spelling "tests" regularly because most children do not seem to fully learn conventional spelling without efforts to deliberately focus attention on it. On Mondays the teacher gives an example of a spelling rule, and the children are asked to think of words that might fit it. At the end of the week, the children get a spelling test and are asked to write their misspelled words (a maximum of five) five times each. To enable the children to learn to spell without becoming inhibited writers, we do more than simply count up the number of spelling mistakes. As a group, we analyze the kinds of mistakes the children made on the test so they can see what spelling rules they need to work on, and that is the end of the "test." The children know that the results of spelling tests are relatively unimportant because the real tests are in their daily writing. Like everything else children learn, learning how to spell is a developmental process.

In general, the teacher discusses errors or problems in written work done by the Olds or pencils in comments and questions. These take various forms: an open-ended question; a reminder about a recently discussed spelling rule; a suggestion about where to find the proper spelling of a word; a question aimed at pinpointing lack of clarity in the writing; a question about a choice of words; or a suggestion to supply further information, to insert punctuation marks, and so forth. The teacher always uses pencil and writes in the margin so that the comments and questions are not seen as permanent, and if they are in a neat copy, they can be erased after the child has made the improvements. In this way, the children can benefit from the help but still retain authorship. The same is true of oral comments and questions. They are not visible, and so the written work remains the child's work rather than becoming the teacher's.

We make sure that our penciled remarks do not dominate a child's written work, or else it becomes no different from the red marking pen. In both cases, attention is inevitably drawn to the teacher's negative criticism of the child and away from what the child is able to do. Even for final drafts, in which we encourage children to work to their best standard, we expect just that—*their* best standard—which means that there will still be some spelling, punctuation, and grammar errors. If we did not accept their work, we would be telling the children, in effect, that they can work to their own standards for everything but the most important occasions, which ultimately debunks the children's efforts and encourages dependence on adults.

Therefore, when visitors look at neat copies, particularly when the children have been dealing with new content, we point out the quality of thought expressed and the vocabulary used because these, not spelling or punctuation, are most indicative of what the children have learned.

How can children revise and edit each other's work?

Usually this question means: "How can you be sure that all mistakes are noticed when children correct each other's work?" The answer is, you can't. However, correcting mistakes is not the purpose of having the children help each other revise and edit their work. The purpose of working with partners, for this activity as well as others, is to help each other articulate questions, to identify what has been learned, and to become critical in a constructive way. We have found that when children are placed in situations of responsibility for themselves and others, their own work improves, and they mature.

Learning to give constructive criticism is tricky, but it is one of the most important aspects of working together. It is learned through experience in an environment that minimizes competition for self-advancement and maximizes cooperation and trust in others. Everyone is expected to exchange ideas. Everyone is responsible for giving positive feedback because everyone is entitled to receive it; it is part and parcel of problem solving. Positive feedback is first given in a group setting with teacher direction. After a while, the children come to expect helpful feedback from each other.

To help children learn to give constructive criticism, the teachers discuss what happens if someone does the opposite. Everyone, adults and children alike, knows what destructive criticism is—an emphasis on what is wrong, inadequate, and incompetent. Everyone knows how such criticism feels.

If a child makes negative remarks about someone's work, uttering comments such as "That's stupid," or "Don't you even know that?" the child is immediately admonished either by the other children or by the teacher: "That's not true." "That's not helpful." If such remarks are repeated, the teacher tells the child to leave the group while the others continue with their work. As soon as she can, the teacher has a private talk with the child. This discussion is calm and as brief as possible. The child is asked to explain the behavior, to decide if it was appropriate, what could have been done instead, what could be done next time, and what must be done now. The child usually apologizes to the group or occasionally the child or the teacher gives an explanation of the behavior. The teacher asks the others whether the apology is acceptable, and when everyone agrees that the problem is solved, we resume work. Everyone, especially the teacher, makes sure that the child is forgiven.

Although this pattern has to be repeated many times with some children and may even require class discussions to help the child unlearn the unfriendly behavior, the child eventually learns to be more appropriate and helpful. When such children are able to be constructive, the teacher makes positive comments about the change. Occasionally the child's name is mentioned for special encouragement. The children have become so accustomed to expecting constructive criticism that when the Olds developed their list of evaluation criteria for presenting and discussing book reports, it included behavior of the audience: ''Were we helpful?''

Isn't it inefficient to let children make mistakes first and then teach them how to do their work properly?

In our experience, the opposite is true. To tell children everything about how to do their work is similar to giving them a recipe to follow. In the end, the work may be completed, but they will not be able to deviate from the recipe in future situations. Instead we tell them that when they experience difficulties, they should articulate them and think of ways to overcome them. Such discussions take place in a group so that it becomes obvious that many of the problems are shared by others. The suggestions for solutions sometimes result in guidelines for particular tasks. After trying out the guidelines formulated by the group, revisions and additions may be made until the guidelines are clear and logical. Then they are posted in the classroom for future reference.

To develop guidelines with the help of a teacher, the children have to think about their difficulties, try to come up with possible solutions, test the tentative solutions, and examine the results. All this is done with the help of a partner with whom they must discuss the whole process. Although at first this process may appear inefficient and a waste of time, guidelines for carrying out tasks are much easier to understand, accept, and remember when they are one's own solutions to one's own problems. Meanwhile, the children develop self-confidence and independence, help each other, and gain experience thinking for themselves and solving problems.

How do you teach math?

The basic premise is that children are at a very concrete level of thought and, therefore, need the experience of many hands-on activities in math. Thus, new concepts are discussed and demonstrated through the use of hands-on activities— children manipulating concrete materials. Essentially a math problem is just another kind of problem to solve. We use the familiar approach of trying to think of different ways to solve the problem and checking out each one. We find that an important part of teaching, whether it concerns math or other problems, is helping the children look for patterns in a variety of forms and situations. The fact that everything can be done with a partner facilitates this kind of learning. It is in these ways that the children acquire insights into math and become confident math students.

There is not enough time for the children to get sufficient practice solving math problems during theme time, and they don't always know enough math to do the mathematical aspects of the theme study. Furthermore, some themes or subtopics do not lend themselves to incorporating math as much as others. For all these reasons, we have separate daily math periods. However, whenever we can, we include theme study in the math periods just as we include math in our theme study.

Your emphasis on factual material seems to ignore the development of creativity in children. What do you do to foster creativity?

In our view, creativity in children develops from being exposed to a variety of ideas, insights, viewpoints, skills, techniques, and experiences as well as the creativity of others. It comes from practice in making decisions and trying things out for oneself. These exposures and experiences, combined with the fact that all work is original because the children are never asked to fill in blanks, answer a standard set of questions, or color in pictures that other people have drawn, all contribute to developing creativity.

Do you give homework?

All theme study work is done in school. Homework assignments entail only work outside of theme study and are required only of the Middles and Olds. Over the years, we have developed homework assignments to complement the work done in school. They consist of such activities as storywriting, book reports, and math. Because, in each case, homework is further used in school, assignments assume more importance to the children than they would if there were no follow-up. The kinds of homework assigned remain the same over the entire year so that the children can learn to plan their time and to work responsibly.

Without textbooks, how do you know if you've covered enough material in the various subjects? What about the provincial curriculum guidelines?

Our objectives are phrased in terms of learnings to be achieved rather than material covered. The children should learn how to learn, how to think for themselves, how to be active learners who dare to try new things when solving problems, and how to accept and apply constructive criticism. We want them to develop self-confidence and to freely use their own abilities and resources.

We use the government guidelines for the math curriculum because these are based on a philosophy similar to that of our school. However, the material may be dealt with somewhat earlier or later than prescribed. As for the other subject areas, we find that the children learn more language arts, social studies, and science through our in-depth theme studies than is expected in the provincial guidelines.

Teacher's Role

How can teachers have time to do theme studies when they already have a full schedule of subjects they are responsible for covering?

If teachers do theme studies, they don't need to teach most other subjects separately. To look again at the example of oceans as a possible theme, one could study plants and animals in the ocean, including the evolution of fish, and continue by studying how people use the ocean, which might include such areas as fishing methods, fishing in underdeveloped countries, farming the sea, or undersea oil. Alternatively one might continue by investigating the discovery of continents, the history of shipbuilding, the development of oceans, different parts of the ocean, or weather, tides, waves, and so on. To study such topics as these obviously involves a natural integration of just about the full range of subjects required by most boards of education—language arts, social studies, science, art, music, and some math. Therefore, teaching a theme is not really extra work but just a different way of viewing traditional subject areas and a different way of organizing the work and the time. Theme studies require extended, concentrated periods of time if they are to be successful. Trying to squeeze them into a small corner of the weekly schedule is frustrating for teachers and children alike.

A theme approach might be manageable for a teacher with a science or history background, but how can someone who doesn't have any particular content strength teach theme?

No special background is required. To teach a theme, a teacher needs to be curious and enthusiastic enough to be willing to carry out the necessary background investigation to prepare for the theme study. At the end of the advance preparation, a teacher certainly can't know everything; enough knowledge to launch the theme is all that is required, along with an interest in learning more about the theme with the children. During the school year, the preparation continues (as it does with any teaching) as various possibilities, needs, and interests emerge.

How do you group children? What are some problems of children working in groups?

At the beginning of the year, children who are new to teamwork can choose their own partners. After some preparatory discussion, they start working on their projects; problems are discussed as they arise. Children who have worked in teams before also choose their own partners, but only after a brief review, with the teacher, of how to choose a partner and what makes someone a good partner. Occasionally, the teacher decides who should work together. No matter how partners are selected, the teacher always asks, "What would you do if it turned out that you had trouble working together?" Another brief discussion then ensues about the need to investigate the reasons for lack of cooperation and the need to exert efforts to solve such problems. Only as a last recourse should the children turn to the teacher for help. In actual fact, however, even though the children are expected to solve their own problems by themselves, the security of knowing that the teacher is there in case of trouble is a necessary condition for the success of their independent problem solving.

Before the teams start working, the teacher asks, "Why and how do you work together?" It is not difficult for the children to come up with answers: "You help each other read by taking turns. Then you talk about what you have read to make sure you understand it." "We work together because it's easier and faster that way." "Two people know more than one."

In our experience with a great variety of children, the expectation that they will help solve each other's problems has been fulfilled because nobody is allowed to give up on another person. A person always gets another chance but not without a serious discussion that includes concrete examples of the problem and suggestions for improvement. Although the children may not give up on anyone, we let them know that, by the same token, they need not necessarily like everyone or want to work with everyone; there are ways of avoiding those we don't get along with without making life difficult for everyone around. Sometimes, if there is no improvement in a problematic situation, the teacher or the children will change the teams temporarily.

Because certain behaviors are a problem for the group, it is the group's responsibility to find appropriate ways of changing those behaviors. For example, it has happened that a couple of children have been so difficult for all of us that they have had to be excluded from the group until they eventually earned their way back in. By such means, even the most difficult children make tremendous progress although it may take as long as a full year, or even two years. When it happens everyone is aware of this kind of progress. A child once remarked to a newcomer with a problem, "You can get better. You know X? Well, he used to have lots of problems, but now he's nice again."

Group work allows children to copy and cheat. What do you do if a child cheats?

As was already discussed, the children learn more and faster by working together and by talking about their work because feedback is important. We tell them that people know something only if they can say it in their own words and can explain it to others. Copying is evidence of not comprehending and of letting others do your thinking for you. We discuss the difference between helping your partner on the one hand, and doing the thinking for your partner by giving the answers on the other. As a result, the children remind each other of the distinction, and the very idea of cheating loses its meaning.

On those occasions when copying does occur, the team involved might break up temporarily, which the children find threatening and unpleasant. Sometimes children have been asked to explain why their work showed the very same sentence, and they have reported that they talked about it and could not think of any other way to say it. Such cases are not a problem. Children have even asked what to do if two people can think of only one way to say something. Basically the children know that they are expected to ask for help if they need it. Therefore, they rarely copy.

Are children ever allowed to work by themselves?

We have had a few children with such serious social problems that it was necessary to limit their work with a partner to short-term tasks lasting about half an hour at a time. These instances have shown that they don't like working alone for a long period of time. In general, when children work alone, they realize that they miss not only help, but a great deal of fun as well. Consequently, everyone wants to participate in a team.

There are, however, certain kinds of tasks that are more suited for individual work than group effort. These tend to fall outside of the theme study. In journal writing, for example, the children usually work on their own although ideas for stories, spellings, and so on are frequently exchanged.

What do you do if a child doesn't find anything interesting enough to study?

We hardly ever have such a child, but it does happen once in a while. The reason the child gives is not necessarily the real one. Sometimes, the problem stems not so much from disinterest as from being left out of a group because of poor work habits or poor social skills, or because a friend chose to work with another person. When we know that the professed disinterest is due to some such reason, we include the child in a team that is working on a topic the child likes. This move requires discussion with the excluded child and the selected team about possible ways of dealing with the situation and about the need to give others a chance to try again. We also make it clear that if the new team is not able to sort out the problems, the child will eventually have to do the project alone. In general, if the child is given support and encouragement, this approach is successful because nobody wants to be an outcast and have to suffer the difficulties of doing a project alone.

The child who insists that the list of topics offered is of no interest is given the option of thinking of a related topic and writing a proposal for a project to be discussed with the teacher. To help the child think of alternatives, the teacher brainstorms with the child, tries to recollect what has been of particular interest to the child before, or suggests a form that a project on a topic from the existing list might take that would make the assignment more attractive. These approaches solve most such problems because the child is taken seriously and is treated fairly.

What do you do if a child is lazy and doesn't want to work? What do you do about children who don't work up to their potential?

In our experience, children who don't work are not lazy; they have reasons for not working. It is up to the teacher to help such children discover the causes for not working and solve the problem somehow. We do this by observing them closely and having discussions with them and, if necessary, with their parents. We treat home and school as a unit and therefore involve the parents and sometimes even other children in the search for suggestions to help such children deal with their problems.

Children who waste time or socialize too much are warned, not only by the teacher, but also by the other children, that play during work time means work during play time. When this happens, the work is closely supervised by the teacher. Not pulling your weight in teamwork has the additional unpleasant result of having to do everything alone, which is harder and less enjoyable. For these reasons, rarely does anyone try to get away with inadequate amounts of work for long.

What about the child who does not finish the work because it is just too difficult?

We stress individual progress. Even though children work for roughly the same amount of time on particular tasks, they produce very different work because they have different abilities. What is too difficult for whom becomes obvious early in the year, and we therefore guide the children to do their maximum but not to worry about what others can do. Regardless of how little they accomplish or whether assistance was necessary, we praise children when they make genuine efforts. As usual we provide follow-up to help them articulate how they did their assignment, what the problems were, how they tried to solve them, and what strategies proved to be successful. With all of these precautions, children don't often take on work that is too difficult for them.

Occasionally newcomers give the impression of being able to do more than they really can. The problem, however, soon surfaces: such children are either not accustomed to open-ended tasks or they are overwhelmed by the many decisions they have to make or they are afraid of making mistakes or worst of all, they think that help from others amounts to cheating. We help such children find work at an appropriate level of difficulty and then make it clear that they must work on the assignment to the extent that they feel it has been completed. A lot of help may be necessary at the beginning, but it is gradually withdrawn as such children become more independent. However, their efforts continue to be monitored from a distance, and at appropriate moments, we tactfully ask other children to offer help.

If the children are allowed to work on different topics, how do you organize all their activities and keep track of their work?

We do quite a bit of advance preparation, and once the theme study is under way, we still continue to prepare. After several years of doing theme studies with the children, however, their interests and the types of difficulties they are likely to encounter become fairly predictable, and, as a result, our preparation time becomes more productive than it was at first. Still, questions and problems come up that we hadn't anticipated. But if we don't know something, we just say so; there is no reason to make children believe that the teacher knows everything. At any rate, to admit ignorance is a good teaching tactic because then we can enlist the children to think of ways to solve the problem. In fact, we sometimes feign ignorance to stimulate children to find answers themselves. Our job is to help the children locate information, not to tell them everything. When a child asks a question, we might well say, "I'm not sure, but I'll look around for you," and then later, we might produce a book or article or picture and tell the child, "This might answer your question."

Thus, it can be said that we serve as overseers and resource persons. Since we don't stand in the front of the room (come to think of it, there are no ''fronts'' to our classrooms) and give traditional lessons, we have more time to keep tabs on who is doing what and how their work is progressing.

We also help both ourselves and the children keep track of their work by means of a large chart that we post on the wall. The chart lists the children's names vertically and the different tasks horizontally. The teacher records each child's assignment and makes note of each stage as it is finished. For example, when we studied fishing methods, each child did a project on one kind of fishing method. The square following a child's name would say, for example, ''longlining'' and would contain certain notations (''Notes'' for note-taking, ''R'' for rough copy, ''RE'' for revised and edited, and ''N'' for neat copy). When all the tasks have been completed, the teacher initials the square. That way, the children can see how far along they are. Whether the assignment is large or small, we keep track of the children's work in this manner. The only kind of task that does not get recorded on this chart is work that we do together, such as reading and taking notes with the whole group.

If the children have to learn everything from experience, what is the teacher's role?

In our view, teaching is not a matter of pouring knowledge into children's heads; it is not a matter of controlling what they learn at every moment. Our experience bears out the findings of many studies: children learn what they are ready for, what they are exposed to, and what interests them. However, left to themselves, they obviously will not learn all that they can learn. People who are more knowledgeable and experienced—teachers—have to assist in this process. We provide the behind-the-scenes organization, and we make sure that they experience a great variety of facts and interpretations so that they can follow their interests and discover what they are ready to learn. We give feedback, guidance, and encouragement. All of this, in our view, constitutes responsible teaching.

Other Sundry Matters

To get jobs and become contributing members of society later in life, children have to learn how to work hard and get a job done. But the theme study approach seems to teach them to expect to be entertained.

We don't agree with this assessment of the theme study approach. Quite the contrary; this approach demands a lot of hard work from the children. Nobody gives them anything on a silver platter. They have to think about, plan, and actually do a lot of work, and they have to take the initiative. If a child doesn't initiate anything, nothing will get accomplished, and the child will be left behind. Hence, the children have to develop responsibility and independence, which again, is hard work. But hard work and enjoyment are not incompatible. Indeed, enjoying the work is essential if the children are to persist and develop all the good qualities expected of them.

Competition seems to be almost totally absent in the theme study approach. Does this affect the children's motivation to learn?

If we begin with a theme that is interesting, relevant, and has substance and then add a supportive and cooperative learning environment and an enthusiatic teacher, it is bound to be more than any five- to ten-year-old can resist. Because all our work is carried out for a purpose, there is no busywork or endless repetition for children to contend with. There are also other factors that contribute to motivating the children. The fact that they work together makes for pleasant working conditions; the fact that the teacher studies with the children drives home the importance of their work; and the fact that everyone is studying the same theme, although at different levels and with different emphases, allows children to have a community of interests and to help each other. We have had very few children (and usually they come to us after having attended different schools) who are not motivated from the start. But, given some extra attention and encouragement, these children also become motivated before long.

How do the children find out what is expected of them?

Before addressing this question, we might consider, "Why do students need to know what is expected of them?" Traditionally at least part of the answer lies in the need to know course requirements in order to prepare for tests, quizzes, or projects on which they will be graded. Though this is not our reason, we do believe that all people, adults as much as children, need to know what is expected of them whenever they are in situations in which they must interrelate with others if they are to know how to function.

How they find out what is expected of them is another matter. We primarily expect effort and cooperation, and we constantly communicate these expectations to the children through what we say and do. It is not quite as clear-cut as this, however, because part of our expectation is that the children establish their own expectations of themselves. For their overall development, children must have insights into how the different things they are learning are interrelated. They must come to realize that they have to be able to apply their knowledge to new situations, and that understanding implies an ability to articulate their knowledge to others. The need for these insights becomes apparent to the children when they try to produce a project and find that because they don't understand certain aspects of it, the project is seen to be incomplete, incorrect, or illogical by others. Gradually the children learn to assess their own learning, so that they can see the strengths and weaknesses of their work, and they begin to take responsibility for improving it. Therefore, over a period of time, the children learn what is expected of them by participating in setting their own standards and expectations.

To help them raise their standards so they can establish high but attainable goals, we sometimes initiate group discussions on questions such as, "How do you know when a project/book/article/movie is good?" The children soon learn that standards are not cut-and-dried but often depend on the purpose of an activity. In spite of all the uncertainties, it is important for children to know that there is no limit to what they can learn and produce. The goal is not to become perfect but to grow.

The theme study approach might be beneficial for the above-average student, but can it also help the average or poor student?

The theme study approach fosters skills that everyone should know: how to locate and use resources and information; how to solve problems; and how to carry out tasks. Therefore, this approach is appropriate for all children. Because there are no minimum or maximum specifications of how broadly or deeply any one child should pursue a study and because there is a tremendous choice of possible subtopics, children at different levels and with different abilities never have to feel inadequate.

The range of subtopics studied in a class also makes it difficult and, therefore, unlikely that the children will make invidious distinctions about the quality of their work. Moreover, because the children work together and therefore must cooperate and because we put great stock in trying to establish a stimulating and encouraging environment, the school is relatively free of the negative competition that pits children against each other and publicly rates them on a scale from "stupid" to "smart." For these reasons, children who learn slowly have no cause to feel inhibited or incapable. In our experience, children with learning problems have benefited from the theme study approach at least as much as those who learn quickly and easily.

Aren't some themes too difficult for primary/kindergarten children?

We have been asked the same question for each age group. Given the opportunity, children are able to do a great deal more than they are often given credit for. Their own lives are touched by many important events and situations that adults often avoid discussing with them until they have reached the "proper" age. Our task, however, is to expand children's horizons, not to limit their learnings. We must introduce them to challenging subjects that are meaty and important at an early age so that their thinking skills can improve and their concentration spans can increase.

One reason for choosing broad themes is that they offer so many potential subtopics, some of which will appeal to and be within the capabilities of young children while others will be more suitable for older children. In addition, each subtopic can be studied to varying depths, again depending on the children's maturity. However, if children get into a topic deeper than they can handle, we help them finish the study to their satisfaction and turn to something else.

If every classroom is studying different subtopics of a theme, how can there be any organization to the education system?

Right now we're a long way from such a problem. But assuming for a moment that an entire school or district wanted to incorporate theme studies into the curriculum, how could that be coordinated? One possibility would be to organize themes into a three- or four-year cycle so that a child who was studying a particular theme in grade two, for example, would be exposed to the same theme again in grade five or six. That is, in fact, how we do it. We are on a four-year cycle with the following themes: living things, people and their work, oceans, and Nova Scotia and other places in the world.

We find that the children who are in the school for the full five years benefit a great deal in their last year when they are in the Olds group and study the same theme they studied when they were in the Youngs, because there is very little overlap or repetition even if some of the same subtopics are dealt with. For example, the theme studies on "Houses" described in these pages are subtopics of the "People and Their Work" theme. The five-year-olds learned to become observant about their own houses and houses in their neighborhoods and gained an elementary appreciation of building structures, materials, and tools. If we were to deal with some of the same subtopics four years later when this theme comes up again, these former five-year-olds would study such issues as are usually explored by the Olds; for example, the history of building, the development of technology, resulting social aspects of people's lives, and the development of communities. That is assuming we decide to study the same subtopics, but we could, of course, branch in any number of other, totally different directions, such as farming, mining, health occupations, industrialization, work in Third World countries, and on and on. In any case, repeating the "People and Their Work" theme is not a problem for those who have studied aspects of it before because their interests, abilities, and maturity have changed. Quite the contrary; their knowledge and understanding can only deepen.

Are most of the children in your school professors' kids?

Only a small percentage of the children have parents who teach at the university. The only criterion for attending the school is, unfortunately, the ability to pay the fees. Nevertheless, the children come from a variety of backgrounds, and some parents sacrifice a great deal to send their children to the school.

How do parents react to the program?

Those parents who know about our program and are attracted to the school because of it react very well. They generally cooperate, often lending assistance and trying to coordinate their efforts at home with what we do in school.

There are others who are less clear about the program. We spend quite a bit of time with them explaining what we do and why, and answering their questions. Sometimes these parents are concerned about the more technical aspects of their child's work, such as neatness or spelling. In that case, we show them their child's file of work (we keep all work in school) comparing work done early in the school year with what the child was able to do a couple of months later. The more recent work is always much longer and better. Such visible evidence and the accompanying careful explanations are generally useful in allaying the parents' concerns.

Parents who enroll children with definite problems of one kind or another (we get a number of them because we have had success in turning discouraged children into active learners) are fully informed of our thoughts on the possibilities for change in their child's learning and behavior and of the usually long waiting period before we can expect improvements. Some parents, however, become impatient or have unrealistic expectations of their children. Others emphasize accuracy and perfection and think that children should have daily drills, learn to read by sounding out, and so on, all of which contribute to the child's difficulties in making progress in school. Therefore, we have to let the parents know that their efforts to help the child are not really helpful. We usually have long discussions with them, explaining what the child is experiencing in school, why progress may be slow, what signs of development (if any) we have noticed, and our views on how learning takes place. We then suggest supportive activities and responses they might try, and we make it clear that it is important for them to refrain from doing things that are contrary to what happens in school. We also encourage them to be patient.

Once they see progress, parents usually accept what we are doing in school. There are, however, cases where it is very difficult for them to change their expectations and activities at home, which, of course, serves to confuse and discourage the child. All that we can do is continue to talk to the parents and work with the child using all the possibilities that our school can offer: help from other children who used to have difficulties and from partners who can have a positive influence, development of strategies in problem solving, encouragement from other children who comment on how well the child is doing, recognition of progress and effort from the teacher, extra lessons, and so on.

Sometimes children develop behavioral problems after coming to our school. Becoming responsible and independent requires making mistakes and learning from them, but some children, confronted with choices and decisions, push the limits of the school and test everyone in sight. They sometimes go home and report school problems in a way that puts the onus of doing something about it on their parents. If the parents come to see us, we suggest that the child be encouraged to raise the problem in school and that, in the future, all problems should be brought up by the child in school as they arise. In that way, they can be discussed and dealt with by the children or teacher involved. We make it known to both children and parents that everyone in the school has to learn self-control and how to deal with problems and that it won't do to expect only the teacher to rule misbehavior out of order. When children get into difficulties with others, they are expected by the other children and the teacher to discuss their reasons for misbehaving, to suggest alternative behavior, and to apologize. Parents almost always find this a reasonable approach.

In general, we keep in very close contact with parents. As a result, most of them understand and hold a high opinion of the program. Many of them ask us for suggestions for work or other activities they might do with their children at home. Such positive responses are a great help.

Is it expensive to have a theme studies program?

The cost of doing theme studies is no greater and perhaps even less than a conventional curriculum. The only expense that would significantly be affected would be the cost of materials. In many schools, the perception is that twenty-five children require twenty-five readers, twenty-five math books, twenty-five science books, and perhaps the same number of spelling and social studies texts. That's a great many books. In a theme studies classroom, the same number of children use a wide variety of materials that they share. Thus, a single volume or small number of copies suffice. Furthermore, not all materials need to be purchased; some can be borrowed from libraries and individuals. Over a period of time, teachers can build up substantial collections of print materials (especially if themes are repeated) such that it becomes increasingly less expensive to carry out a theme studies program. At any rate, books are only one of many resources used in a theme studies classroom. Once we look to the community, potential resources become almost infinite, and most of these are free.

What about Evaluation?

Traditional marking systems are inconsistent with theme studies. Nonetheless, as is true of any systematically organized learning/teaching process, it is still important for teachers to conduct evaluations. However, our reasons for and methods of evaluation are very different from traditional ones and flow from the purposes and objectives inherent in the theme studies approach.

The Why, What, and How of It

We need to evaluate in order to know what level of development a child has reached in various aspects of learning, what attempts the child has made to learn, and what areas the child has mastered. Evaluation helps us see what experiences the child needs in order to make progress and in what areas the most effort should be put. Basically, evaluation helps provide us with a plan for teaching.

All aspects of learning within theme studies are open to evaluation. Thus, in addition to content learning, we evaluate a number of other areas, including reading, writing, oral communication skills, math, thinking ability, and social skills. Even though these components are integrated for theme study, they must be separated for analysis and evaluation. If we lump them all together when we try to analyze them, we will get only a very crude picture. Evaluation needs to be much more refined if it is to be useful to teachers and children. Accordingly, as with any analysis, the aspects involved have to be isolated and scrutinized. To do so does not mean that they are seen or taught as separate entities. For example, social skills must be evaluated using a set of criteria far different from those used to evaluate reading, but both social skills and reading are important parts of the same larger framework—the theme study. Both of them were learned within the same context. They must be removed from the context and separated from each other only partially and briefly for evaluation purposes.

For our evaluation of the traditional subject areas, we combine the knowledge gained from research on the reading and writing processes and on math with the ideas derived from our own experience working with and observing children reading, writing, and doing math. We translate these insights into lists of criteria that cover broad stages of development. We then use these lists to evaluate the children's work. We also prepare checklists for the other areas we evaluate; they too are based on our experience with children.* In addition to written checklists, our evaluation also takes the form of ongoing verbal feedback to the children. The following should illustrate how we evaluate.

To evaluate children's reading, we used to do full miscue analyses.[1] These analyses were tremendously time-consuming, but with experience, we eventually learned what kinds of reading materials are best for evaluation purposes and what aspects of reading are most central for our age groups. We each use a somewhat different, but short (usually one page) reading evaluation summary, generally in the form of a checklist. These summaries are based on miscue analysis principles and are each appropriate for the particular levels we teach. In all cases we consider the types of reading strategies a particular child uses for both fiction and nonfiction at a variety of levels. We also keep track of each child's choice of reading material and attitude toward reading.

The evaluation of writing for the Youngs and Middles has required designing lists of criteria based on the teachers' observations over the past several years. For the Olds, the analysis provided by Wilkinson, Barnsley, Hanna, and Swan in *Assessing Language Development* (Oxford University Press, London & Toronto, 1980) has proved useful. Basing their analysis on a great number of writing samples of children from seven to fifteen, the authors describe many aspects of broad stages in the development of writing. For example, some of the aspects of writing style that they discuss are syntax, structure and organization, cohesion, awareness of audience, appropriateness, verbal competence, and affective development. These aspects are only part of one category; there are others, and the authors supply criteria for each aspect of writing at each stage of development. Consequently, the

---

* We are not including any of our checklists here because they are not fully enough developed. We make changes in them every year, and while we find them useful for our own evaluation purposes, they have not been tested beyond our classrooms.

teacher has found it too cumbersome, complicated, and time-consuming to apply on a regular basis. However, she was able to translate these lists of criteria into lists of examples of what is meant by them. By omitting those stages of development in writing that she does not encounter in the Olds, she has managed to design usable checklists that enable her to summarize her evaluation of a child's writing all on one page, which she can then attach to the analyzed writing sample. At our present stage, our evaluation of writing still takes a fair amount of work, but we know that more experience will help us to further improve the process and narrow down the range of criteria to what is more appropriate for the age groups we teach as well as more manageable for us.

Proficiency in oral communication skills is an important foundation for most of the written work the children do. Some of the questions we ask ourselves when assessing the children's oral communication are: Do they contribute in group sessions? When they have ideas, can they explain them clearly? Do they depend on someone else to do their verbalizing for them, especially when a situation becomes complicated? Can they listen to someone else's ideas and build on them? When new ideas are introduced, are they able to internalize the new language associated with these ideas quickly or do they require a lot of repetition?

For evaluating math, we use ideas from the Nuffield Mathematics Teaching Projects in England and publications such as Mary Baratta-Lorton's book, *Mathematics Their Way* (Addison-Wesley Publishing Company, Reading, Massachusetts, 1976). The basic idea is to observe whether a child is in the concrete, the transitional, or the symbolic stage of development for each mathematical concept. At each stage, it is important to note whether a child is still working at the concept or has mastered it. Here again, we have found it helpful to add some criteria of our own.

Thinking ability is obviously interwoven with all the other areas discussed above. To evaluate development in thinking, we look at the child's ability to generate ideas about a topic, to categorize them, to consider suitable resources, to plan work, to ask good questions, to articulate viewpoints and problems, to organize information, to make notes that are intelligible and usable, to integrate information and ideas, and to see problems from other people's point of view.

In evaluating social skills, we ask: Does the child know how to work and play cooperatively with others? Is the child too domineering or too passive? Does the child show tolerance toward others when they make mistakes and find constructive ways to help them? What about the child's frustration level? Does the child suffer from low self-esteem? And so on.

These, then, are the sorts of things we evaluate and how we go about trying to figure out how to do it. We are particularly fortunate because our situation allows us to coordinate our efforts. We can help each other refine the criteria we use for evaluating children, and we can keep each other up to date on the children's overall development, their school work, their playground behavior, and changes at home. But even without that special advantage, we believe that it is only through constant evaluation that we can develop more efficient and effective teaching strategies.

If we don't know how the children are doing, how can we know what we ought to do to help them? Evaluation is so essential to good teaching that it must be built into the daily routine.

Instead of Quizzes and Tests . . .

Quizzes and tests necessitate the presentation of a narrow range of information that is to be mastered by the majority of children in a group. This process makes learning dull for the most advanced children and a losing struggle for those furthest behind.

Generally one of the main reasons for giving tests and quizzes is to force students to review their work. But surely students should study out of interest rather than being motivated by the threat of dreaded tests and the fear of incurring the teacher's displeasure. With a theme studies curriculum, there is no need to resort to tests because theme studies require children to constantly take stock of what they have learned and find out where the gaps in their knowledge are, to uncover more information, and to make connections among different bits of information and ideas. First the children get the information; then they review it when they write about it; then they review it again when they rewrite the information using a new format, and again, when they revise and edit it; and again, when they prepare a neat copy; and again, when they illustrate the information; and yet again, when they present it publicly. Each review takes a new form, and so neither the material nor the process becomes boring. By the time it is all over, the learnings have been so well consolidated and integrated that they are not likely to be forgotten.

When we speak about quizzes and tests, we should consider the consequences of the kind of correction that these usually entail. For the teacher to point out each and every mistake serves only to discourage risk-taking. When a child has open-ended tasks where the amount and variety of knowledge and skills are not limited by the teacher, as is true with theme studies, such correction would be even more devastating. In addition, if it is the teacher who points out the mistakes, children will not learn to become critical of their own work. The effects of this kind of correction are that the teacher focuses on the children's weaknesses only, and the children focus on their score and do not feel the need to try to really understand their weaknesses. On both counts, because of the emphasis on end-products, such an evaluation system is not effective in helping either the teacher or the children pay attention to strategies for improvement.

In contrast, if children look over their work with someone who raises questions about it—a partner or the teacher—they learn to be more critical of it themselves and, with practice, to improve the quality of the work. It is the children who have to do the learning; no one else can do it for them. Therefore, they have to find their own mistakes and make their own corrections.

If there is sufficient indication that children are doing their best, then their mistakes are accepted. Rather than giving children low marks and creating a feeling of failure, the teacher must analyze the uncorrected mistakes in order to find the reasons for them and be able to plan future learning experiences to correct them. Such an analysis is not difficult because the teacher spends so much time working directly with the children every day, thereby getting to know their strengths and weaknesses. There is little new that a test can tell an observant teacher. Moreover, with children engaged in interesting work, tests are superfluous as a means of making sure that they work as hard as they can. Therefore, at least at the elementary level, there is no reason for tests.

Instead of Grades and Report Cards . . .

We not only do not give quizzes and tests, we also do not issue grades and report cards. One might well wonder how, without marks on individual papers or grades and report cards indicating overall assessment, any of the interested parties—the children, their parents, and other schools the children will one day attend—become informed about how the children are doing in school.

It is not very difficult for the children to figure out how they are doing. They do it in many ways. The first way is the most important and most direct. One of the teachers' major tasks is to help the children identify their strengths and weaknesses and to ensure that they are aware of their progress by showing them earlier efforts and comparing them with later ones. Another direct way is through recognition of good effort and good work by teachers and peers.

Another sign of progress is the very fact of being expected to do increasingly more difficult work. The children have no problem discerning this expectation. Because they work in cross-age groups, they have the opportunity to observe some children doing easier work and others doing more difficult work. They also know that during their first year in the Middles or Olds, they cannot do the same quality work as those who are there for the second year. However, during this time they also get a clear idea of what they are working toward. Still another way of knowing about their progress is by moving from one group to the next, from Youngs to Middles and from Middles to Olds. This happens only when they are ready for such a move and may occur at any time of the year—at the end, near the beginning, at Christmas, and so on. The children know the possibilities and often put even more effort into their work when they know they are close to being ready for a move.

Although competition is discouraged, another way the children can evaluate their own progress comes from working together, which makes them aware of how their work compares with that of others. They cannot help but find out because they consult each other at almost every point in their work. They discover in no time whom to consult for what difficulties. They know that some are better in reading, others in writing, and still others in experimenting, drawing, or spelling. By the same token, they realize when their strengths are being used by others.

The parents are kept informed of their children's progress through a variety of means as well. We have individual parent-teacher conferences during which we discuss the children's progress. These are scheduled three times a year for all parents and more often, as needed, for those whose children are having academic or social problems. These conferences proceed in systematic fashion because we use our lists of evaluation criteria, which we have checked off. We also show the parents examples of the children's work that illustrate the points we wish to make. Because we keep all the children's work, including their many rough copies, on file for the entire school year, we can show the parents what their children did in September and then in January and May. These work samples give the parents a concrete understanding of their children's progress and problems and are, therefore, very useful for evaluation purposes.

It is only when a child leaves the school that we write a report and then only to assist the teachers in the child's new school. The report includes a description of the themes studied, the child's strengths and weaknesses, both academic and social, the kinds of support that proved helpful to the child, and a recommendation for placement. We also offer to go over the report in person with the teacher in the child's new school. When we think it useful, we discuss the child's placement with the parents in order to help them become more sensitive to their child's learning needs as we see them.

Faring in Other Schools

There has been no systematic follow-up study of the children's performance after they leave our school. However, we have received a great deal of informal feedback from parents and children over the years about those children who were among the weaker students as well as those who were more capable. In almost all cases, these reports have been very positive, especially when they were about children who had attended the school for at least two years. The reports are usually phrased in terms of the enthusiasm and solid foundation provided by our school in the "basics," in the attitude toward problem-solving, and in self-confidence, independence, and responsibility. In general, the children tend to find the work in their new school easier.

Children with minor learning difficulties have had to work hard in their new surroundings—as they did in our school—but they have done well. Those with more serious learning problems who, through the theme approach, developed some self-confidence and some strategies for overcoming their weaknesses have sometimes slid back, particularly if they have had to contend with a lot of drills and busywork. The progress that such children make through studying themes and learning to think for themselves can be seriously eroded by an approach that focuses primarily on accuracy and end-products.

This is not to suggest that the other children do not face a period of adjustment to other schools. Usually it takes them time to get used to sitting at their desk most of the day, taking tests and receiving marks, working alone without consulting with others, experiencing competition, following stringent rules about sharpening their pencils, going to the bathroom, and other such details, performing tasks when the purpose is not always clear, and so forth. However, when the children leave our school after being there for a number of years, they have enough self-confidence to be able to make the best of it. Also involved, perhaps, is that when children leave D. U. E. S. to enter fifth grade elsewhere, they have often outgrown our school and are eager to go to a bigger school where they can participate in extracurricular activities and meet a wider circle of children from among whom they can choose their friends. From all reports, adjustment to their new schools takes from about six weeks to three months.

What about Discipline?

As with evaluation, it is impossible to impose a traditional approach to discipline in a theme studies classroom. The nature of the work requires children to move about freely, to consult with each other, and to work on different projects. The kind of discipline that is used must be one that facilitates such activity so that it flows smoothly and productively. Ultimately, of course, this means that the children must learn to be responsible for their own and their classmates' behavior; the development of strong self-discipline is our aim.

The children's ability to handle freedom of movement and activity ranges from those with well-developed self-discipline to those who behave acceptably only when discipline is imposed by the teacher. The former function well in a theme study setting and are capable of producing work that is often far beyond the level usually expected of children their age. The latter need a lot of help to learn to handle their freedom responsibly. Much of our time and energy as teachers is spent moving children along the continuum from external discipline to internal discipline.

Structure and Rules

Many people equate structure in the classroom only with that which is plainly visible: children sitting down, quietly working by themselves all at the same assignment, and doing as they are told. If that is structure, then it is clearly missing in our classrooms. However, although it may appear otherwise to the casual observer, our classrooms very definitely have a structure, but it is quite different from the structure found in more traditional classrooms. Ours is a structure that flows from the educational and social objectives and the needs of educational practice, not the other way around. Thus, there are rules, procedures, routines, and clear expectations, all of which are developed with the aim of accomplishing the educational and social tasks undertaken.

The need for permission to carry out minor details of a learning task, be it to make a comment, to check information, to help another child, or to get a piece of paper, amounts to lack of trust in children (to say nothing of wasting far too much of everyone's time). This way of doing things would make a theme studies program virtually impossible. To physically and mentally constrain children is to inhibit them; if they are not allowed to think or to make decisions, they are not being allowed to learn. The children in our school are task-bound not seat-bound and must, therefore, talk and walk around in order to do their work. This kind of sound and movement is purposeful and quite different from chaos.

The distinction is ultimately one between teacher-centered classrooms and child-centered classrooms. In the former, all learning depends on the teacher's knowledge and ability to organize and control what is being learned, when it is learned, and under what conditions it is learned. By implication, the children must be fully dependent on the teacher for their learning and even their actions, including when they can speak and move.

Our purpose is the opposite: to make the children independent of us. Theme study requires a fair amount of self-reliance. Certainly we provide the framework: we do the background work of organizing and planning; we set the stage for what will happen; and we make clear what the general tone and decorum of the classroom will be. But within this framework, our classrooms are child-centered. The children, who are not streamed and must all work together regardless of their levels of academic and social development, have to make their own decisions and mistakes. They have to learn to become independent learners and to develop self-discipline. Therefore, the focus is on them and what they are doing. We can only help them in these endeavors by observing them closely and providing guidance and assistance as needed. The result, at least most of the time, is that the children become immersed in their work because they are truly interested in it. Some even become impatient with antics in the class that divert them from their interests, and after a time, with encouragement from the teacher, the children begin to monitor each other. Therefore, while they are allowed a great deal of movement and decision-making, the classroom does not become a free-for-all. Moreover, because the children are not rewarded for their antics, those inclined to act up eventually turn to more productive pursuits. All the children gain a measure of self-discipline.

We have two basic rules to foster self-discipline. The first one is that the children must be considerate of the people around them. Although other, more specific rules have been developed over the years, they can all be traced back to this general rule.

We make a point of explicitly and repeatedly connecting the more specific rules to this one so that the children will understand the concept in all its fullness and will eventually internalize the principles of considerate behavior. To help each other develop consideration, the children learn that they must communicate what they are thinking and feeling.

Before settling down to do their work in small groups or pairs, the children are periodically reminded of the need to be considerate, which means to work as quietly as possible, to whisper to their partners, and not to talk to someone across the room or do anything else that distracts others. Everyone is expected to remind others of the need to be considerate, and they do.

Most children learn to ignore the sounds and movement in the classroom and to focus on their work. Those who have a low tolerance for noise have to let others know that it is too noisy or have to move to a quieter place to work. We find that children usually become absorbed in their work and do not notice what others are doing in another part of the same room regardless of the noise, movement, or number of visitors watching them do their work.

The second basic "rule" is to remember that school is for learning. Therefore, the children are encouraged to make decisions that will help them make the best use of their work time. Those who consistently misuse work time are required to spend their play time on work.

Actually, both rules are about learning responsibility. Children are expected to help each other be responsible in all aspects of school life. They remind each other to get back to work and to remember that teasing can be unfriendly, that an eraser is to be shared with others who need it, and that the box of pencil crayons should be placed where everyone can reach it. If someone is hurt, others should feel responsible for helping until the injury is taken care of. Children rotate through a series of small housekeeping jobs throughout the year, such as wiping tables after lunch, and reminding others if too much of a mess is left behind, because if so it will cut down on the cleaners' play time.

Encouraging this kind of development in children clearly is a departure from traditional discipline methods. Although there are still times when the law must be laid down, it is always followed by the question, "Why is this important?" so that the children's understanding of the rules will grow and their ability to articulate them themselves will increase.

Problems: Some Causes and Solutions

Our first task in dealing with behavioral problems is to try to identify factors that interfere with the development of self-discipline. These usually can be corrected or worked around so that our objective becomes to help the children to progressively substitute successful behavior patterns for poor ones. In our experience, there are certain causes inhibiting the development of self-discipline that seem to crop up repeatedly.

First, children with learning difficulties might feel constantly frustrated; they might see themselves as unable to learn and as different from other children. Once learning strategies are identified that work for them and it is demonstrated to them over a period of time that they can learn, the need to gain attention through inappropriate behavior can be rechanneled into confidence in their abilities. While the change is occurring, we make it clear that we expect the children to be responsible for their actions, and we always make sure that they are aware of the reasons for the expected behavior. Of course changes occur over a period of weeks and months rather than hours and days.

Ongoing medical or health-related problems are frequently a significant cause of behaviorial difficulties. We have found this to be especially true of allergies, which quite often go undiagnosed. Other common health problems are insufficient sleep on a regular basis and poor eating habits.

Child-rearing patterns that contradict those implemented in the school can make for problematic behavior. When children receive opposite messages about what is expected of them, they become confused. We find that these problems are usually based on parents' well-intentioned but erroneous understandings of what practices in actual fact result in a happy, well-adjusted, and constructive childhood. In these situations, we spend a great deal of time explaining how we do things in school and how things can be done at home to support children's learning in school (all the time communicating to the parents that it has also taken us time to achieve these understandings). We try to be open to parents' concerns and to build on their knowledge of their children.

Children also sometimes experience behavioral problems as a result of dramatic changes in their family situations—a separation or divorce, a new baby in the family, or the death of a relative. We try, of course, to provide support to children and to other family members in such situations as much as we can.

A smaller but often sticky problem is presented by children who are perfectionists. They set unrealistic standards for themselves, and as soon as they begin a task, they see that they will not achieve these standards. Their reaction sometimes takes the form of ''I can't,'' but often children cover up their feelings of inadequacy with misbehavior. Because constructive criticism, risk-taking, and repetition are built into our theme studies, all with the understanding that gradual improvement (not perfection) will result, such children can begin to set realistic goals and not be afraid of, or discouraged by, mistakes.

Some children are unable to understand the behavior of others, which makes it difficult for them to internalize appropriate social behavior themselves. They cannot adapt their behavior to suit the situations they find themselves in, and it does no good to expect them to change automatically because of the school environment. What they require is calm, repeated verbal analysis of their behavior, explanations of how it affects others around them, and suggestions for alternative acceptable behavior. We show them how to think through what they do step by step; gradually they begin to do the analysis themselves and make some changes. We have found that it takes a long time for children who hurt others physically and psychologically and who are disruptive, uncooperative, alienated, and unhappy to change. Even then, they are usually still very "lively," but at least they have some self-control.

In addition to the children who can be easily identified as having difficulties with others, there are those who are extremely passive. Theirs may not be a discipline problem in the usual sense, but their passivity is a behavioral problem nevertheless. Such children need to learn how to say no, and to do so emphatically; they need to learn to decide for themselves whether they want to play a game or do work in a way that is different from what is being planned by their friends.

Theme study is an excellent approach for children with these sorts of problems because the learning focus is not on skills at which they are often unsuccessful or on facts that they have to memorize. Instead, they get caught up in investigating topics of real interest to them. And, at last it is legitimate for them to be active: they make up the questions, and they do the thinking—often orally, which is almost always an easier mode for them. There is no stigma attached to getting help from others because even the best readers and writers often need help. Thus, the differences between children's abilities do not seem as significant. It also helps that our focus is always concrete because learning about the world around them makes sense to children.

Involving the Children in Analyzing and Solving Problems

When a problem occurs between children, even if one child clearly appears to be at fault, both are asked to explain the situation to each other from their own points of view and to come to an agreement about what will prevent the problem from happening another time. When children have poor social skills, the teacher stays with them to facilitate the process. Gradually they learn to carry out this process themselves.

Some problems are discussed during meetings of the whole school. These meetings are held after lunch four days a week. An agenda is drawn up and recorded on the board. It lists the daily chores, announcements, and a limited number of issues that different children may wish to discuss. The name of the person suggesting an agenda item is also recorded. The meetings are generally chaired by a teacher who, when necessary, reminds the children why we hold meetings, how these meetings can be most productive (take turns speaking and raise your hand for a turn to speak), and how to discuss problems (describe what happened or what the concern is without mentioning names). The only problems discussed at meetings are those that are of general importance; these meetings, after all, are not public humiliation sessions.

After a child has described a problem, the teacher always asks: "Why do you think this happened?" "What did you do about it?" "Did it work?" "What else could you have tried?" "What would you do if it happened again?" Others at the meeting can help by making suggestions about how to better understand the prob-

**A Teacher Chairs the Meeting. Children and Teachers
Contribute Items for the Agenda.**

lem, the reasons for it, and how to arrive at appropriate solutions. Those children who are not in tune with other people's feelings and expectations need clear, repeated discussions to learn social skills. Although some problems such as teasing may come up in our meetings every week of the year, and it is easy to feel discouraged about the lack of progress, in actual fact, it is often different children each time dealing with a problem that is new to them.

With problems involving general misbehavior during work time, the teacher assumes that children who have these problems perceive the work as being too difficult, and, therefore, she helps them identify strategies to work around the difficulty. Because of specific problems (e.g., poor short-term memory or high distractability) that cause learning to be more difficult for some children than it is for most, these children react with destructive behavior when they reach their frustration level. When this happens, the teacher always conveys one of the following messages. It's okay not to know something; just ask for help. People learn only by trying things out, and often their first efforts are dismal; the important thing is to keep on trying. Mistakes are to be learned from, not avoided at all costs. The teacher tries to help these children realize that they misbehave when they are upset about their work or their ability to learn and that, with help, they can develop strategies that will make them more effective learners.

Once children understand the source of their problems, it is sometimes necessary for the teacher to impose consequences for repeated habitual difficulties. Some of the measures we find necessary to use are: working by themselves in another room if they have been disrupting others; writing down, for example, how a discussion should proceed if they persist in not taking turns; practicing an activity that presented a problem, such as sitting quietly if they were distracting others; and finishing work at lunch time or recess if they were dawdling or playing when they should have been working. In all cases, the consequence must clearly flow from the problem. Mere punishment unrelated to any particular problem does not teach children how to solve their problems; it merely breeds hostility. Therefore, we always try to make certain that the expectations make sense to the children and that they are internalizing the reasons behind the rules and developing the strength of character necessary to work and play pleasantly, sensibly, and productively.

When problems appear to be unrelated to work, we try to help the children concerned to identify the causes, and then we often discuss with the whole group what others can do to be supportive. We usually do this in the presence of the children with the problematic behavior and with them contributing to the discussion. This can be a great relief to them as well as to the other children who sometimes become very concerned and anxious about the misbehavior. To cite just one example, one day a child in the Youngs who had not had much success playing with others at recess left the group after a few minutes of fidgeting and began tipping over chairs. Rather than removing him from the classroom or reprimanding him, his teacher stopped the discussion and said to the group, "X seems to have a problem. Can anyone figure out what it is?" After several serious suggestions, one child said, "Maybe he doesn't think anyone is his friend." The chair-tipping activity immediately stopped and X responded curtly, "I don't." After a spontaneous chorus of "Well, I'm your friend," and "I like you," we proceeded to discuss aspects of the children's behavior that made X feel disliked and aspects of X's behavior that made it difficult for the others to tolerate him in their games. The children began to realize how it feels to be excluded and decided to delineate boundaries of games more clearly so that those with socially difficult behavior would not need to deal with so many unspoken rules.

When teachers encourage problem solving and independence, it is inevitable that some children will test the rules in an effort to discover the limits. In addition, there are some children who, in spite of all the help, have problems that are particularly intractable. For them, further measures are sometimes necessary. This is especially true of children who are unkind to others. Thus, after an uncalled-for incident, the child who was unkind might have to write an account of what happened, what some of the alternatives might have been, and an apology to the appropriate person.

Essentially, we treat behavior in the same way as we treat work. When children are working on a theme study project, they are expected to discuss and help each other analyze the problems they encounter and to cooperate in working out solutions. The same applies to behavioral problems. We try to make sure that all the children know that those with problems can change and that others can play an important part in providing support and encouragement in this process. They are usually eager to help, whether it be with reading and writing or just to play a game with such children when they are too frustrated to continue an activity. This help often provides a bridge back to work.

Involving the children in this process has many benefits. Because their suggestions and help are taken seriously, the children are capable of great efforts in assisting others. Their involvement provides thirty-five extra minds and bodies to help change behavior. The children learn to understand the motivation behind other people's behavior, which also makes them aware that their own problems are often similar. "Nobody likes me." "My work is terrible." "I can't draw." Such comments show them that other children are also complex people who have a variety of strengths and weaknesses.

As with theme study work, underlying the whole process of discipline, then, is the teacher's agenda of how to help children become independent, both in getting along with others and in learning how to handle their own problems effectively. Therefore, when a child comes to us with a problem, be it academic or behavioral, we do not provide the solution. Instead, we get them to do the thinking by asking them questions about the problem. At first children often have no idea whatsoever about how to solve their problems. After a time, they begin to be able to articulate possibilities, but sometimes they still seem unable to carry them out. Eventually they try new strategies on their own. Whenever this happens, we try our hardest to catch children in the act of solving their own problems so that we can encourage their efforts. Over time, we can all see change in the kinds of problems the children present, the ways they discuss them, and the solutions that they develop and apply.

In essence, our approach to discipline has the same objectives as the theme study approach—learning to solve problems, developing thinking ability, and building self-confidence, responsibility, and independence. We also employ the same means to achieve these objectives—mutual help and cooperation. These similarities in our handling of discipline and theme studies provide children with consistency in all aspects of their school life. It is this view and application of discipline that enables us to carry out a successful theme studies program.

(Kids and teachers all learn together.)

Theme Study—Can Anybody Do It?

When we give workshops to teachers on the theme study approach, it never fails that someone will remark, "That's all well and good, but you teach in an extraordinary school. The school where I work is nothing like yours. It's very ordinary, but I think it's probably a lot more typical. How can a teacher like me do theme study?"

It is true. As a small nongraded school where we work closely with each other, have almost total freedom to develop the curriculum, combine children in cross-age groupings, and organize the timetable as we see fit, ours is an unusual school. It is an ideal setup for developing innovative teaching approaches.

But it is not the only school in which the theme study approach will work. A school need not necessarily be small or nongraded; cross-age grouping, while desirable, is not essential. Although it is clearly preferable for a group of two or three teachers to work together in developing and implementing theme studies, this approach can also be used by one teacher. In fact, in the beginning, we left

each other alone and worked mostly on our own. It simply takes longer to identify weaknesses and develop a deeper understanding of the approach when there
are no others with whom to consult.

The features of Dalhousie University Elementary School that are necessary for
a theme studies program, although not to the extent found in our school, are a
degree of freedom to develop curriculum and some flexibility to combine chunks
of time in the timetable. Nothing more is required other than the teacher's willingness to take the risk of trying something new, which precisely describes our
situation when we started doing theme studies. None of us had any experience
with the approach; we had never developed a curriculum before; and our budget
for materials was nonexistent. Theme study, nevertheless, made so much sense
to us in theory that we decided to take a chance and try it.

A person interested in learning how to do theme studies can expect a certain
workload. A fair amount of preparation must be done, especially before introducing a theme study but also once it is under way. However, the same can be said
of any good teaching. To gain the background knowledge needed to conduct a
theme study does not mean that teachers have to learn everything about the theme
and become experts. In fact, much of the preparation time is spent ferreting out
and deciding how to best use existing expertise in the form of teaching/learning
materials and people who have something to offer on the subject. In many schools,
frequent field trips present too many obstacles and complications to be realistic.
It is still possible, however, for people with expertise to come to the classroom.
These preparations, along with some rearrangements in the schedule, which most
elementary schools are flexible enough to accept, are all that need to happen before
meeting with the children.

The next problem that arises is how one teacher, even with some preparation,
can carry out a theme study with twenty-five or thirty children. This seems to be
a far cry from Dalhousie University Elementary School where three teachers work
with thirty-six children. However, since two of the teachers share one job, the ratio
is not as favorable as it may at first appear.* Furthermore, because of our situation, we have more responsibilities than we would have if we were in a more conventional school.†

---

* The ratio of eighteen to one is just an average. In actual practice, depending on the
work being done, it varies from twelve to one to twenty-four to one and for our
almost daily school meetings, at which only one teacher is usually present, it is
thirty-six to one. Moreover, the thirty-six children span five grades—Primary through
four.

† Serving as a learning laboratory for adults involved in education, the school fulfills
many unusual functions: several dozen student teachers, practicing teachers, and
school administrators visit the school every year and spend many hours observing it
in action and later discussing the program with us; we give a number of workshops
during the year for teachers and administrators at other schools, for student teachers
at other teacher education institutions, for teachers' organizations, and for interested

Nonetheless, twenty-five children and one teacher in a classroom are twenty-five children and one teacher in a classroom. Part of the secret of doing theme studies successfully, regardless of the size of the class, lies in dividing the class into groups of two or at most three (not four or five because a group that size can easily be unwieldy for the children, and, therefore, almost certainly unproductive). Thus, instead of twenty-five individuals, the teacher has only ten to twelve groups to deal with. That does not mean that ten or twelve different subtopics and projects are required; usually the children define four to eight projects, which is fine because more than one group can be working on the same one. Therefore, once a theme study is under way and working with some success, the limited number of groups and the small number of subtopics allow the teacher to keep tabs on everyone, to circulate and observe, and to give help as needed.

Another part of the secret of successful theme studies with a class of any size is that the children who learn more quickly and complete their work more easily never just bide their time waiting for the others to finish. Because we do not attempt to have everyone end up with the same amount of content knowledge, there is no need to hinder the progress of the fast workers. The teacher can introduce a new related subtopic to the whole class. Then, as children approach the end of one project, they can begin another, and because the work is purposeful, they are eager to get on with it. To have two or more projects going at the same time is not confusing to the children because all of the subtopics are closely related.

The third part of the secret is to be sure the children assume some responsibility. They will be better off and the class will function more smoothly and productively when they take on some of the load. There are always children who are having problems, be they academic or social or both, and there are always other children who can provide assistance. However, a sense of responsibility is not automatic. Children learn it through example, through experiencing the consequences of irresponsibility, through discussion, and through a great deal of patience on the part of the teacher. The obvious benefits of cooperation extend also to the teacher, who can always use an extra pair of hands to assist those who need help.

Thus, teachers can spread the workload around during class. After school, they likewise need not be overworked by taking home the work of twenty-five or more children every night. Because theme study proceeds slowly and because teachers know their children well from observing them so much and so closely, they can look over the children's work on a rotating basis. If they take home only a few

members of the public; student teachers practice teach in the school; and they, along with university faculty members, also conduct research in the school. In addition, because we are a small school operating on a shoestring budget, the only specialists we have are part-time French and music teachers. There are no resource teachers to help children with learning problems, no nurse to look after them if they fall sick, and not even a principal to oversee the whole operation of the school. We are the resource teachers, the nurse, the principal, and the secretary.

notebooks or papers every night, they can keep up with the children's progress and make useful written comments on the work without being overburdened.

Once convinced that this approach is a good one and that it can be carried out in more normal settings, teachers' next concern, understandably, is how they can learn to do theme studies. Perhaps some of our experiences in trying to figure out why certain things went wrong and what we did about them when we were new to this approach will be instructive.

The transition from teacher-centered and accuracy-oriented teaching to child-centered and problem-solving teaching was not easy and did not happen overnight. It took us nearly three years to learn one of the most difficult aspects of this transition: how to guide children as opposed to telling them what to do, how to watch them make mistakes without worrying about wasting time, how to provide choices without turning the classroom into chaos, and how to make sure that they were learning even though they were moving around and talking to others—in short, how to trust that children can learn to be responsible.

We had some ideas about this kind of teaching before we began, but we had never seen it in practice. We knew that what we had been doing in our classrooms did not fit currently held theories of how children learn. Furthermore, these new concepts about teaching and learning seemed so reasonable that we felt compelled to try to incorporate them into our classrooms as much as possible.

Although all three of us were involved in this changeover and were theoretically there to support and help each other solve problems, in practice that is not what happened. The feeling that this approach would be easy to implement was one we all shared. Because we were not accustomed to working closely with other teachers and, therefore, carried on in relative isolation from each other and because we expected the change to be almost automatic, each of us often felt discouraged when we repeatedly encountered situations that did not seem to be developing according to plan. This seeming failure was hard on our self-esteem, but gradually we sorted out the problems, each in our own ways.

In retrospect, strange as it may seem, the fact that we went more or less our own separate ways in those early months and years had a very positive side to it. None of us was critical of the others, even when things obviously were not going well and what we were doing did not fit the theory. In effect, our lack of consultation gave each of us space and time to work out our own solutions. As we became more successful, we began to turn to each other to discuss and sort out our problems. It became easier to admit to having problems as we each became better at identifying and articulating them and once we knew the approach was finally working.

Since each of the three of us experienced the transition somewhat differently, we have singled out some of the experiences of one of us—the teacher of the Olds—to illustrate what we went through and how we learned from our mistakes.

To begin with, she made a list of points that should characterize her new program. The list was to serve as a reminder of the principles and objectives that should guide her work; they became her criteria for measuring her progress. The list stated:

- children are motivated to learn when they are interested in the subject;
- they should always be encouraged to do the thinking and take the initiative;
- they should have choices at many points in their learning, including how to do their work;
- they should work in groups and help each other;
- children should participate in the evaluation of their work;
- the teacher's role is to respond to and guide the children's efforts, which means offering only constructive questions and comments and providing encouragement;
- the teacher must be a "kid-watcher," that is, someone who closely observes the children's learning processes.

That first year the theme was "Living Things." The teacher brainstormed with the children about the differences between living and inorganic things. Then they brainstormed about the functions of living things. All the children had a great deal to contribute, and the discussions were quite lively. After the first week and a half of brainstorms, discussions, making up questions, and doing some reading about the topic, she concluded that the new approach was successful.

She prepared a list of activities on what happens in the fall to living things in our northern climate, and then each child selected one. This work continued for a few weeks with the teacher preparing more activities every week and the children doing one after another. The time was filled with many small tasks that kept both the children and the teacher working very hard. However, they weren't working toward any specific goal. The work consisted of just a collection of interesting small activities that were all over the place. This was a shortcoming that she did not recognize at the time.

One problem she did recognize, however, was that by mid-October, she was already exhausted from organizing so many activities every week. She realized that she needed to let the children do more of the work and assume a larger share of the responsibility. Somehow she should try to give up the need to feel in control of each thing that was happening and concentrate instead on guiding the children. So in the next part of the study, she let each child choose an animal to learn about. Everyone had to start with a brainstorm and then do the research. Amid a lot of discussion and comparison of ideas, each child did a brainstorm and then more or less attacked the bookshelves and the teacher-prepared files, carrying great loads of information to their tables, chatting a bit with friends, and getting to work.

This was great, the teacher thought. But not for long. After two or three days, the seemingly enthusiastic and motivated learners had, for reasons unknown to her, changed into restless, bored, and frustrated children, some of whom acted scared, others obnoxious. They weren't learning! What had gone wrong?

The teacher was in a panic: it should have been working, but it wasn't. After analyzing what was going on in the class by watching the children and putting herself in their shoes, it dawned on her that the children did not know what to do with the information they were reading. She, therefore, decided to redo the introduction to the individual projects. The following day she apologized to the children for not having properly taught them how to do a project and then proceeded to explain the steps such an undertaking involves. The children seemed relieved, and the teacher felt particularly happy to have cleared up this knotty problem. They went back to their piles of information and worked. The problem, it seemed, was solved.

However, well into the projects, the teacher vaguely sensed that something was still wrong. It seemed that the children were not learning all that much. She pondered what they had been doing and checked her list of criteria. Eventually it occurred to her that the children had not really figured out how to do a project. They were merely following a recipe that she had given them. They were, in fact, learning very little from the experience because the teacher had been doing all the important work for them. The problem was how to guide children to think, not how to give them formulas. However, because the opportunity had gone, that issue was put on the back burner.

It was not long before another problem began to gnaw at her. Although the children were free to consult with one another, the help they offered seemed to be very limited. Their discussions consisted mainly of enthusiastic reports about the interesting things they were picking up from their readings. Questions were raised but usually not answered. Problems about work were generally not articulated, and when they were, they were not always solved. Some children were bored, and others even decided that it was all too difficult and gave up. Needless to say, the teacher kept smiling and working hard to help everyone. Somehow all the children eventually got their projects finished.

After the dust had settled, the teacher tried to evaluate this first theme study. Despite the many problems, there had indeed been some success in implementing the new approach. The children had tried to work together and had learned some interesting things. Although it seemed that they should have been able to do more work by themselves and with each other, they had, in fact, learned, to varying degrees, that they had to help themselves and each other. They had begun to realize that the teacher could not possibly help everyone with all their problems whenever they needed it. Out of necessity, the teacher had frequently said, "Please ask X or Y for help. I'm busy working with Z now," or "You decide whatever you think is best." This turned out to be a better tactic than she realized at the time because it forced the children to take initiative and do more of the thinking.

Nevertheless, there was still a problem with the quality of the help the children gave each other and their willingness to accept each other's suggestions. During the daily round of helping the children, the teacher noticed many similarities in the kinds of problems they encountered. Yet the variety in their reactions to the problems was remarkable. Some children panicked without even trying to think of ways of solving their problems and without turning to the other children for help; others relied only on themselves for solutions to their problems; and still others shopped around for ideas, went back to their seats, tried a few things, and somehow solved their problems.

The children's lack of confidence in each other's advice and a lingering reluctance to take initiative were demonstrated by the fact that when one child asked another child a question, and the answer suggested that a decision of some kind had to be made, the first child would often not implement the decision without consulting the teacher first. As soon as she noticed this, her standard reply became, "You decide," leaving the children with no option but to make decisions independently. This reply also eventually had the effect of cutting down on questions and of giving the teacher more time to help those with greater problems.

Despite the progress, whenever she checked her list of criteria, she had the same nagging feeling that she was still doing too much of the thinking and not enough guiding. Why couldn't the children help each other to a greater extent? What was wrong? This problem took her a couple of years to solve satisfactorily.

As a result of the first experience doing project work, the teacher organized the next year's projects differently. Instead of telling the children how to do a project, she had them collect information after the brainstorm. As soon as a number of children became restless, she called the group together and asked if they had a problem with their work. The response was immediate and came from most children, "What do we do with the information? Are we supposed to write it down? Where do we put it?" The teacher then asked the children for their ideas. It did not take them long to suggest that there was a need to organize information and that they could use the categories from the brainstorm. She then showed them a chart format for organizing their information. The immediate response was, "There's not enough room for all the writing," which revealed another entirely new problem: it turned out that the children did not know how to take notes.

Still, by December of the second year, the teacher had made a lot of progress in her own learning. She could anticipate the children's difficulties with project work, but she also made sure that they experienced the difficulties as well so that they would learn to articulate their problems and discuss ways of solving them. Mistakes were used as positive experiences to learn from. At last she was beginning to learn how to guide the children.

Nevertheless, she had fallen into the same error with note taking as she had with organizing information. Using a few examples, she had demonstrated note taking after which she had simply expected the children to do it by themselves. Again she had done the work and the thinking, and of course, the children had not learned much. In no time this problem began to surface. Now the children had charts to put notes into, but in spite of the teacher's demonstration, they still did not have enough space to write them in. This happened to every single child in the class. Many had to squeeze whole sentences or even paragraphs into the charts. Obviously, they did not know how to take notes or even what notes were supposed to look like.

The teacher stopped and asked why the charts were not working. The children suggested that the problem could be solved by making larger boxes in the charts or by writing less. Both suggestions presented new problems. The charts could not be bigger than the paper they were written on—an insuperable problem. On the other hand, the children could not write less, because they did not know how—a problem with a solution. To solve this problem, the teacher read aloud to the entire class some material that was relevant to all the projects. She read it section by section stopping after each one and asking the children what information was important to write down and how much would suffice. This way, the children had to do the thinking and make the decisions instead of watching the teacher do everything. The result was that they learned how to take notes.

From then on each time an aspect of project work or any other activity became a problem for the children, usually signaled by a general restlessness in the room, the teacher called a meeting to help the children articulate the problem and develop solutions.

Upon completion of the project, the teacher asked the class how they had gone about doing their work. The various successful steps were written down and posted for future reference in doing project work. The children could use the guidelines they had developed themselves. But this process has to be repeated with each new group every year.

The teacher discovered with each successive class that note taking is very difficult for children, and because it is so important, a great deal of guided practice is necessary. To provide this guidance, she has continued the practice of reading together with the whole class, taking one section of a text at a time, discussing it, getting the children to decide what the most important information is and how to write it down. Sometimes the text has to be outlined, and sometimes the children read a few texts together and put the information on charts using categories derived from a brainstorm. The material selected for this kind of reading and discussion pertains to the topic to be studied and provides some general background on the topic. Thus, this activity serves the triple purpose of getting the children started on the topic while at the same time equipping them to deal with the information independently and in ways that will enable them to use it later.

Gradually, the teacher decreases her involvement until the children can continue on their own. She looks over their notes every day to be able to guide them better the next day. Only occasionally does she respond to lack of clarity or a mistake by asking the child a question about it. The children learn from their own observations as well. It becomes easier for them to see their shortcomings when they need to use their notes to write them into prose.

The process of reading and note taking with the whole class is painfully slow. At first, there were times when the teacher almost gave up on it. She was afraid this process was inefficient and worried that not enough material would be "covered." Referring every so often to her checklist of criteria helped her to persist because it made her realize that the children were indeed learning a great deal: they were having to think and, in the long run, they could do it by themselves.

As for the problem of children working together, the situation had improved, but the children continued to find it very difficult. It took the teacher about two years to fully realize that this was because they still did not have enough of a common knowledge base to be able to help each other with their work. In the meantime, the improvements that the children were making were due to the increased discussion and preparation of the topic, including the increased amount of reading that the whole class had done with the teacher (work initially intended to improve the skill of note taking).

She now does even more preparation and more reading about the topic with the whole group than she used to so that the children can work together more effectively. At some point she asks what aspects of the topic would be interesting and worthwhile to study, and after suggesting several, the children choose the topics for their projects. Each project now includes information that everyone has learned as well as information that pertains only to the chosen project. With this method the children have more guided practice in note taking while also building a great deal of knowledge in common, which, in turn, facilitates discussion of their projects with each other.

And last but not least, there is finally cohesion in the program because the projects are aspects of the main topic and fit together in ways that are apparent to the children.

Hindsight makes the mistakes easy to see, but when a person is in the middle of a situation and is trying to make fairly major changes, things often become blurred. Certainly, one cannot be aware of all the problems and solutions all at once. The analysis develops piecemeal with one point coming into sharper focus at one time and others at other times until eventually the whole picture is clear. It has taken us a few years to reach this stage. Now that we feel at home with this approach, we still make mistakes, but the difference is that we no longer worry about them. Learning from mistakes is as much a part of the learning process for teachers as it is for children. If we were able to recognize and correct our mistakes when the approach was new to us and when we were unsure of ourselves, we certainly can do so now.

The most important single lesson we have learned from our experiences is that it takes time and practice to develop this approach. Therefore, our advice to teachers new to theme studies is to begin slowly and not be discouraged by mistakes. Perhaps the first study should extend over a shorter period of time and deal with a smaller chunk of work than those described in previous chapters. Those theme studies stand simply as examples of the kind of work that can be accomplished through this approach. They demonstrate the process. Any theme study must be adapted to what the teacher feels comfortable attempting and to the realities of the particular classroom involved. Nonetheless, two things are certain: virtually all children benefit from the theme study approach, and it is realizable in just about any elementary school classroom.

Notes

Chapter 1
Introduction

1. "Standardized Testing—in Whose Interests?" *Mudpie* 5(8):5 (October 1984).
2. *How Children Fail*, by John Holt. Pitman Publishing Corp. (Delta), New York, 1964.
   Death at an Early Age, by Jonathan Kozol. Houghton Mifflin (Bantam), Boston, 1967.
   Education for Alienation, by Nathaniel Hickerson. Prentice-Hall, Inc., Englewood Cliffs, N.J., 1966.
   Schools Against Children: The Case for Community Control, Annette T. Rubinstein (ed.). Monthly Review Press, New York, 1970.
   Crisis in the Classroom: The Remaking of American Education, by Charles E. Silberman. Random House (Vintage), New York, 1970.
3. Malcolm Levin, "The Back to Basics Scam, or . . . Why Progressive Education Has Never Been Tried." *Mudpie* 3(6):8–16 (June 1983).

Chapter 2
Theme Study: What It Is and How to Do It

1. Impressions of a student teacher working in the school: Christine Cudmore-Kear. "An Investigation into the Role of the Teacher." Unpublished paper, 1986.

Chapter 3
Around the World in Sixty Days: A Theme Study about Houses with the Middles (Ages Six to Eight)

1. Among the books that contained useful portions for these files were:
   Houses, by Irving and Ruth Adler. John Day, New York, 1964.
   Houses and Homes, by Carol Bowyer. Usborne, London, 1978.
   A New True Book: Houses, by Katherine Carter. Children's Press, Chicago, 1957.
   A True Book of Houses, by Katherine Carter. Children's Press, Chicago, 1957.
   All About Houses, by William Dugan. Golden Press, New York, 1975.
   History of Houses, by F. Jupo. Dodd, Mead, New York, 1974.
   Simple Shelters, by L.P. Huntington. Coward, McCann, & Geoghegan, New York, 1979.
   Bedouins, by Fidelity Lancaster. Gloucester, New York, 1978.
   Zulus, by John Mack. Macdonald, London, 1980.
   Growing Up Masai, by Tom Shachtman. Macmillan, New York, 1981.
   Shelters from Prehistoric Times to Today, by Ann Siberell. Holt, Rinehart, and Winston, New York, 1979.

The American Indian Habitats, by N. Simon and E. Wolfson. David McKay, New York, 1978.

Building an Igloo, by Uli Steltzer. Douglas & McIntyre, Vancouver, 1981.

A History of Houses, by R.J. Unstead. A. & C. Black, Ltd., London, 1958.

The Micmac, by R.H. Whitehead and H. McGree. Nimbus, Halifax, 1983.

Chapter 4
The History of Buildings: A Theme Study with the Olds (Ages Eight to Ten)

1. I supplemented that with information from:

   Men, Machines and History: The story of tools and machines in relation to social progress, by Samuel Lilley. International Publishers, New York, 1966.

   All the Ways of Building: A new story of architecture, by L. Lamprey. The Macmillan Company, Toronto, 1954.

   People and Spaces: A view of history through architecture, by Anita Abramovitz. The Viking Press, New York, 1979.

   From Stones to Skyscrapers: A book about architecture, by Thea and Richard Bergere. Dodd, Mead & Company, New York, 1960.

   Master Builders of the Middle Ages, by David Jacobs. Horizon Caravel Books, Harper & Row, New York, 1969.

2. See:

   Beginning Experiences in Architecture: A guide for the elementary school teacher, by George E. Trogler. Van Nostrand Reinhold Company, Toronto and New York, 1972.

   Bridges: A project book, by Anne and Scott MacGregor. Lothrop, Lee, & Shepard Books Ltd., New York, 1980.

   Structures and Forces, Stages 1 & 2. A Unit for Teachers. Series: Science 5/13. MacDonald Educational, London and New York, 1974.

   Architecture: A book of projects for young adults, by Forrest Wilson. Van Nostrand Reinhold Company, Toronto and New York, 1968.

   Building: The fight against gravity, by Mario Salvadori. Atheneum, New York, 1979.

3. Of the numerous books that deal with building materials and structures, the following ones include good reading material for children to use:

   Man the Builder, by John Harvey. Priory Press Ltd., London, 1973.

   The Magic Stones: The story of the arch, by Alaine. Faber & Faber, London, 1957.

   Looking at Architecture, by Roberta M. Paine. Lothrop, Lee, & Shepard Co., New York, 1974.

   Bridges: A project book, by Anne and Scott MacGregory. Lothrop, Lee, & Shepard Books Ltd., New York, 1980.

   Building Wonders of the World, by Patricia Bahree. MacDonald Series Eye Openers, MacDonald Educational, London, 1982.

   Your Book of Architecture, by Agnes Allen. Faber & Faber, London, 1958.

4. For this social history study, the children read sections of the following books:

   A World Full of Homes, by William A. Burns. Whittlesey House, McGraw-Hill Book Co., Inc., New York and Toronto, 1953.

   All About Houses, by William Dugan. Golden Press, New York and Western Publishing Co. Inc., Racine, Wisc., 1975.

   A History of Houses, by R.J. Unstead. A Black's Junior Reference Book. A. & C. Black Ltd., London, 1958.

The Children's Book of Houses and Homes, by Carol Bowyer. Usborne Publishing Ltd., London, 1978.

The First Civilizations, by Anne Millard. The Children's Picture World History. Usborne Publishing Ltd., London, 1977.

The Time Traveller Book of Pharaohs & Pyramids, by Tony Allan and Vivienne Henry. Usborne Publishing Ltd. and Hayes Books, Burlington, Ont., 1977.

Homes in History, by Molly Harrison. Series: Picture History. Wayland Publishers Ltd., Hove, East Sussex, 1983.

The Story of Your Home, by Agnes Allen. Faber & Faber Ltd., London, 1972.

Houses, by Irving and Ruth Adler. The "Reason Why" Books, John Day Co., New York, 1965.

The Roman Engineers, by L.A. and J.A. Hamey. A Cambridge Topic Book. Lerner Publications Company, Minneapolis, 1981.

The Buildings of Ancient Man, by Helen and Richard Leacroft. Addison-Wesley Publishing Co., Reading, Mass., 1973.

By the same authors, Helen and Richard Leacroft, and the same publisher, Addison-Wesley Publishing Co., Reading, Mass.:

The Buildings of Ancient Mesopotamia, 1970.

The Buildings of Ancient Greece, 1966.

The Buildings of Early Islam, 1976.

5. The books used for this assignment were:

The Houses of Mankind, by Colin Duly. Thames & Hudson, London, 1979.

Simple Shelters, by Lee Pennock Huntington. Coward, McCann & Geoghegan, New York, 1979.

Tents: Architecture of the nomads, by Torvald Faegre. Anchor Press/Doubleday, Garden City, N.Y., 1979.

Issues of the *National Geographic* magazine that were used mainly for the pictures and the captions.

6. Unfortunately I could not get two other films on time:

Medieval Times: Role of the Church, Coronet Films. 20 minutes, color, 1961.

Jabberwocky, A Monty Python Film. Directed by Terry Gilliam. 104 minutes, color, 1977. I wanted to show this one to offset the unrealistic, immaculately clean and lifeless portrayal of the Middle Ages so typical of many school films.

7. Sections of the following books were used:

Monasteries, by R.J. Unstead. A Black's Junior Reference Book. A. & C. Black Ltd., London, 1961.

Churches and Cathedrals, by Helen and Richard Leacroft. Lutterworth Press, London, 1972.

Building the Medieval Cathedral, by Percy Watson. A Cambridge Topic Book. Lerner Publications Company, Minneapolis (1976), 1979.

Life in a Fifteenth-Century Monastery, by Anne Boyd. A Cambridge Topic Book. Lerner Publications Company, Minneapolis, 1975.

Faces on Places: About gargoyles and other stone creatures, by Suzanne Haldome. The Viking Press, New York, 1980.

I Carve Stone, by Joan Fine. Thomas Y. Crowell, New York, 1979.

8. See the list of books in note 4.

9. Meanwhile, the children also started to read and discuss sections from:

Castles, by R.J. Unstead. A. & C. Black Ltd., London, 1970.

Castles, A MacDonald Topic Book. MacDonald Educational, London, 1976.

The Castle Story, by Sheila Sancha. Thomas Y. Crowell, New York, 1979.

Castles and Fortresses, by R.R. Selsam. Methuen & Co., Ltd., London, 1954.

Chapter 5
Building Learning, Learning from Building: The Olds and Middles Cooperate—With Impressive Results

1. The following proved to be useful reading materials on building houses:
   How a House Happens, by Jan Adkins. Walker and Company Inc., New York and Fitzhenry & Whiteside, Toronto, 1971.
   Tools in Your Life, by Irving Adler. John Day Company, New York, 1956.
   Myra Builds a House, Women at Work, by Beverly Allison and Judith Lawrence. D.C. Heath, Lexington, Mass., 1975.
   Canadian Wood-Frame House Construction. Central Mortgage and Housing Corporation, NHA 5031, Ottawa, n.d.
   Building a House, A Wonder Book, by Brian Read. Transworld Publications Ltd., Orange, Calif., 1977.
   Building a House, by K. Robbins, Four Winds Press, New York, 1984.
   House Building for Children: Six different houses that children can build by themselves, by Les Walker. The Overlook Press, New York, 1977.

Chapter 6
From Stones to Bricks: A Study of Housing with the Youngs (Ages Five and Six)

1. Some of the books I used were:
   The New Flats, by David Mackay. Penguin Books, Ipswich, 1972.
   Old Houses, by David Mackay. Penguin Books, Ipswich, 1972.
   Homes, by Peter Usborne. Macdonald & Company, London, 1971.

Chapter 9
What about "The Basics"? And Other Sundry Matters

1. One such book is *Reading Without Nonsense* (2nd ed.), by Frank Smith. Teachers College Press, Columbia University, New York, 1985.
2. To mention just one such source: *Writing: Teachers and Children at Work*, by Donald Graves. Heinemann Educational Books, Portsmouth, N.H., 1983.

Chapter 10
What about Evaluation?

1. See *Reading Miscue Inventory Manual: Procedure for Diagnosis and Evaluation*, by Yetta M. Goodman and Carolyn L. Burke. Macmillan Publishing Co., New York, 1972.